Leading With
TRUST

How to Build Strong School Teams

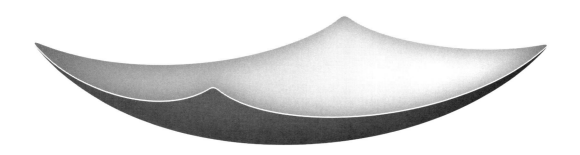

Susan Stephenson

Solution Tree | Press

a division of

Solution Tree

555 North Morton Street
Bloomington, IN 47404

(800) 733-6786 (toll free)
(812) 336-7700
FAX: (812) 336-7790

email: info@solution-tree.com
solution-tree.com

Printed in the United States of America

13 12 11 10 09   1 2 3 4 5

    Library of Congress Cataloging-in-Publication Data
Stephenson, Susan.
    Leading with trust : how to build strong school teams / Susan Stephenson.
       p. cm.
    ISBN 978-1-935249-12-2 (lib. bdg.) -- ISBN 978-1-934009-46-8
  1. School personnel management. 2. School employees--Professional relationships. 3. Group work in education. 4. Trust. I. Title.
    LB2831.5.S8 2009
    371.2'01--dc22
                                             2008056147

President: Douglas Rife

Publisher: Robert D. Clouse

Director of Production: Gretchen Knapp

Managing Editor of Production: Caroline Wise

Senior Production Editor: Edward Levy

Proofreader: Elisabeth Abrams

Cover and Text Designer: Orlando Angel

To Brenda Martin—a trusted friend to so many

1952–2007

Known to all as "Madame" at North Kipling Junior Middle School,

her motto was "Be kind to people and do your job well."

Acknowledgments

The research in this book is based on the work of many key authors who have written about trust in schools and the workplace. I am indebted to Suzanne Bailey for her mentoring throughout the 1990s at many workshops, in private conversations, and in correspondence based on her unpublished teaching materials. Anthony S. Bryk and Barbara Schneider, with Julie Reed Kochanek, published a foundational case study of four hundred Chicago elementary schools, *Trust in Schools* (2002), which established the centrality of relational trust as a social resource for school improvement. Stephen M. R. Covey's *The Speed of Trust* (2006), building on the work of his father's *The 7 Habits of Highly Effective People*, applies just as much to schools as it does to the corporate world.

I am deeply indebted to the passionate message and extensive print resources of Rebecca DuFour, Richard DuFour, and Robert Eaker, who continue to empower educators to work as professional learning communities. Andy Hargreaves has written numerous books on culture, change, and leadership in education. His article "Teaching and Betrayal" was especially relevant to my understanding of barriers to trust.

Julie Reed Kochanek, coauthor of Bryk and Schneider's *Trust in Schools*, continued the theme in her *Building Trust for Better Schools: Research-Based Practices* (2005), which presented a series of valuable processes for building trust in a school community. Roy Lewicki, a leading scholar in the study of trust development, negotiation, and conflict-management processes, has written many helpful articles, among them "Models of Interpersonal Trust Development: Theoretical Approaches, Empirical Evidence, and Future Directions."

The Canadian educational researchers Coral Mitchell and Larry Sackney, authors of *Profound Improvement: Building Capacity for a Learning Community* (2000), base their work on a wholeness perspective. In taking a capacity-building approach to school improvement, they have recognized the importance of creating a trusting climate. Megan Tschannen-Moran's *Trust Matters: Leadership for Successful Schools* (2004), is based on extensive review of the literature and her own research in hundreds of schools and offers excellent, practical, hands-on advice.

Many authors have of course influenced my writing, but these provided key insights. This book takes all their research into account and links it together with strategies and activities designed to first confront distrust and then build trust, from its early stages to the highest levels of mature, high-performing trust.

In the many months it took to write this book, I experienced firsthand what collaboration, teamwork, and trust are all about. In addition to my colleagues in the Peel District School Board (DSB), York Region DSB, and Toronto DSB (all in Ontario, Canada), I wish to acknowledge the following learning partners.

Monique Mili, Bridget Harrison, and Paul Thibault collaborated with me to delve deeper into the issue of trust as we developed workshops for administrators, teachers, and support staff. Paul Thibault also worked with me examining how laughter and humor could be nurtured in schools where morale was low to facilitate staff and student learning and increase achievement. I realized then that a culture of good humor was one part of the bigger issue of building trusting relationships. The Learning Together project in the Halton DSB led me to collaborate with a wonderful group of administrators and teachers as we honed the strategies that would work to make their projects successful.

Susan Chisholm, my primary editor, kept my writing clear and relevant with her gentle feedback and wizardry with words. I am deeply indebted to her. Helen Evans, a critical friend, offered her experience and research as we discussed the complex issues facing schools. Don Marshall developed the critically important surveys and gave advice on making their results accurate and meaningful. A turning point in my writing happened when Helen and I talked candidly with Lori Foote and Sharon O'Halloran, two trusted union leaders, about the possibilities of union representatives and administrators working more as partners and less as adversaries.

My relationship with Solution Tree has allowed me to work with many amazing people. Gretchen Knapp encouraged me to dig deeper into the barriers to trust and guided me through the process with her wise counsel and support. She introduced me to Ed Levy, who has been my wonderful editor and patient guide through the final phase.

I deeply thank all of these people who have collaborated with me with the goal of making school relationships more trusting. They complete the picture, along with all the students I taught and staff members I worked with in my career who have taught me lessons about trust.

Finally, thanks to my husband Tom, my best friend, who understood my commitment and gave me the support I needed to keep going.

Visit **go.solution-tree.com/leadership** to download the reproducibles and read other materials associated with this book.

Table of Contents

About the Author

Susan Stephenson (M.Ed.) enjoyed thirty-six years as a family studies classroom teacher. From 1986 to 2002 she assumed various leadership roles in three Canadian school districts as well as with the Ontario Secondary School Teachers' Federation. The recipient of two awards for distinction in professional learning, Sue retired as a school principal in 2002, "reinvented herself" as a freelance consultant and staff developer, and was elected to the Provincial Executive of the Retired Teachers of Ontario.

Sue has published numerous articles and resource books and, with Paul Thibault, has written *Laughing Matters: Strategies for Building a Joyful Learning Community* (2006). Sue is a speaker across Canada and the United States to both corporate and educational audiences on teamwork, leadership, morale, humor—and trust. She has the unique distinction of being a Certified Laughter Leader with the World Laughter Tour. Sue credits much of her success to her sense of humor and an ability to engage audiences in lively, informative presentations.

Sue lives with her husband Tom in Ontario, Canada, where she is a proud stepgrandmother with a passion for family, friends, colleagues, and creativity.

Introduction

People are at the heart of schooling. No matter how innovative a school reform may be, it is unlikely to succeed unless people on the front lines of schooling are working well together to implement it. Studies have shown that growth in trust predicts a growth in teacher commitment to the school and a greater openness to innovation. The latest work on trust in schools ties the growth of trust to gains in school productivity or increased school achievement.

—Julie Reed Kochanek

Years ago, in my role as a staff development consultant for a large school district, I was asked to identify the most crucial elements of school improvement and effectiveness. After much reflection, I decided that these key characteristics must be present:

- The staff must believe that they are "good but growing"; that is, they see continuous improvement as an integral part of their work.

- The staff must be willing to take risks inside and outside the classroom in order to be innovative.

- Teachers must see that working together is pleasurable and even joyful. Leaders must model this behavior.

All of these characteristics are dependent on staff members trusting one another.

Even though at the time there wasn't much research being done about the importance of trust in work relationships, my experiences working with many different staffs told me that if trust isn't there, schools can't move forward. So I began to explore the barriers to trust and the strategies needed to build relationships, teams, and learning communities based on trust. I knew that if administrators aren't trusted, and if staff don't trust one another, it is very difficult even to identify the real challenges of a school, let alone address them.

Then, in 1996, I was invited to help high school staff members improve their levels of trust. The results of a schoolwide survey had revealed very low levels of trust among the staff, and they were concerned—even surprised—

about it. I attended several planning meetings with a large group on their professional development committee, and together we planned an offsite staff retreat. The retreat would fall on a professional development day and use the evening before it to set the stage. The principal would cover some of the expenses, and staff would pay part of the costs themselves. As an outside facilitator, I wanted to assist them with a process but let them take ownership of the task and the actions arising out of their decisions.

Holding a retreat that acknowledged that there were low levels of trust and mutual respect was a gutsy, high-risk step, but though attendance was voluntary, almost all of the staff attended. Social activities were planned for the first evening, including informal storytelling about the memories people had of the school's history—some funny and some sad. This served to stimulate deeper discussion, and back in their rooms many staff members talked for hours into the night. The following morning they worked collaboratively in groups, focusing on signs of the low trust visible in the school and signs of high-trust that could be possible in the future. The attention shifted in the afternoon to action planning and making recommendations to the planning team and principal. These were the action areas that resulted from the retreat:

- Use of the staff room/dining room
- Professionalism and conflict
- Improvement of communication
- Format of staff meetings
- Interpersonal and social relationships
- Meeting teachers' needs

This was a rare example of a school tackling its low trust head-on and doing something tangible about it. Specific, long-lasting changes occurred because of their honesty and willingness to put real issues on the table. For example, they formed six work teams following the retreat. One of their documents, called "What Does Trust Look Like, Feel Like, and Sound Like?" listed their Ten Commandments of Trust:

> Specific, long-lasting changes occurred because of their honesty and willingness to put real issues on the table.

1. Have no fear.
2. Manifest mutual admiration.
3. Open thy door.
4. Open thy mind.
5. Radiate energy.
6. Speak with a straight tongue.
7. Live your dreams.
8. Free thy turf.
9. Embrace time-sharing.
10. Be interdependent.

This retreat was pivotal in beginning my action research about building trust in schools. It taught me that a large school, led by a trusted group of staff members who had their principal's encouragement and involvement, could talk intensely about trust issues and take ownership for creating a healthier, more caring climate. These staffers understood that feelings of discomfort were a natural part of the growth process.

The role of trust in continuous school improvement remains just as, if not more, relevant today because of increased accountability for universal student success. As Paul Thibault and I have written, laughter and joy are also crucial to improving school morale for staff and achievement levels for students:

> Without laughter and a culture of good humor to make continuous school improvement an enjoyable process, rather than an exhausting chore, we have little chance of achieving success—let alone sustaining it. . . . A culture of distrust, low morale and resistance to change often blocks teamwork and collaboration. (Stephenson & Thibault, 2006, p. 2)

School leaders usually have a sound educational vision and a plan for achieving it. However, if their plan doesn't include the necessary groundwork to build a trusting climate and positive relationships with staff and parents, they risk both the vision itself and their professional relationships. Trust is a crucial ingredient for building a successful school. Yet it is rarely addressed on its own as a core issue, even though we know that mature levels of trust are required in high-performing teams that are the heart of any learning community.

Leading With Trust will help educators see why succeeding with school improvement initiatives depends on the level of trust in schools. It will help them identify the level of trust in their organization, the causes of distrust if it exists, and the right strategies for moving into a more productive, high-performing, trusting environment. It also connects the stages of trust to school effectiveness by helping educators see how their school's history has an impact—positive or negative—on its chances of future success.

"If you do what you've always done, you'll get what you've always gotten."

—Anthony Robbins

Intended Audience

You may find that what you are learning while you are wearing one hat helps you to see what you need to do while wearing the other.

—Kathleen D. Ryan and Daniel K. Oestreich

Schools rely on many different people for leadership. Some have formal roles, such as principal, union representative, teacher leader, and curriculum or literacy leader. Many informal leaders also make a significant impact, including teachers and classified or support staff. This book is written for all of these leaders. People dealing with trust issues in other organizations will also find the book's strategies and activities useful. The general reader may also find that *Leading With Trust* can help with an understanding of his or her personal relationships.

If you belong to one of the groups listed here, however, you will find this book especially useful:

- Anyone in a leadership role who takes action to make a school better for student learning, such as an administrator, teacher leader, union steward, mentor, member of a parent council, or parent teacher association

- Experienced administrators and teacher leaders who have been transferred and are developing an entry plan for an existing or newly opened school

- Newly appointed administrators and teacher leaders looking for ways to assess the trust-culture of their new school placement or to develop their own personal trust capacity

- Staff development and professional learning leaders at the local, district, state, or provincial levels in collaborative study groups or courses with school boards and unions

Organization

One of my frustrations with books about school change has always been that they provide the "why"—the theory—in great detail, but not the "how"—the practice. *Leading With Trust* focuses on the *how* of building trust—how to do things that make a difference, rather than just plan and talk about them.

This book has been organized around stages of trust building along a continuum, from low levels of malignant distrust to high levels of mature trust. At each stage, trust has a different face and poses different challenges. No matter how good or bad the trust-culture is, selecting an appropriate plan of action at each level takes skill in observation, assessment, and collaboration.

Building Capacity

Personal capacity is an amalgam of all the embedded values, assumptions, beliefs, and practical knowledge that teachers carry with them and the professional networks and knowledge bases with which they connect.

—Coral Mitchell and Larry Sackney

We know that professional learning that is mandated or forced upon educators without providing them with the skills and knowledge for such growth and development has few long-term benefits and often meets with resistance. Each staff member's growth plan should be unique and based on the notion of continuous growth.

Each stage of trust building therefore involves strategies for building personal, interpersonal, and organizational capacity. These strategies are sequenced and include specific activities. The activities ensure that a loosely based group can become a high-functioning team and that, at the same time, each individual on that team can increase his or her personal capacity for

"There was no point in waiting around for the system to improve. . . . I urged principals to take charge and to assume that on any given day the system may not know what it is doing."

—Michael Fullan

At each stage, trust has a different face and poses different challenges.

trust as well. Building high levels of trust and shared leadership takes time and planning, but the outcome is well worth the effort!

The Scope of This Book

It is the intent of this book to focus on the school as the unit of change. It is true that the school district and school community, as well as the state or province and perhaps even the national government, have an impact on an individual school. But while school leaders need to be aware of "the outside world" and are tied to a larger system, their greatest impact on student learning is within their own school. For this reason, this book will focus only on the personal, interpersonal, and intraorganizational aspects of trust, as shown in figure I.1.

> "Capacity for a learning community needs deliberately and explicitly to be built within schools and school systems."
>
> —Larry Sackney

Personal Trust

Interpersonal/Staff Trust

Organizational Trust

Trust Beyond the School

Figure I.1: The spheres of personal, interpersonal, and organizational trust

Chapter Structure

Chapter 1, The Courage to Confront Distrust, identifies the core barriers to trust development, including fear and betrayal. How can a leader or a group recognize and then have the courage to begin the discussion about problems with trust? Are there cultures in which the levels of distrust are so deep that they cannot be helped?

Chapter 2, Lower-Risk Strategies to Deal With Distrust, provides strategies and activities to begin to overcome the barriers to trust and start the healing process. The strategies are organized into two categories: personal and interpersonal. A core organizational feature of the interpersonal strategies is the formation of a facilitation team of five or six teacher leaders to assist the principal and other administrators.

Chapter 3, The Courage to Begin Building Trust, provides a deeper understanding about what trust in its beginning and developing stages means specifically in schools. If trust is evident—but in low levels—how can a leader begin to lay the groundwork for growth in relationships? If this is a new school, how can staff members get to know each other and begin to trust? With an eye on a high-performing trust culture as a goal, how can groups continue to move through the process of trust building without giving up?

Chapter 4, Medium-Risk Strategies to Develop Trust, builds on the strategies introduced in chapter 2 and continues in a sequenced manner to outline personal and then interpersonal strategies with specific activities to move from early trust to developing trust levels.

Chapter 5, The Courage to Create High-Trust Cultures, deals with the rare, mature stage of trust building using two corporate case studies as models. Is it possible for a school to reach this level of high-trusting relationships? What does it look like when it happens? How is learning enhanced for staff and students?

Chapter 6, Higher-Risk Strategies for High-Trust Cultures, adds to the strategies in chapter 4 three additional strategies that are appropriate at this high-trust level. This chapter also summarizes key messages from the book and identifies areas of possible future exploration. What can we learn from corporate high-trust cultures? If schools were ever to reach this rare level of high-trust, what would be different and how would they sustain it?

Print and Online Resources

At the end of most chapters is a list of resources relevant to the topics in that chapter. Supporting, supplementary, and reproducible materials for *Leading With Trust* can also be found online. These include customizable activity pages and charts to introduce the key messages and activities to larger groups.

An Invitation

Leading With Trust will enable school leaders to accomplish the vision and goals they seek. It will help to create a team of educators who trust one another enough to be open, to share information about their own vulnerabilities, hopes, and ideas for the future. That kind of trust allows people to feel they can work "without a net"—that is, that they can take the risks that lead to the best they can do.

Visit **go.solution-tree .com/leadership** to download resources.

Make the book as useful as you can:

- Scribble in the margins.
- Use sticky notes to mark special places.
- Use stickers or colored dots for highlights.
- Share the book with colleagues.
- Sit down after work with a friend to talk about it.
- Start a journal for personal reflection.

Embellish, adapt, or tailor it to make it your own, and above all, relax and enjoy learning about trust.

The Courage to Confront Distrust

A substantial barrier is the lack of trust among educators and poor quality relationships that exist in many schools, particularly those most challenged by poverty and social problems. Consequently, it is critical that leaders of learning communities make the establishment of high quality relationships and trust a high priority.

—Dennis Sparks

Newspaper headlines attest to a crisis of trust in society brought on by the failure of some of our institutions to warrant our faith in them. Is our pet food contaminated? Are our children's toys safe? Can we trust our savings and pension plans to the people who supposedly work on our behalf? Do our politicians tell the truth about the most profound issues that we face?

Consider the following statistics:

- In the United States, a 2005 Harris poll revealed that only 22 percent of those surveyed tend to trust the media, only 8 percent trust political parties, only 27 percent trust the government, and only 12 percent trust big companies (Covey, 2006).

- A survey of over 7,000 executives, managers, and employees identified a "trust gap" between employees and their organization.

Only 20 percent of people strongly trust the top management of their organization and 36 percent moderately trust their top management. The remaining 44 percent range from not trusting to strongly distrusting their top management (Katz, 2007).

When our institutions fail us, even when the failures represent a very small minority, we may come to believe that no one in power will safeguard our well-being. It is the same with our personal lives. Once a friend, partner, spouse, or child in some way betrays the contract we thought we had with that person, all aspects of that relationship must be reexamined and realigned, or it must be terminated.

The high level of distrust in our society is reflected in the enormously popular cartoon strip featuring Dilbert as the main character. Since the cartoon strip began in 1989 in one publication, it has grown to over 2,000 newspapers all around the world. Cartoonist Scott Adams, the necktied, corporate victim once assigned to cubicle 4S700R at Pacific Bell, uses his cartoon to mock current management theories and jargon. His humor draws from that distrust and cynicism that many employees feel. Dilbert feels brainless and undervalued by an inept boss.

The same issues come up in education. Learning communities depend on both formal and informal contracts between and among colleagues. Trust is fragile. If it's been breached, and to the extent that it's been breached, those contracts—both the implicit and explicit ones—must be reexamined and renegotiated.

This chapter examines the research on what distrust is, the barriers we must overcome to create a trusting learning community, and the consequences if we don't.

Educators work in relative isolation. When that factor is coupled with years of downsizing, restructuring, and underfunding, trust within the educational system suffers. Some schools, or groups within schools, may even find themselves completely lacking in trust. In my travels as an educational consultant, I have found that it is not uncommon for educators to describe their trust cultures as dysfunctional, unhealthy, painful, or broken.

In 2002, Andy Hargreaves, a leading educational researcher, author, and speaker, focused his attention on this lack of trust in a startling interview-based study of fifty Canadian teachers in fifteen elementary and secondary schools. These interviews examined the nature of betrayal as a cause of low trust among colleagues in teaching. Research up to that point had shown that, in general, trust between leaders and followers was disappearing. Hargreaves sought to discover what maintained or detracted from a trusting environment:

> In schools and organizations generally, lateral trust among colleagues is as important as vertical trust within the institutional hierarchy. Among teachers, while both personal and professional trust are important in building strong professional communities, they are not always honored equally, nor are they usually treated in a compatible way. Because many schools still operate according to principles of classroom autonomy and norms of professional politeness, trust

Trust is fragile. If it's been breached, and to the extent that it's been breached, those contracts must be reexamined and renegotiated.

in colleagues' commitment or competence tends not to be actively renewed, but to be pushed out of awareness until crises or difficulties draw attention to it.

Teachers, therefore, become aware of trust issues either in emotionally intense relationships with colleagues who are also friends, or when there is a collapse of trust in their professional relationships with colleagues who are also friends, or when there is a collapse of trust in their professional relationships and the existing presumption of trust falls apart.

. . . Issues of trust surface less when trust is honored than when it is breached. It is "difficulties" of trust that are more evident in our data of collegial interactions. (Hargreaves, 2002, p. 396)

The complicated interpersonal dynamics in a school involve many relationships between various stakeholders: leaders (administrators, teachers, or department or division chairs); classified support staff; faculty members; union representatives; parents; and of course students. The causes of distrust can involve any combination of these groups. Certain staff members may not trust other colleagues, the staff as a whole may not trust the administration, or the principal may not trust the union representative. Distrust can also be one-sided. Negative assumptions and stereotypes can lead to the formation of "in-groups" and cliques, causing suspicion and fear in the outsiders. All of this can lead to a complicated web of distrust. No wonder it takes heaps of courage to address issues in the workplace!

The Nature of Distrust

We have all been in either personal or professional relationships or situations that shake or destroy our trust in someone else. Our confidence is weakened, and we may become suspicious and embarrassed if we feel that we've been deliberately fooled. Those feelings reflect the nature of distrust. Roy Lewicki and Edward Tomlinson (2003a) define distrust this way:

Distrust is the confident expectation that another individual's motives, intentions, and behaviors are sinister and harmful to one's own interests. In interdependent relationships, this often entails a sense of fear and anticipation of discomfort or danger. Distrust naturally prompts us to take steps that reduce our vulnerability in an attempt to protect our interests. Accordingly, our distrust of others is likely to evoke a competitive (as opposed to cooperative) orientation that stimulates and exacerbates conflict. (p. 1)

Stephen M. R. Covey (2006) describes trust and distrust this way:

Trust = confidence in integrity and abilities
Distrust = suspicion of integrity and capabilities (p. 5)

The Trust Glass in figure 1.1 (page 10) suggests stages of trust ranging from malignant, deep distrust to mature trust. Schools as institutions may hover at one point on this continuum in a particular school year or semester, but it would be more accurate to think of this scale as applying to every working group in the school. For each, the amount in the glass is different. In the same school, one department may have very low trust while another team of teachers has great camaraderie and a long history of high-trust. Some teachers may be trusted by almost no one, while others may have the trust of everyone.

Where are you on this scale? Where is your school? Try plotting degrees of trust for various groups in your school.

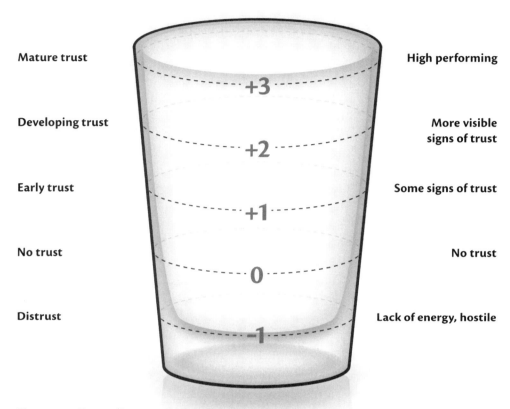

Mature trust — High performing

Developing trust — More visible signs of trust

Early trust — Some signs of trust

No trust — No trust

Distrust — Lack of energy, hostile

+3 +2 +1 0 -1

Figure 1.1: From distrust to mature trust

Distrust isn't always a bad thing. In fact, Lewicki and Tomlinson point out that a "certain level of distrust is vital in preventing excessive group cohesion that precludes sound decision making. It is possible (and even advisable) to have a 'healthy dose' of distrust, particularly with people whom we do not know well" (2003, p. 2). In any organization—even a society—a healthy degree of skepticism can prevent us from falling prey to con artists or being fooled by liars and thieves. We judge how much we can trust a person and decide on the boundaries of our distrust. For example, we may trust a colleague to plan part of a curriculum unit but distrust the same person to keep a secret from our personal life.

On the other hand, dysfunctional distrust can lead to lack of commitment, cynicism, and even revenge. As Lewicki and Tomlinson write:

> Taken to its extreme, distrust can give rise to paranoid cognitions—false or exaggerated cognitions that one is subject to malevolent treatment by others . . . leading to the point of hypervigilance . . . and escalation out of control. (2003b, p. 2)

In an article about leading in cynical times, authors James Kouzes and Barry Posner (2004) make a distinction between cynicism and skepticism:

> Cynicism is the tendency to be close-minded and disillusioned. It differs from skepticism, which is also a tendency to disbelieve; however, skeptics are willing to be convinced if they are presented with persuasive information. Cynics are much less inclined to be influenced, and they have a sneering disbelief in the integrity of others. (p. 1)

We may win over the trust of skeptics, but cynics are the greater challenge.

The Trust Glass shows the range from negative trust (-1, or distrust), to no trust at all (0), to the three stages of trust: early (+1), developing (+2), and mature (+3). Distrust doesn't have to be a permanent state. Schools, and groups within them, can build trust with deliberate planning and action. At first, when relationships improve, there is a common tendency to relax and just try to maintain the feeling of doing better. But as the graphic shows, there are distinct stages to experience beyond maintenance. Trust should be viewed as an active process that can change as a result of events.

Stephen M. R. Covey (2006) talks about the amount of trust or distrust in an organization in terms of assets and liabilities. The upper end of the scale represents the "dividends" that trust can pay, while the lower end represents "taxes" on or withdrawals of trust that cost the school. Schools may move suddenly and significantly down on the Trust Scale. Building trust is much more difficult and time-consuming than its collapse.

Distrust and Learning Communities

Many schools have shifted from cultures of isolation and individual responsibility to ones of collaboration and teamwork. Teachers are required to meet regularly to discuss curriculum expectations, best practices, literacy and numeracy results, and the steps to be taken for universal student success. Administrators are now expected to work as curriculum leaders and to share information, authority, and school governance with teachers, who in turn have taken on added responsibility for aspects of the school outside their classroom.

Collaboration assumes that participants trust each other at some level. Often, well-intentioned administrators and school board officials assume that staff members are prepared and willing to collaborate. Many leaders move too fast and impose a structure of collaboration when staff people may not even know each other very well. The trust level just isn't there.

If there is distrust in a school, it almost certainly will prevent a true learning community from getting off the ground. As Covey (2006) writes, "While high-trust won't necessarily rescue a poor strategy, low trust will almost always derail a good one" (p. 21). It is therefore important to assess the level of trust or distrust, face the seriousness of the distrust if it exists, and do something about it before even thinking about forming a learning community. Trust cannot be assumed.

Several researchers either explicitly or implicitly address the role of trust in achieving a successful learning community.

Coral Mitchell and Larry Sackney describe two components, the cognitive and the affective, that must be in balance in any learning community:

> In a learning community, each person is a worthwhile participant in the tasks, activities, and responsibilities of the community. Each individual works with others in a spirit of experimentation and risk-taking to improve the educational experience of all individuals in the school. This is the task [or cognitive] component. Furthermore, each person deserves the support and care of other school members. People work together in a spirit of trust and mutual respect. This is the emotional [or affective] component. The conjunction of the cognitive and affective aspects adds heart and passion to the work of teachers and students alike. When school people demonstrate passion and fire for what they are doing, that is a sign of a learning community. (2000, p. 8)

See also Affective Interpersonal Trust, page 131, and Cognitive Interpersonal Trust, page 145.

Issues of trust are most closely aligned with the affective or emotional side of the learning community. Just as we are expected to provide a safe learning environment for students, so should we ensure that there is also one for teachers. This means that issues that have never been placed on the table are placed there and that school leaders use the tools they need to work through complex emotional tangles. It takes real courage to confront the potential landmines skillfully.

In his article "Teaching and Betrayal" (2002), Andy Hargreaves presents compelling proof of the vital importance to school success of *teacher collaboration* (a term he considers synonymous with *learning community*). The benefits Hargreaves cites from the research include:

- Increased satisfaction in teaching (Nias, 1989)
- Stronger senses of teaching efficacy (Ashton & Webb, 1986)
- Increased moral support and lessened feelings of guilt and inadequacy (Hargreaves, 1994)
- Lower stress levels (Troman & Woods, 2000)
- Enhanced capacity for coping with change (Little, 1984, 1990)
- Improvements in student achievement (Rosenholtz, 1989; Newman & Wehlage, 1995; McLaughlin & Talbert, 2001)

Collaboration is not achievable without trust, but we must also keep in mind that friendship and collaboration are not necessarily equal. Hargreaves distinguishes between professional collaboration and personal connections this way:

> Professional trust still rests on and affirms social bonds between people. However, these bonds are not based on deep personal knowledge, but in explicit or implicit

norms, principles or understandings of how to work together and what to expect of each other as fellow professionals or as members of the same organization. Trust here is a process, not a state—something that people work toward as a matter of principle and of professional commitment, even if they have little personal relationship with the people in whom their trust is invested. Trust, in other words, helps people move toward creating a measure of shared emotional and intellectual understanding in a larger or complex professional community, instead of presuming that understanding. (Hargreaves, 2002, p. 395)

Let's think about communities in the larger sense. M. Scott Peck, in *The Different Drum: Community Making and Peace* (1987), defines community as:

a group of individuals who have learned to communicate honestly with each other, whose relationships go deeper than their masks of composure and who have developed some significant commitment to rejoice together, mourn together, and to delight in each other, making others' conditions their own. (p. 59)

Hargreaves points out that professional communities are artificial in the sense that trust is a process built over time and that relationships probably stop when people leave work. Peck's definition reminds us more of a workplace modeled on a close neighborhood community. The message in both cases is that trust is the glue that holds relationships together. We must realize that while all communities have infrastructure, bylaws, leaders, and policies, they exist because people want or need to live together in some sort of proximity. The extent to which the relationships of the people who live in those communities are trusting determines the extent to which they are safe and peaceful neighborhoods or hostile and violent ones from which people seek to escape.

DILBERT: © Scott Adams/Dist. by United Feature Syndicate, Inc.

Barriers to Trust

Envision a fun, lighthearted environment. People are cooperative and open to change. Creativity and enthusiasm flow freely. There is a focus on learning, teaching, and success for all students. Such an environment is possible only in a culture of trust, and research suggests that the primary barriers to achieving it are fear and betrayal. Three other barriers to trust are also important—the carousel of leadership, adversarial relationships between unions and school leadership, and inappropriate staff development. Understanding all of these barriers will lead to an understanding of the causes, evidence, and consequences of distrust. Realize as well that in most cases more than one of these barriers is in place at a time, making the challenge of dismantling them even more difficult.

Research suggests that there are two primary barriers to achieving trust: fear and betrayal.

Fear

Fear is an aggressive predator of joy and creativity in the workplace.

—Terrence Deal and M. K. Key

Let's think about the different ways any of us can feel afraid in our workplace. Often our fear has to do with our own insecurities. Will we measure up? Can we meet expectations? This type of fear may be caused by change—in the curriculum, in our job description, in the arrival of a new boss. Some of our fears may have to do with an historical pattern we've experienced: leaders or colleagues who are intimidating, harassing, or bullying; a union representative who maintains an adversarial relationship with management; a school environment that is unsafe physically. Whatever the cause of the fear, it can stand in the way of trust.

When the source of people's fear is someone else, they begin any exchange with that person from a position of distrust. According to Kathleen Ryan and Daniel Oestreich (1998), each side assumes that the other operates from a philosophy of self-interest, and each side is expected to try to achieve its self-interest at the expense of the other party.

There are many specific causes of fear in the school or workplace:

- An overemphasis on (or obsession with) data and accountability exists, leading to fear of being compared with other teachers and schools and vulnerability.
- An atmosphere of secrecy prevails, and information necessary to do the job well is withheld.
- Certain people use rude, degrading reprimands or intimidating gestures.
- Safety procedures are inadequate.
- Inappropriate or ineffective student discipline is the norm, including the nonreporting of serious events to the police.
- The interview and promotion process is intimidating, and the performance appraisal system is arbitrary.
- Changes have caused huge upheavals in curriculum and assessment.
- New colleagues or administrators show a lack of respect for the current culture by taking everything back to zero and starting all over again.

- Power and control are wielded by a few at the top, and the skills and talents of staff members are underutilized.
- There is a history of tolerance for adult bullying. Adult bullies, whether they are supervisors, parents, or co-workers, use fear tactics in the workplace that include yelling, shaming, threatening, intimidating, silencing, and verbally abusing others.

Sometimes these behaviors are both the cause and result of fear.

The Fear of Speaking Up

Apart from being afraid of negative repercussions like embarrassment, harassment, and intimidation, people may also fear that discussions of the performance, competence, or ethical behavior of others may lead to conflict or cause trouble, either for themselves or others. For them, the risk is not worth it, particularly if there has been a pattern of tolerance of incompetence or if revelations have achieved very little in the past. It is the rare professional who has the courage to speak up when facing these day-to-day difficulties.

Hargreaves (2002) talks about teachers having difficulty dealing with conflict because they want to be polite. This reduces teachers' capacity to work through differences and learn from disagreement. Facing conflict and airing disagreement within a profession involve significant risks. Conflict is more likely to be risked when underlying trust already exists.

Even when speaking up about issues seems like the obvious solution, fear often prevents it. These issues are like secrets that everyone knows but no one will confront. Chris Argyris, an organizational theorist from Harvard, calls them the "undiscussables"—the problems or issues that people hesitate to talk about with those who are essential to its resolution. The fear of talking about fear, Argyris says, creates "self-sealing" environments where defensiveness proliferates, because people cannot talk about what they cannot talk about (as cited in Ryan & Oestreich, 1998, p. 77).

Sensitivity is needed to read the warning signs and be on the lookout for evidence of fear. Watch for instances when colleagues exhibit the following behaviors:

- People don't speak up when they are invited to, don't ask obvious questions, or are reluctant to share information.
- People lie or are silent to avoid any awkward subjects and are unenthusiastic.
- Staff are compliant and never question decisions.
- Staff members discuss critical issues in the parking lot, washroom, or hallway, instead of at a meeting.
- An "us vs. them" mentality prevails between the staff and leaders.

If left unattended, issues of fear can have severe consequences, such as:

- Anger and anxiety
- Negativity, cynicism, and a feeling of powerlessness

> Even when speaking up about issues seems like the obvious solution, fear often prevents it.

> "The greater the amount of change and the faster the rate of change, the greater the chance for fear and cynicism to grow."
>
> —Kathleen D. Ryan and Daniel K. Oestreich

- Weakened motivation
- A collection of undiscussables, coupled with an active rumor mill
- Depleted productivity and innovation

All of this encourages a workplace filled with low morale and competition, which stand in the way of any chance of creating a joyful atmosphere where creativity, pride, collaboration, and teamwork flourish.

Betrayal

"Research within organizations has shown that trust violations stifle mutual support and information sharing, and even exert negative effects on organizational citizenship behaviors, job performance, turnover, and profits. The emotional reaction is likely to be composed of some mixture of anger, disappointment, and/or frustration at oneself for trusting and at the offender for exploiting that trust."

—Roy Lewicki and Edward Tomlinson

Andy Hargreaves is credited with focusing educators' attention on prior experiences of betrayal as a specific barrier to trust formation. In his 2002 article, "Teaching and Betrayal," he helps educators understand the existence and effects of betrayal in teaching. According to Hargreaves, betrayal is significant not only in a moral sense, but also because it leads teachers to avoid conflict and interaction with each other and to thereby insulate themselves from opportunities for learning and constructive disagreement.

Much of Hargreaves' 2002 educational study is based on the research of Dennis and Michelle Reina and their book *Trust and Betrayal in the Workplace*. According to Reina and Reina (1998), "Betrayal is the intentional or unintentional breach of trust or the perception of such a breach" (p. 397). It does not have to happen on a large scale. In fact, most betrayals could be characterized as minor and incidental—a failure to fulfill a commitment to supervise a student activity, a breach of a confidence, a meeting that is conducted without a clear agenda. In and of itself, each act may be innocuous or very minor; however, it is often in the accumulation of such acts that the sense of betrayal can take hold and a crisis of trust occur.

Reina and Reina use a betrayal continuum from major to minor and add a distinction between major intentional betrayal such as sabotaging data systems and major unintentional betrayal such as delegating without giving authority (Reina & Reina, 2006). This paradigm might be pictured as in table 1.1.

Table 1.1: Major, Minor, Intentional, and Unintentional Betrayal

	Intentional	**Unintentional**
Major Betrayal	Sabotaging data	Delegating without giving authority
Minor Betrayal	Gossiping	Arriving late for work

It is not just the big things that break trust. Minor and unintentional acts like arriving late for work can break trust when they begin to add up! More significant is a minor intentional betrayal like gossiping.

Gossip

Nine out of ten people experience gossip and backbiting in the workplace. It is the number one destroyer of Communication Trust.

—Dennis and Michelle Reina

It is natural to talk about other people in our daily conversations. When the type of talk becomes malicious, it results in hurtful gossip. Although considered a minor violation, gossip is frequently mentioned by teachers as a concern that can seriously damage collegial relationships. Reina and Reina, as cited by Hargreaves (2002) write:

> Gossip is a strategy people use to achieve status, importance and access to information in cultures or organizations where they do not have access to official channels of involvement and decision-making. . . . While gossip can be an indicator of powerlessness in an individual or organization, it can have disastrous effects on trust among members of the organization as it breaches confidences, twists the truth and discloses information in secretive and suspect ways. (p. 400)

Public Betrayal

Variables that contribute to the severity of betrayal include whether the incident was in public, and therefore more embarrassing, or in private, where fewer people were aware of what happened. Was an apology offered or not? Did the regret expressed seem sincere? Was it a one-time event or a frequent pattern of behavior? Is there any mutual willingness to work on a solution? Betrayal that happens to someone in public is always more humiliating and harder to deal with.

As Hargreaves states, betrayal through shaming is always emotionally disturbing and even sometimes traumatic:

> Shame makes people feel naked, exposed, transparent, and vulnerable in front of others. The pain of shame and humiliation is especially severe when the others who witness it are one's most highly valuable associates or superiors. . . . In education, feelings of shame and the associated senses of hopelessness and helplessness among teachers have been reported in vertical contexts of intrusive, high-stakes inspection and accountability processes and authoritarian leadership styles. (2002, p. 401)

Misunderstandings are another factor in feelings of betrayal. Mistaken perceptions of an intended message or concern over the motive and intent, rather than the message itself, can lead to hurt feelings and tension.

Consider if these causes of betrayal are part of your workplace:

- Fraudulent, dishonest behavior
- Broken confidentiality
- Credit taken for someone else's work
- Failure to meet commitments or keep promises

"After intense or repeated experiences of betrayal, teachers tend to withdraw to their own classrooms, stay away from difficult colleagues, avoid interaction with them, and distance themselves psychologically from what they are experiencing."

—Andy Hargreaves

- Destructive gossip or negative stories, betrayal of secrets and private information
- Lack of acknowledgement or reward for efforts
- Negative memories, reprimands—real or perceived
- Unsubstantiated lack of success in promotion to leadership position
- Rejection, ridicule, disrespect, public shaming

Look for this specific evidence of betrayal:

- Spinning the truth rather than telling it like it is
- Refusal to disclose facts or feelings leaving people "out of the loop" or lacking information
- Decreased cooperation and lack of productive teamwork
- Increased cynicism

The consequences of betrayal can be devastating. Some people transfer to another school. The ones who stay volunteer less and retreat into their workrooms and classrooms. Positive energy is depleted in the school and replaced with bitterness, anxiety, and even spiteful actions. There is no fun, no joy, and no laughter.

The Carousel of Leadership, or "This Too Shall Pass"

In Boards where principals change schools frequently, teachers know that with just a little persistence and tenacity they can easily outlast the administrative interloper in their midst.

—Andy Hargreaves

When schools experience a rapid succession of leaders, the chances of any trust-building and continuity are slim. In their book *Sustainable Leadership,* Hargreaves and Fink (2006) describe a school whose staff had become very cynical, because they had worked for four principals in six years. This pattern of rapid change of leadership is becoming increasingly common. Hargreaves and Fink strongly recommend that all districts and school improvement plans include succession plans and that they slow down the rate of changing leadership, so that teachers do not cynically decide to wait out all their leaders.

Adversarial Relationships: Unions and School Leadership

One of the main reasons unions exist is that there have been repeated breaches of trust in the past. Unions protect their members from unfair management practices and bargain with school districts for salary and benefits. Teacher unions are also involved in high-quality professional development and curriculum design as well as school safety and working conditions. In trusting learning communities, union representatives are included as integral members of the school team.

In other instances, teachers feel that union stewards have overstepped their mandate and taken on a "co-manager" role in direct competition with administrators. While some see this as a natural role for unions to play, it can create angry confrontations, tense political environments, and adversarial relationships. In some cases, unions have been accused of protecting incompetent teachers. There is confusion in the school about who is in charge. Grievances may result in time taken away from a focus on student learning, and the threat of sanctions such as strikes may hover in the air. All of these factors can contribute to a mood of distrust.

Some new teachers report confusion when they are subversively "wooed" by the union representative as they enter their first school. Some don't succumb to the pressure. To them it seems like they have to choose between the two sides—loyalty to the union or loyalty to the principal. A staff cannot build trust with these divisions.

Beyond the school itself, complex political forces are at play during the negotiations of contracts for large groups of teachers. Ken Leithwood, a professor at the Ontario Institute for Studies in Education, had this to say about the effects on a school staff (2006):

> When union-government relationships break down, many teachers experience considerable ambiguity about the direction of their improvement efforts and considerable erosion of their trust in the motives of policy makers and administrators. Such ambiguity and mistrust reduces teachers' organizational commitment and morale, increases teachers' levels of stress, potentially challenges their sense of efficacy, and raises questions about continuing in the professions, especially when the public interprets such troubled relationships as intransigency on the part of teachers. (p. 83)

Inappropriate Staff Development

In spite of the wealth of information and research about the importance of choice and ownership in staff development and professional learning, it is still all too common to find teachers and administrators forced to endure a kind of forced feeding in their learning. Too often staffs have regarded new initiatives begun without their consultation as bandwagons to be endured, without any lasting effect on staff or student learning. When there is no involvement in the planning and delivery, educators rebel and become angry and defiant. Sometimes they even sabotage the efforts of other staff members. They certainly don't support a trusting and collaborative environment.

Improving a Distrustful Situation

Current literature often proposes firing incompetent staff or even outspoken and disruptive personalities as a remedy for the role they play in fostering low trust. While this may have some immediate appeal, realistically it is not a viable choice. Rather than eliminate a problematic staff member (who could be the principal!), we need to give individuals a chance to build

In trusting learning communities, union representatives are included as integral members of the school team.

"If schools are going to become stronger professional learning communities, they must seek not only to establish trust in teaching, but also to avoid the causes of pervasive betrayal and other causes of distrust."

—Andy Hargreaves

a professional growth plan and talk about their experiences, feelings, and opinions about teaching and learning. Application of district review and dismissal policies may be the necessary end result for an incompetent staff member, but I believe many steps can be taken before this.

While it is true that in certain extreme situations trust is lost forever, in most cases, lost trust can be restored. You can be proactive. It takes courage and may be difficult, but it is worth the effort to get relationships back on track. Amazingly, once there is a desire to confront distrust, improvements can come quickly.

When we face issues of distrust, we sometimes need to change our perspective and see the barriers as "walls to be breached," as Coral Mitchell and Larry Sackney put it (2000, p. 79). Sometimes a wall of distrust that seems to be made from bricks ends up being only paper-thin, almost as if it were an imaginary wall in the first place. We need to be careful not to confuse disappointment with betrayal. Disappointments are to be expected in relationships. But betrayal is much more serious. It is an intentional, harmful act. We must also be careful not to make the assumption that failure and betrayal are synonymous. As Megan Tschannen-Moran (2004) writes, "to confuse failure with betrayal is to set yourself up for no creativity, no innovation, no adventure, no intimacy, no trust, no life at all" (p. 130).

> "While restoring trust may take time, both establishing and extending trust can be exceptionally quick."
>
> —Stephen M. R. Covey

Behaviors That Can Rebuild and Repair Trust

Violations of trust alter the glue that holds a relationship together. It is usually a significant event that suggests that the relationship is in trouble. Feelings of anger, frustration, fear, and hurt are all experienced in a swirling sea of emotions. There are three possible outcomes: termination of the relationship, renegotiation of the relationship, or the restoration of it to its original state. If termination of the relationship isn't possible, then sometimes just a shell of it remains.

Here are some questions and principles to keep in mind when seeking to repair trust:

- If the incident was public, more people may need to be involved in the solution.
- It matters whether the incident was inadvertent or intentional.
- An apology or atonement is the most difficult step in repairing trust.
- Apologies are always a good thing.
- Sincerity is a factor, as well as timing.
- It is more difficult to rebuild trust once it is damaged in a mature relationship.
- Trust repair is a bilateral process.

When seeking to repair trust, go back and look at the type of trust that was violated. What stage was the trust in before it was violated? It is easier to rebuild trust in its early stages. People are disappointed but not deeply grieved. The attitude is "Well, you win some, you lose some." If the trust had been developing for some time, people start to question their own perceptions of the situation. There's less willingness to trust again and more tentativeness. For relationships that are well established, a violation can be seen as a transforming event that rips the fabric of the relationship and requires significant reweaving. This is time-consuming and can be very expensive. At this level, the parties involved must answer these questions:

- Do I have the energy?
- Is it worth it to try?
- Are there alternatives?

What Does Trust Repair Do?

According to Lewicki, trust repair accomplishes the following:

- Speaks to the importance of the relationship
- Owns responsibility for the violation
- Provides an account/explanation
- Rebalances the power relationship
- Reduces uncertainty about others' ability, benevolence, integrity (2006, p. 12)

Figure 1.2 shows Lewicki's diagram of the stages of trust repair after a violation of trust.

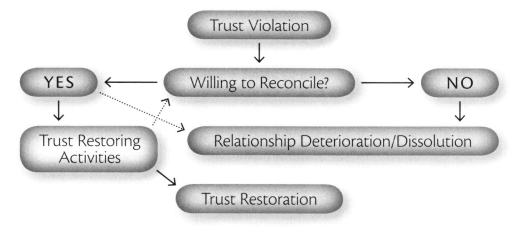

Figure 1.2: Trust repair after a violation

Adapted from Roy J. Lewicki's Trust Development Model. Used with permission of Roy. J. Lewicki.

Lewicki notes that:

- Smaller trust violations can be more easily resolved than bigger ones.
- Apologies are more effective:
  - If the violator takes responsibility rather than displaces the responsibility
  - When conveyed sincerely

- When conveyed quickly
- If the parties involved have had a violation-free history
- When the parties expect a violation-free future (2006, p. 16)

Distrust is common in many schools, or parts of many schools. Whenever we experience fear and betrayal in relationships, even at work, it is hard to trust again. Fear of being duped, feelings of suspicion about all new relationships, and wariness of ever opening up and being vulnerable again—these are all to be expected. But to solve problems and become better for the sake of the students, we need one another, and that shared community working together is worth the risk. Barack Obama wrote about this same principle as it applies to politics in his book *The Audacity of Hope* (2006):

> I understood the skepticism, but that there was—and always had been—another tradition to politics, a tradition that stretched from the days of the country's founding to the glory of the civil rights movement, a tradition based on the simple idea that we have a stake in one another, and that what binds us together is greater than what drives us apart, and that if enough people believe in the truth of the proposition and act on it, then we might not solve every problem, but we can get something meaningful done. (p. 2)

Key Messages

1. Distrust is a substantial barrier to productive relationships and learning in schools.
2. The cynicism found in society plays itself out in schools and classrooms.
3. Lateral trust between colleagues is as important as vertical trust in leaders.
4. The web of distrust in schools is complicated and often based on deep suspicion, negative stereotypes, and inaccurate assumptions.
5. Distrust can be both valuable and dysfunctional.
6. True learning communities are not possible in distrusting cultures.
7. The five main barriers to trust in schools are fear, betrayal, frequently changing leadership, inappropriate staff development, and adversarial relationships between unions and school leadership.
8. There is hope for raising the levels of trust in a school and directly dealing with distrust.

Questions

1. Which barriers to trust have you personally experienced?
2. How has cynicism affected the trust level in your relationships at work?
3. Do you believe lateral trust among colleagues is as important as vertical trust of leaders? Does lateral trust matter that much?

4. Describe a situation where a colleague has earned your distrust.

5. Where would you place your work environment on the Trust-Distrust Scale? Where are you? Where is your school?

6. Can you ever think of a time when distrust was a good thing at work?

7. Do you agree that trust is a process and not a state? Does it follow that distrust is a process and not a state as well?

8. Have you experienced the fear of speaking up about an issue? Why were you afraid? Afterward, did you regret not speaking up?

9. Do you think educators try to be polite and avoid conflict more than other professionals?

10. Are you hopeful that adversarial relationships between some union representatives and some administrators and teachers can improve and be more collaborative? How important is this barrier to trust?

VIPs

Take time and reflect on the Very Important Points you feel were made in this chapter. What resonated with you the most?

Visit **go.solution-tree.com/leadership** to download and print the resources and activities discussed in this book.

Lower-Risk Strategies to Deal With Distrust

The behaviors that build trust vary depending on the stage of the relationship.

—Julie Reed Kochanek

Having looked at distrust, we turn our focus now to what to do if barriers to trust exist in your school. What strategies and activities can you use or adapt for your particular situation? This will be an evolving, learning process for everyone.

Readers of this book will approach trust building from different perspectives:

- You may have a gut feeling that all is not well and that people aren't trusting.

- You may be a new leader to a school inheriting a culture of distrust.

- You may be examining whether trust is a key factor in your situation. Maybe it is laziness, incompetence, or something other than trust. You may be wondering if you yourself must take partial responsibility for the low trust in the first place.

In the worst-case scenario, you have concrete evidence of sabotage and fear and betrayal in a toxic environment to confront.

The stage first needs to be set with lower-risk activities that will acknowledge the distrust and invite people to collaboratively plan how to build trust together. This may slow down the speed you would like to work at to attain the progress you want.

Many innovations fail because deeper, higher-risk implementation strategies are demanded of people who don't know each other well, let alone trust each other. One of the best ways to ensure failure is to ask people who don't trust each other to become involved in an activity that is high risk. For example, an activity to develop or revise a school mission or vision scenario may be received with a high degree of suspicion and resistance when there is low trust. Very often, high-risk strategies are initiated too early and have little chance of success.

In order to increase trust, capacity for growth must be built both at the personal and interpersonal levels with small and large groups within the organization. To reflect this, the strategies in this book have been structured in two groups, personal and interpersonal. For each strategy there are hundreds of potential activities you can use; the ones presented here will help you start to approach the issue of distrust in your school.

Above all, do no more harm. There are no quick fixes in dealing with distrust. It won't be easy, but it will be worth it. Do not make these strategies another example of inappropriate staff development in which staff have no choice and are asked for buy in without adequate research and conversation. Take the time to let people work through the process.

> One of the best ways to ensure failure is to ask people who don't trust each other to become involved in an activity that is high risk.

What Are Personal Capacity Strategies?

If at all possible, personal reflection needs to take place before interpersonal work, so that so you can decide what role you played in creating the distrustful environment. There will be many personal insights as groups gain insight into and ownership of their culture of distrust, but starting with yourself will give you time for valuable introspection.

The personal strategies at the distrust level will build your own capacity and understanding of distrust issues as you react to and reflect on the findings. Some readers may feel that these personal strategies are too much like self-help fads they have run across, but you skip them at your own peril. If you seriously want to improve trust, you *must* start with yourself. You may find that even after you have started focusing on the interpersonal strategies, you are still focusing on yourself and your personal trust issues. Building trust is an ongoing process, and each person has to find his or her own path.

What Are Interpersonal Capacity Strategies?

The interpersonal strategies and suggested activities are intended for small or large groups. Decide if you can facilitate the activity yourself or require a third party to help you. You may want to be the facilitator if you feel confident in your skills to do this and if the discussion will not involve the quality of your leadership. You may want to share this role with a facilitation team, which will allow you to dialogue with staff members as a member, but not the most important member, of that group. Or you may feel you are part of the problem and need to step aside and listen.

In most cases, strategies will be initiated by the formal group leader, although it is possible, though less usual, for a member of a group to suggest a strategy to the formal leader and facilitate the process.

The Wheel of Change

This continuous growth process goes through stages over time and lasts for months and sometimes even years. Progress will be experienced as steps forward, although sometimes you will experience regression. This is the wheel of change—both within yourself and the group. Think of this wheel as having five spokes, as shown in figure 2.1:

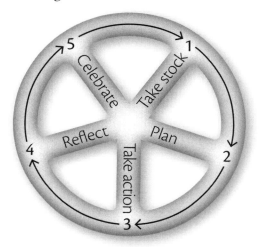

Figure 2.1: The continuous growth process depicted as a wheel

1. **Take stock** of the current situation by talking about it.
2. **Plan** the next step in the process by getting agreement from the group.
3. **Take action** to move the process forward and build toward success.
4. **Reflect** on how well the action you decided on actually turned out. Did you make progress or not? Consolidate what you learned from doing this.
5. **Celebrate** for even trying something new. Start the process again with planning next steps.

Beware of overplanning. It's very easy to get so involved with planning that nothing ever gets done. Avoid "paralysis by analysis" by regularly asking the group about its sense of progress. Make sure that you listen carefully to the answers. In groups that lack trust, overplanning can exacerbate cynicism.

The very same strategy can be highly effective and move a group forward in one situation and yet fail or become a destructive force in a different situation. In cases of deep distrust, outcomes are highly unpredictable and reactions often volatile.

Remember that group strategies vary in effectiveness depending on the group. In my years of working within schools, I have found that the very same strategy can be highly effective and move a group forward in one situation and yet fail or become a destructive force in a different situation. In cases of deep distrust, outcomes are highly unpredictable and reactions often volatile. Careful preplanning is necessary to increase the chances of success.

Another thing to keep in mind is that even the clearest instructions often have several interpretations. All of the strategies work under the following conditions:

- The conditions are right.
- The leadership is supportive.
- The staff feels ownership.
- Their feelings are listened to.
- There is a long-term plan.
- Things start to change.

None of the strategies work under these conditions:

- There is a failure to confront.
- The conditions are too toxic.
- They are seen as a quick fix.
- It is done to people rather than with them.
- There is sabotage.
- The administration isn't involved.
- Things stay the same after all.

Start cautiously. Don't wait too long.

Worth Remembering

According to Edgar Dale (1969), we learn about:

- 10 percent of what we read
- 20 percent of what we hear
- 30 percent of what we see
- 50 percent of what we see and hear
- 70 percent of what we discuss
- 80 percent of what we experience
- 95 percent of what we teach others

As you can see, learning must be discussed, experienced, and shared. That is the rationale behind the strategies in this book—discuss and share what you read here, and it will have a far greater impact!

Personal Capacity Strategies

We will be looking at two personal capacity strategies at this stage, each with two activities:

1. Face your fears.
2. Ask for feedback.

Face Your Fears

Facing your own fear and talking about it is a therapeutic first step in making progress. If you are starting a new group, it is natural to be anxious about getting off to a positive start. A lot of energy and planning go into forming new groups. That is stressful in itself. You may fear criticism and rejection if you open up a discussion of these issues. The fear or anxiety you are experiencing might also be a fear of change itself. It is natural to feel uncomfortable or insecure in this situation. A very useful book on this topic is *Feel the Fear and Do It Anyway* (1988), by Susan Jeffers. She writes, "At the bottom of every one of your fears is simply the fear that you can't handle whatever life may bring you" (p. 7). You need to try to shift your thinking from "I can't do this" to "I can handle it." This growth process, in some cases, will be long and tough. Following are two activities to help you start to make the shift.

Make a Pain-to-Power Chart

Fear can be a powerful source of pain. The distress and hurt that result can seem like a jumbled mixture of emotions if unexamined. By gaining the clarity that comes from making the Pain-to-Power Chart, you will be motivated to take action.

Jeffers suggests these steps to help you start (Jeffers, 1988):

1. Take out a piece of paper and map out what the sources of fear are for you. Draw figure 2.2 in the center of the page:

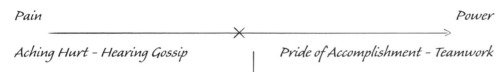

The bearers of fear will always be there to tell you it's impossible. The professional dream-exterminators will try to kill your dream.—Jack Canfield

Take the first step. The bridge will be there.—Betty Hill Crowson

I learned that courage was not the absence of fear, but the triumph over it. The brave man is not he who does not feel afraid, but he who conquers that fear.—Nelson Mandela

Figure 2.2: Pain-to-power chart

2. On the left side, list the painful feelings you've experienced and their causes, such as "aching hurt/hearing gossip." On the right side, note positive powerful feelings and their causes, such as "pride of accomplishment/real teamwork."

3. Write some motivating quotations, like these, on the page:

    · "The best way out is through."—Helen Keller

    · "The joy is in the journey."—Betty Hill Crowson

    · "Courage is not freedom from fear. It's being afraid and going on anyway."—Anonymous

4. Mark an *X* on the Pain-to-Power line to indicate where your current level of fear lies.

As the days and weeks go by, reflect on what has caused the mark to move forward or backward along the line. For example, a step forward comes when you face your fears about raising an important issue at a meeting that you have wanted to mention for a long time. Other people agree with you that your issue has merit. You feel more confident to do more of this.

Don't forget to use your mistakes as learning experiences. Write reflections on this page. As time goes on, the Pain-to-Power Chart may even become the basis for a journal.

As you use the chart, look for shifts in attitude such as these:

• From "It's a problem" to "It's an opportunity"

• From "Life's a struggle" to "Life's an adventure"

What attitude shifts would you add to this list?

Dialogue With a Trusted Colleague

Now that you've personally reflected on your fears, sit down with a trusted friend, colleague, or mentor and talk about what you are afraid of in your current situation. Most likely, you are describing it from the viewpoint of the pain. Jeffers (1998) says we need to shift this thinking from pain to power. Here are some examples of what that shift looks like:

Pain	Power
helplessness	choice
depression	energy
paralysis	action

(Jeffers, 1989, p. 26)

Identify Your Realm of Control

The Serenity Prayer offers a useful perspective in the face of fear:

Grant me the serenity to accept the things I cannot change,
The courage to change the things I can,
And the wisdom to know the difference.

(Anonymous)

What do you think you can change? That is, what is within your control or sphere of influence? Are you afraid of things that you cannot change? Are there aspects of the problem that you could change on your own or with some help from outside? Do you have the courage to?

What Now?

After taking the time for this reflection about your fears, you need to make a decision about whether or not you can proceed. It can be very uncomfortable to identify and face your fears head on. Talking with a close friend always helps to get some perspective. If your fears and anxiety are deeply embedded in the past and are stressful, you may want to get professional help.

If you believe that the fears are manageable, proceed with the next steps, which involve reaching out to others for feedback about your leadership.

Ask for Feedback

The next step is to get some reliable feedback about yourself. This feedback process has two levels: self-reflection and feedback from the staff.

As scary as it may seem, getting feedback about yourself is a powerful step to finding out the reality of your situation as you begin to build trust. You need to check any assumptions you have about how much your group actually trusts you. Your intuition may be right, but until you find out for sure, you don't know where you really stand.

Megan Tschannen-Moran, author of *Trust Matters*, cautions that the results could be hard to take:

> Principals have described feeling hurt and disappointed, even like they have been "kicked in the stomach," on receiving results that reveal a lack of trust in their leadership. Teachers may have similar feelings. It is important not to lash out in reaction to this perceived insult but to seek to understand the perceptions and feelings that are revealed on the surveys. If you don't want to know the truth, don't administer the surveys in the first place. . . . Suppressing negative results will only lead to greater distrust, so do not administer the surveys if you do not intend to share the results with those who offered their opinions. (Tschannen-Moran, 2004, p. 208)

You will eventually want to get some feedback from the whole group about how much they trust each other. This step will be described in the Interpersonal Capacity Strategies (page 37). But to ensure future buy-in, take the first step yourself, and show everyone that you are willing to do this, too.

Self-Reflect: Feedback, Not Failure

The first level involves being honest with yourself and entering into a process requiring some serious soul searching. View this step as feedback, not failure. Read the statements, and rate yourself from one (never) to

"Broken trust presents an opportunity for you to make huge leaps in building your own self-trust and personal credibility. You will grow in character and competence."

—Stephen M. R. Covey

Activity

ten (always). Table 2.1 will get you started. What conclusions can you draw? How would other people answer these questions about you?

Table 2.1: My Reflections

My Reflections	1	2	3	4	5	6	7	8	9	10
	NEVER								ALWAYS	
I am predictable (not erratic).										
I communicate clearly (not carelessly).										
I treat promises seriously (not lightly).										
I am forthright (not dishonest).										

Visit **go.solution-tree .com/leadership** to download and print My Reflections.

Adapted from *Credibility: How Leaders Gain and Lose It, Why People Demand It.* Revised Ed., by James M. Kouzes and Barry Z. Posner. Copyright © 2003. Reproduced with permission of John Wiley & Sons, Inc.

Now use the additional statements shown in the reproducible Leader Self-Assessment (page 208) to challenge or confirm the responses you gave here.

Ask Your Staff for Feedback

The next step is to go to the whole staff for feedback. This step needs to be carefully planned and sensitively introduced to ensure that both the process and the results are meaningful. As Megan Tschannen-Moran (n.d.) reminds us, "The study of trust has been likened to the study of the roots of a delicate plant. Without great care, the examination can damage or even destroy the very thing about which greater understanding is sought."

This type of feedback helps you solve what has been termed the *IDKWIS problem.* This acronym refers to the feeling of being in the dark about how we are seen by our colleagues and staff members. IDKWIS is like a chemical formula:

NETMA + NEAMO + INA = IDKWIS

NETMA (Nobody ever tells me anything.)

NEAMO (Nobody ever asks my opinion.)

INA (I never ask.)

IDKWIS (I don't know where I stand.)

(Jones & Bearley, 1996, p. 9)

Anonymity and Confidentiality

These two issues generally create more concern for research participants than any other. Anonymity is the right of persons to remain unidentifiable in all forms of response, and confidentiality is the obligation to keep information that has been collected from being inappropriately shared with others. An essential part of the research protocol is to protect the privacy of participants and provide adequate means for confidential research response.

Fostering and promoting the sense of confidentiality and anonymity requires taking reasonable steps in regard to collecting, storing, and collating data. While viewed by some as making things more difficult, technology can offer ways of promoting a sense of confidential response and enabling participation rates.

Web-based survey applications, through a common and open access link, provide a level of anonymity beyond that of a paper survey. Some data collection procedures collect the IP address of the computer the data was sent from, but it is usually difficult and impractical to match that address with any one individual. If participants share a common computer or access site, it would be particularly difficult to identify the individual respondents. People are also more likely to complete electronic surveys, because they eliminate the fear of handwriting identification.

In all circumstances, promote participation as voluntary. Any measure that can be taken to foster both anonymity and confidentiality, and the belief in it by the respondents, is key to the success of the process. I know this from my own experience. As a rookie vice principal, I decided to get some feedback about my leadership, especially about how trustworthy I was regarded by the teachers. I chose to give a survey to staff members during a parent-teacher interview night, when everyone was assembled in the school cafeteria. To ensure that I didn't miss anyone, I wrote each person's name in pencil on the envelopes containing their surveys. To my surprise, those little innocent pencil marks caused some of the staff to think that this was my way of tracking the responses. The next day I heard about this suspicion through the grapevine and tried to resolve it, but matters only got worse from there. This well-intentioned yet naïve gesture on my part to get some feedback taught me that anonymity is of utmost importance. While I did receive some useful information from that survey, I jeopardized and diminished my results by the method I chose to use for distributing the surveys in the first place.

Third-Party Assistance

Enlist the help of a neutral third party who will meet with your group and work through the feedback process for you. This person will assist you in administering the survey, collaboratively score, review, and summarize the results, and assist in developing a plan for the sharing of information back to the staff. Sharing the results will in itself demonstrate integrity and commitment to the process and provide a foundation that will begin to build trust.

An essential part of the research protocol is to protect the privacy of participants and provide adequate means for confidential research response.

"The moment there is suspicion about a person's motives, everything he does becomes tainted."

—Mahatma Gandhi

Here are some further tips for implementation success:

- If possible, consider using web-based survey software for this feedback process. By using a web-based link on a common site, participants may feel a greater level of anonymity in responding honestly to the questions. Most survey programs allow for multiple-choice formats as well as open-text commentary, and some also provide a data summary at the completion of the survey.

- Tell the participants that the purpose of the survey is your own professional growth. Acknowledge that you feel you are venturing into unknown territory.

- Ask them to be honest. Explain that asking for personal feedback is your first step with them. Based on the results, you will be inviting them to join you in the planning and implementation of other strategies for building or rebuilding trust together in the whole group.

- Emphasize that participation in the survey is voluntary, but that the greater the participation, the more "valid" the results will be.

- Ensure anonymity and promise confidentiality. There must be no way to trace the results back to anyone. If surveys are completed in paper format, providing a neutral and secure drop-off box for the completed forms will foster confidence in the anonymity of the responses.

- Offer the survey to everyone on staff. If you select certain individuals, you can be sure the word will get around, and there may be suspicion about why the others weren't included. This is not a good way to start building trust.

- Tell participants they can skip questions that they are uncomfortable with.

For the first stage of the feedback process, consider the Staff Feedback About Leader questions (page 209). Visit **go.solution-tree.com/leadership** to download and print this survey. Note the similarity of these questions to those of My Reflections (page 32).

You may want to develop your own questions. Keep in mind that it takes time and skill to get the right questions to elicit useful feedback.

Anecdotal Commentary

In addition to the questions requiring responses on a six-point scale, you might also consider asking for anecdotal commentary. Ask participants for the following:

- Three strengths, three concerns, and three possible actions with regard to how the leader builds trust with teachers and staff

- Five words that describe the current culture of the school

Include a section after the questions for general comments.

The Results

Better the devil you know, than the devil you don't.

—English proverb

After the results are processed, you will have a clearer idea of the issues and will need to come to some conclusions and prepare for how and when to share these with the staff who participated.

Numeric scores are faster to tabulate, but anecdotal comments take more time. Try to group responses under four or five categories or headings. To ensure that this is a trustworthy process, capture exact phrasing from participants rather than paraphrasing or condensing. People will be looking for their own comments in the results.

Try to identify three to five things you are doing well and five to seven things you could do differently to lessen distrust and build more trust. In addition to the positive and negative attributes, also look for "action" suggestions from the respondents that are specifically noteworthy—as well as possible. These may be organized on a scale from easier-to-accomplish to more-time-consuming-and-difficult-to-achieve.

You may decide that you need more than one meeting to share the results. Presenting the information through a series of meetings may allow the staff to more carefully review the presentation, invite dialogue, and privately formulate questions for consideration at the next stage. The first meeting could be a factual sharing of the data you received. At the second, a week or so later, you can share your conclusions. You might also distribute the data in advance of the meeting, along with a copy of the intended agenda.

These will most likely be uncomfortable meetings for you, especially if the results of the staff survey are less than you expected. You could ask the third party who helped you to present the feedback or give the report, and then you could add your comments at the end of the session. Here is a suggested six-step process to follow:

> Capture exact phrasing from participants rather than paraphrasing or condensing. People will be looking for their own comments in the results.

1. Invite all of the participants to attend.

2. Start by thanking everyone for participating. This will reduce the awkwardness of the situation.

3. Give attendees an overview, explaining why you have asked for this feedback.

4. Tell them what you learned from it. Give people printed results after translating the overall score into these categories:

   -1 Distrust

   0 No trust

   +1 Early trust

   +2 Developing trust

   +3 Mature trust

5. Emphasize that this is an important part of your personal growth plan and that you will take the results seriously and think through their implications.

6. Suggest to the staff that they may want to use this process either for themselves as individuals or together. The participants will be more likely to participate and invite feedback about themselves in the future when they see how you model this process with grace and dignity.

This process will provide a lot of insights and some criticism. I have found the Seven Steps for Healing, as suggested by Reina and Reina (2006), to be helpful at this point in the process.

1. Observe and acknowledge what has happened. For healing to begin, you must acknowledge the loss.

2. Allow all feelings to surface. Honor emotions such as pain, anger, and confusion.

3. Get support. Support helps you shift from being "the victim" to taking responsibility for yourself, your job, and your life.

4. Reframe the experience. Consider the bigger picture and what you have learned.

5. Take responsibility. What part did you play? What actions can you take now?

6. Forgive yourself and others. Release yourself from the burden of carrying these feelings.

7. Let go and move on. Take action and put the experience behind you, looking forward rather than backward.

You could also survey students and parents. Refer to Megan Tschannen-Moran's website (www.megantm.com) for sample surveys about trust that she offers for use with these two groups.

After you have done this survey once, you can repeat it each year or at some suitable interval, such as a term or semester. If the staff trusts the process you used and you found it manageable to administer and assess, subsequent implementation will be a lot easier.

What Now?

With this feedback, you will identify your strengths and your stretches—where you intend to improve in trust areas. Encourage specific suggestions regarding what you do well and suggestions for what could be better. You may even pick up information about other leadership areas in addition to trust.

View this experience as a step in the process of gaining self-knowledge and building your self-confidence. From this experience, synthesize your key personal learnings, or trust reminders.

continued >

Adult learning is a continuous, lifelong process. Occasionally we need to stop, sit back, and just be proud of who we are and the progress we have made. Affirmations can be helpful when we need to be reminded of our own inner wisdom, strengths, and areas of growth. You should be proud of the progress you have made examining your capacity to grow and be appropriately trusting of others. This was a difficult beginning for you—more difficult than you thought it might be. Now it is time to apply your trust reminders to your interpersonal work. The learning process will continue as you share your thoughts with others and listen to their feelings and ideas.

Interpersonal Capacity Strategies

This section will discuss nine interpersonal capacity strategies. As with the personal capacity strategies, each will be followed by one or more activities designed to implement the strategy:

1. Start with student learning.
2. Build relationships one conversation at a time.
3. Involve a facilitation team.
4. Invite feedback on staff trust.
5. Give permission to have some fun.
6. Agree on norms of acceptable conduct.
7. Share personal stories.
8. Put the real issues "on the table."
9. Move from issues to actions.

Start With Student Learning

This first interpersonal strategy for use with other staff members focuses on beliefs about student learning. If you have not already shared your beliefs about student learning, now is the time. Talking about doing what is best for all children never fails to unite any group of educators.

But don't just talk about yourself. Invite teachers to be part of a dialogue about the reason they became teachers and why they choose to stay in this career.

This discussion will remain at the forefront of all planning from now on. It isn't a one-time event, but the beginning of uniting the staff around a common goal. Don't be tempted to go further by discussing a vision of success yet. Save this higher-risk strategy until there is greater trust and the staff is ready for it.

The sole purpose of the existence of schools is the education of students. Sometimes this seems to be forgotten in the busy day-to-day life of classrooms and schools. Now is the time to focus on your core purpose.

"By 1997, schools with strong positive trust reports had a one in two chance of being in the improving group. In contrast, the likelihood of improving for schools with very weak trust reports was only one in seven."

—Anthony Bryk and Barbara Schneider

I've Been Framed

This activity invites all staff to become very specific, with a tangible end product for each person. It was designed by Helen Evans when she was a principal in Toronto, Canada.

1. Open the activity by telling participants that trust is a key issue for all schools and that higher levels of trust can actually lead to increased achievement for students.

2. Ask staff to take a few moments to reflect on paper about their personal beliefs about student learning.

3. Ask them to include why they became teachers (or counselors or school secretaries, and so on).

4. Then ask them why they have chosen to stay in this career in a school.

5. In pairs and then in groups of two pairs, ask staff to share their responses and reactions to these questions. This is just a sharing period, without debate or question.

6. Invite staff to give any overall comments on the process and results.

7. As leader of the whole group, wait your turn and articulate your responses *after* others have had the floor. Everyone will be interested in your beliefs, but if you share yours first, your ideas may seem more important and others may feel the need to mimic you.

8. At the end of the discussion, give everyone ten to fifteen minutes to compose and display their beliefs on cardstock that could be framed in a small glass picture frame or a paper frame. Have marker pens handy. Ask participants to write each belief on a different card. They should use their own words but could also use symbols or graphics. (Participants usually produce about two or three cards each.) Invite staff to display these beliefs on their desks in their work areas, so they are always at the forefront. You should do this as well.

Save the "Vision Discussion" for Later

While these belief statements could form the basis of a vision scenario discussion, it is too early in the process to even mention the word *vision*. It can seem jargon-like and may be too risky for the group. Vision discussions focus on an optimistic, future-oriented description of a successful scenario for the students, the staff, and the system as a whole and serve as a future goal or endpoint in a process. Visions act like magnets, pulling us forward, but when the staff is still dealing with basic issues of trust, it is too early for a grand vision.

Many educators have found this to be a very powerful activity. They often report never having been asked what their own beliefs are in their careers. One individual said to me, "I never thought my beliefs were important. I thought they came from the central authorities. Now I know *my* beliefs are valued! How refreshing!"

> Visions act like magnets, pulling us forward, but when the staff is still dealing with basic issues of trust, it is too early for a grand vision.

Action Plans

Out of the I've Been Framed activity, specific areas of professional growth and staff development will start to become apparent. People may even say, "At this moment I don't know how I would make this become reality, but I still believe in it." It could spark the beginning of some mentoring of younger teachers by more experienced staff. Some very tough issues may be mentioned and put out on the table for discussion. Requests for help from outside the group or school may surface. These are all positive developments.

Here are some specific action plans that could emerge from this activity:

- Institute school ceremonies and rituals recognizing and celebrating student growth and achievement.

- Personally greet students and parents when they arrive in the morning.

- Pay more attention to those who seem unhappy by complimenting them or engaging them with a smile.

Whatever happens, focusing on children's needs brings out the best in everyone.

What Now?

As new initiatives continue to come from outside the school, the staff can now start to collectively ask, What does this have to do with students and learning? If the answer is hard to come up with, or even impossible, then the staff should possibly commit to more urgent plans. Staff members will begin to sense more of an overall purpose, revolving around doing what is best for students. This is the beginning of building trust with staff members and valuing their beliefs.

Build Relationships One Conversation at a Time

Now that the staff know more about each others' beliefs about student learning and realize that you are committed to this focus, you are ready to continue building relationships. We all need more opportunities to just be with each other and talk. You might begin with purely social activities with the goal of including more professional dialogue time at staff meetings and even in the staff room.

These conversations may not be easy for you. You may feel uncomfortable, but holding them communicates you are willing to improve the level of trust. Then, if you do something because of what you have heard, however small, it will show that you are listening.

Your conversations must include all staff—beginning teachers, veteran staff, even the weaker ones, and, yes, even those whom you know to be incompetent.

You will have to consider how supportive you are in your relationships. Do you share the leadership with others? Are your actions trustworthy?

Staff members will begin to sense there is more of an overall purpose, revolving around doing what is best for students. This is the beginning of building trust with staff members and valuing their beliefs.

As you turn your focus to the quality and kinds of relationships on your staff, you need to consider asking a few trusted staff to join with you as advisors as you plan each step and review its success. Although this idea is described in the strategy named Involve a Facilitation Team (page 43), you could start to mention it in conversation informally now. As Roland Barth writes, relationships have a huge impact on student learning:

> One incontrovertible finding emerges from my career spent working in and around schools: The nature of relationships among adults within a school has a greater influence on the character and quality of that school and on student accomplishment than anything else. If the relationships between administrators and teachers are trusting, generous, helpful and co-operative, then the relationships between teachers and students, between students and students, and between teachers and parents are likely to be trusting, generous, helpful and co-operative. If, on the other hand, relationships between administrators and teachers are fearful, competitive, suspicious and corrosive, then *these* qualities will disseminate throughout the school community. (2006, p. 8)

Revive Social Activities

Many schools report that their social activities are dwindling in numbers, and attendance is falling at activities that are held. Schools that used to have thriving social committees are having a hard time finding participants. These committees traditionally made sure that in some tangible way, the staff acknowledged colleagues who had a prolonged illness or lost a close family member. They also looked after the coffee in the staff room and planned parties and special occasion get-togethers for staff members—sometimes inviting spouses, partners, and children to attend. The diminishment or death of these committees reminds us of the loss of congeniality in schools. Perhaps we need to make an effort to resurrect them in whatever form works best for the organization.

Gather together staff members who play these social roles, either formally or informally, and talk with them about how these activities are going and how you can contribute to any needed improvements or enhancements.

Here are some discussion starters:

- What kind of purely social activities do we plan?
- Does the staff get together in smaller groups? Are these groups seen as cliques?
- Do we collect monetary contributions to cover the expenses?
- Has the principal ever contributed funds?
- What is the history of these events?
- Are social activities incorporated into staff meetings?
- What could we do to bring people together and give them a chance to get to know each other better and encourage conversation?

Although many of these activities are spontaneous and require no planning, here are some examples of organized social activities:

- Potluck dinners at the homes of staff members
- Bowling nights
- Holiday dinner dances
- Trivial Pursuit nights
- Soup in the staff room during winter lunchtimes

What activities could you add to this list?

Helen Evans, a principal colleague, shared with me one of her strategies for birthdays. For each staff member's birthday, one person had the responsibility of purchasing a birthday card and chocolate bar. All staff signed the card. A notice was put into the staff weekly bulletin. An alternative is to arrange for a large cake with candles to be delivered to the staff room each month, and those staff members who celebrate a birthday that month are honored at that point. When teachers are treated like competent professionals who are respected and cared for, they are more likely to treat each other with respect and personal regard.

A note of caution: Even when these plans are well intentioned and carefully thought out, they can backfire. For example, some plans may be offensive to certain cultures or ages, or a few staff members may not have paid their dues, and as a result no one knows whether to include them in schoolwide activities. In general, plan with sensitivity, and don't let the problems scuttle the enthusiasm and positive benefits.

> When teachers are treated like competent professionals who are respected and cared for, they are more likely to treat each other with respect and personal regard.

Listen, Learn, and Then Do Something Tangible

Listen carefully when staff are together socially to pick up ideas that will make a real difference. Here are two examples:

1. Provide some basic items in the staff room that will bring people there, such as a microwave oven, comfortable furniture, and a notice board for good news.

2. Design the front office to make it welcoming to staff, students, and parents.

As your interactions are repeated, trust will grow over time. Listening to others outside the workplace can ease their feelings of vulnerability and shyness.

Counsel New and Weak Teachers

Administrators need to begin to build trusting relationships and make connections with underachieving, weaker staff members. It takes considerable time to commit long term to helping improve the performance of the weaker staff. Offering your help in a coaching rather than an evaluative manner will build trust. This is easier said than done in most school boards. You may find that some teachers are very defensive about assistance from an administrator, because they fear professional embarrassment or even the loss of their job. Some of the current literature on trust in schools focuses on the principal's taking the definitive steps to fire and replace incompetent staff. But focusing on individual growth plans and providing assistance can often help teachers turn around their performance and save you from the lengthy process of documentation and review leading to dismissal. If this fails, then important discussions need to take place about the incompetent person's resigning or entering into a formal review process and leaving that way.

The needs of beginning teachers as well as any weak teachers have to be addressed. Focusing on these two groups will make the rest of the staff feel more trusting, because they will know you understand all students need the benefit of good teaching.

Share Leadership

If everybody is thinking the same, not much thinking is getting done.

—Madeline Hunter

One of the most effective ways to build trust is to invite staff members to share in the leadership and decision making of the school. However, in a situation of low trust, it is always a refreshing move to offer others a chance to speak up. Extend an invitation to those who may be seen as divisive on staff to share their views. Many times the angriest staff members feel they have never been acknowledged as having worthwhile opinions and have taken leadership positions underground. Union leaders should also be invited to join in decision making as partners. All issues need to be put on the table. The principal needs to be seen as taking the first risk in building trust by sharing power with teachers. All of the conversations need to be built on the premise that students will benefit from the final outcomes.

Kochanek (2005) uses the term *supportive leadership* in much the same way in terms of building trust. She defines it as:

> friendly, open, guided by norms of equality. The supportive principal (leader) is approachable, helpful and concerned about the social and professional needs of the staff. He/she motivates the faculty to improve with constructive criticism. Teachers feel respected as people and as professionals. This positive principal-teacher trust also leads the way for teacher-teacher trust improvements. (p. 21)

Building these types of shared relationships takes time. When there are low levels of trust, focus on decisions that can have quick payoffs and are in the best interests of students. To increase your chances of success, keep to smaller issues that you can tackle together at this stage.

Another positive effect of a principal's sharing leadership with teachers is that it builds trust between teachers too. Kochanek emphasizes the following:

> Observations from the case studies indicate that many of the same mechanisms that were used to build trust between the principal and teachers were also useful

in building trust between the teachers. The authors used analyses conducted on all schools in the Chicago sample. The findings show that the growth of trust between teachers and principal has a positive, significant relationship with the growth of trust between teachers. (p. 77)

This is good news. By working to build relationships between the staff and the school leader, principals can also build relationships between teachers (Kochanek, 2005).

Be Trustworthy

Trust grows out of trustworthiness, out of the character to make and keep commitments, to share resources, to be caring and responsible, to belong, to love unconditionally.

—Stephen R. Covey

One of the surest ways to establish and maintain trust is to be trustworthy yourself. When you want to increase trust, increase your trustworthiness. This is your single most important strategy and has the highest leverage.

> When you want to increase trust, increase your trust-worthiness. This is your single most important strategy and has the highest leverage.

- Be sensitive to and aware of any actions that might be perceived as making you seem untrustworthy or untrusting.
- Set the example; walk your talk, and speak the truth.
- Be nondefensive and quit taking it personally (QTIP).
- Remember that trustworthiness is a direct function of character, credibility, commitment, and competence.
- Deliver on promises, and tell people if you cannot.
- Be punctual.
- Get back to people if you said you would.

Being trustworthy builds loyalty with employees. Building relationships and listening to employees' problems will make them stay longer.

What Now?

In an educational work setting, trusting relationships are the key to success. Staff who know each other and have fun together at work achieve greater results.

It's time now to build a special support team to guide the planning. This is the next strategy—involving a facilitation team.

Involve a Facilitation Team

Even in the best of times, it is extremely challenging for one person to lead and manage an entire staff, but it is particularly difficult to do so in a low-trust situation. The creation of a small facilitation team, like a steering committee of internal advisors, makes one group responsible for planning

> "Relationships among educators within a school range from vigorously healthy to dangerously competitive. Strengthen those relationships, and you improve professional practice."
>
> —Roland Barth

the trust-building process with the principal and other administrators. Sometimes known as a *process implementation team* or a *coordinating council*, it is a team that commits to work with the principal in a leadership role to design strategies and activities that will build trusting relationships in order to improve staff and student learning.

As you continue to build relationships with staff members, keep an eye out for people who could share the leadership role with you and that you could work with. Perhaps they have already volunteered to help on certain projects.

This strategy describes what a facilitation team does, how to create one, and how to build its capacity.

Purpose of the Facilitation Team

As a leader, once you have committed to using a team approach to assess the present and design the road to the future, you must communicate the purpose of the facilitation team clearly to the staff.

The facilitation team will have responsibility for:

- Working to become a team themselves
- Discussing and assessing the culture of the staff and its readiness for certain tasks
- Initiating, managing, and facilitating all aspects of the trust-building process
- Constantly monitoring and adjusting the process
- Establishing and maintaining open communication
- Ensuring that the process remains active from year to year
- Welcoming new team members

Activity

Composition and Selection of the Facilitation Team

Chances of success are greater when a cross section of the staff is represented on the facilitation team. Smaller teams of four or five members are more effective. With more members there is greater complexity of communication. If you want to involve more staff, keep the team small, but open the meetings to anyone who wants to attend. Another option is to have a core team and an expanded advisory group.

Resist the impulse to simply create a team from those on staff already established as leaders, such as department heads or grade representatives. Sometimes these groups have established agendas that get in the way of building trust.

In order to be transparent and build trust, don't appoint team members by yourself; you will need to involve the staff in the selection process. Here is one simple team formation procedure:

1. Ask the staff to nominate people. Tell them you are looking for about four or five people who are representative of the staff and will speak on their behalf. I recommend that each staff member be limited to naming one person who represents them and their beliefs.

2. Explain that facilitation teams traditionally had a mandate to gather information, analyze it, and recommend ways to be more effective. However, this model was too slow and often caused the team to become isolated from the rest of the staff. Instead, the facilitation team will be facilitators of the process, but staff will make major decisions together.

3. Place a secure box in the office or staffroom for names to be submitted in writing.

4. Emphasize that everyone on staff is eligible, including union representatives as well as support staff, such as caretakers, teaching assistants, and secretaries. Encourage new staff members as well as veterans. In a low-trust situation that involves union issues, it may be seen as a risk to include the union steward. You will have to decide if the situation is appropriate. If at all possible, encourage the union representative to stand for the position of facilitation team member if no one nominates him or her.

5. Once you have a list of nominees, seek a commitment from each of them to join the facilitation team. Encourage them to accept the nomination of their peers for this vital leadership role.

6. Try to include everyone who is nominated—even those who weren't your own first choice. You must accept the people that the staff nominates for your intentions to be believable. They are going to help you make this work, so don't balk at the names—get on with it. Trust the staff.

7. If more than five or six people are nominated, hold an election. If you don't get four or five names, even two or three people will be a big help. Perhaps more will step forward over time when they see how it's working.

8. If you don't get any names, you will have to go back to the staff and try again. Emphasize that the purpose of the team is to build trust among staff with the ultimate goal of improving student learning. The staff might be testing you to see how serious you are; but it's more likely that informal leaders who are trusted by the staff just need to be encouraged to step forward.

If all of these efforts fail to form the facilitation team, introduce the strategy called Invite Feedback on Staff Trust (page 47), and then come back to this request.

Build the Capacity and Trust Level of the Facilitation Team

Activity

Once chosen, this group of people need to get to know each other. Time spent building the capacity and trust level of the facilitation team will have huge payoffs when they begin to share all of this process with the rest of the staff. Consider holding the inaugural meeting in a different setting, one that is perhaps more relaxed and conducive to congeniality. Set some rudimentary ground rules for meeting and communicating. These can be revised later as the group becomes more cohesive. They will also need to agree on a facilitation team leader.

Begin by ensuring that each person on the facilitation team has read the introduction and first chapter of this book. The group needs to understand the chief underpinnings of the work they will be doing.

Ask for their opinions on how well they and other staff members have received previous activities. Focus on:

- The I've Been Framed activity (page 38)

- Results of the Staff Feedback About Leader survey (page 209)

- Social activities already underway

Share Roland Barth's "Improving Relationships Within the Schoolhouse" with the facilitation team members. (Visit **go.solution-tree.com/leadership** to download and print the full text.)

In the article, Barth discusses the courage educators need to talk about the "nondiscussable issues" that everybody knows about but no one talks about in public. He outlines four types of relationships among adults in schools: parallel play, adversarial relationships, congenial relationships, and collegial relationships.

Give the facilitation team members time to read and discuss the content and the issues it raises both for them as a team and for the whole staff.

Then ask them to look ahead to the strategies they will be using with the staff as outlined in the next sections of this book, and explain that they will first go through the strategies themselves for their own team-building and to prepare themselves to use them with the larger group. Use the following strategies with them, and after they have experienced all of them, they can decide the best order in which to use them with the whole staff:

- Share Personal Stories (page 63)

- Agree on Norms of Acceptable Conduct (page 58). Their norms need to include where and how often they will meet, how agendas will be developed, and their method of record keeping. They will also need to discuss how they will draw out any introverts, who tend to speak less.

- Give Permission to Have Some Fun (page 53). Start by getting them to come up with a name for themselves so they start to form an identity.

- Invite Feedback on Staff Trust (page 47). The facilitation team will need to discuss how they will collect and report this information back to their constituents.

Record Keeping

The facilitation team will need to keep track of their decisions and progress. They should set up a system of recording notes from each meeting with an action list noting who, what, and when for each action.

They also need to keep and store all the visual charts and outcomes from meetings with the whole staff. Find a safe place for these important records.

A Cautionary Note

You will have to use caution to prevent the facilitation team from being viewed with suspicion by the skeptics and cynics as the "inside group." Facilitation team members need to be connected with the larger group at the same time they serve as advisors to the principal. This is a unique role for staff members to play, and the stakes are high. In a way, they are the pipeline between the principal and the staff as a whole.

The facilitation team members need to constantly be checking back and forth with the whole staff. They need to be ready and willing to talk with people in hallways, in the lunchroom and, yes, even in the parking lot.

It is important for staff members to know that these people are representing them and can be approached to share information or answer questions at any time. Of course staff members will still be interacting with the principal to talk, but with these new communication routes opened, there is the potential for trust to grow and spread across the staff.

What Now?

Once the facilitation team has had some time to get to know each other and set ground rules for themselves, they can begin to work with the facilitation team leader to plan the next step. Just as the principal asked for feedback about his or her leadership around trust issues, the whole staff needs to work through a similar process about the level of staff trust. This will be a delicate and important step. With the facilitation team's wisdom and input, the whole staff should now be supportive. Without such a representative team as the keystone, success in the future may be more tentative.

Invite Feedback on Staff Trust

Now it's time to put the issue of trust *among* staff members on the table in a deliberate way. You have already assessed the trust relationship between yourself and teachers in Ask for Feedback (page 31), so the ice has been broken. You have set the stage to ask people to look more deeply at their relationships with each other.

This is the first task in which the facilitation team can really get involved. They will collaboratively plan how to take the "trust temperature" of the whole staff. This information will become the baseline for all future planning. Ideally, it should be done on an annual basis, so that they can make comparisons with baseline data and growth.

This strategy includes three activities:

1. Start the trust discussion with the article by Roland Barth.

2. Introduce the research on trust with the staff.

3. Administer a Staff Trust Survey (page 210) and share the results.

Activity Start the Trust Discussion

The facilitation team's first task is to decide with the principal or leader how and when to put the issue of trust on the table with all staff members. After the team has read the Barth article, they need to discuss it among themselves. Because this team represents the interests of the staff, everything they do together is a trial run of how it might work with the whole staff.

They then need to plan how to introduce the article to the staff. (A word of caution: Although this step needs careful planning, in most cases it's better to do something and get it going than to spend too much time discussing how to start.) Whatever the strategy used, it must engage the interests and feelings of the staff and answer the question, Why is this important to us? Possible strategies include presenting this article either with the whole staff at one meeting or at smaller division or department meetings.

Both formats have advantages. The smaller meetings may be more intimate and encourage more dialogue. The larger meeting will save time, and everyone will hear every comment.

Copy and distribute Barth's article to staff members to read ahead of time, or divide the staff into groups and use the Jigsaw Method to read the article.

The Jigsaw Method

Form groups of five, called "home groups." Then divide the Barth article into five sections and ask each person from the home group to be responsible for reading a different one of the five sections. Ask all the people reading the same section to gather together into what is called an "expert group." Give these expert groups time to read and discuss the content, and then ask each of the experts to move back to their home groups and share what they learned. Ask the home groups to reflect on these topics:

- The "nondiscussables" that need to be put on the table

- The connections between the ideas in the article and what was revealed in the leader feedback session

Barth states that the types of relationships among adults in schools include:

- Parallel play relationships—working in isolation in our own classrooms or work areas
- Adversarial relationships—competitive and sometimes blatantly hostile
- Congenial relationships—personal and friendly
- Collegial relationships—a real learning community

Here are some possible discussion questions:

- Which relationships are you experiencing?
- Which one is predominant?

- Are there specific examples of any of the four relationships in the school?

- What's going well? (even one example of a good thing that's happened)

- How might staff move from parallel play and adversarial relationships to congenial and even collegial relationships?

Emphasize that this is a continuation of the process that began with feedback about the administrator or leader. The purpose of this step is to determine the level of trust in the school among the staff members themselves. This is a critical step in seriously confronting the issues for the benefit of staff, student learning, and relationships. There will be many more chances for deeper discussion over the coming months. Knowing that it is a process and not a one-time event will in itself build trust.

Introduce the Research on Trust

Activity

Staff members would benefit from having a short handout to read with some key information from the research section of chapter 1. This factual content meets the needs of the abstract learner, justifies the validity of the topic in the literature, and answers the question, what are the facts I need to know about this?

The contents of the handout could include:

- Definition of distrust (page 9)

- Definition of trust (page 9)

- The Trust Glass (page 10)

- Correlation to Roland Barth's four types of relationships

- Importance of trust in student achievement (pages 99–101)

Use the discussion from this research base and from Barth's article as a springboard to introduce the next activity—the Staff Trust Survey.

Administer the Staff Trust Survey

Activity

A critical purpose of this survey is to investigate the level of trust throughout the whole school by looking at the relationships among staff members. It is important that the staff survey align itself to the elements structured within the feedback process, but also address issues specific to the collegial nature of the nonadministrative school staff.

The reproducible Staff Trust Survey (page 210) provides a limited sample of questions. You may wish to use these as a first-level approach or have the facilitation team investigate alternate questions by doing web-based research for survey-question samples. Questions from the previous section of this book may also be adapted to meet the needs of a staff-to-staff survey format.

Visit **go.solution-tree .com/leadership** to download and print this survey.

Use Tried and True Questions

When searching for appropriate questions to use with your survey design, it is important to make use of questions that have already proven their validity in a survey process. They are both "tried" and "true." Essentially, this means that the questions have been previously used and demonstrated success not only in garnering the types of responses expected, but also in demonstrating consistent response patterns.

While it is both interesting and fun to design your own questions, most items found within, or adapted from, a formal survey process, like those in the reproducible Staff Trust Survey (page 210), have already proven their capacity to be both *valid* and *reliable*.

Remember these additional tips for success—similar to those in "Ask for Feedback" (page 31).

Introduce the Survey

To introduce this survey in a nonthreatening way, refer the staff to the Staff Feedback About Leader (page 209) survey, which they have already completed. The principal could personalize the experience by sharing a significant insight gleaned from their feedback. In addition:

- Show them this book. Sometimes showing a book on the topic reduces fear and lends more validity for the conversation about trust.

- Explain to the participants that the purpose of the survey is to get honest input from everyone on staff about the current level of trust in the school.

- Explain that you are not looking to blame people but to improve trust in order to benefit student and staff learning and teamwork by asking for honest feedback.

- Emphasize that participation in the survey is voluntary, but that the more people who participate, the better the results will be.

Administer the Survey

If possible, consider using web-based survey software for this feedback process. By using a web-based link on a common site, participants can respond anonymously. Most survey programs allow for multiple-choice formats as well as open-text commentary and provide a data summary process at the completion of the survey. The questions contained within the sample survey above may be edited into a software program, or you may enter your own questions.

The facilitation team could split up and meet individually or in pairs with small groups of the staff to distribute the survey and answer questions about it.

Again, there must be no way to trace the results back to anyone. (See Anonymity and Confidentiality, page 33.) If the surveys are not done online, remember to provide a location for confidential and anonymous drop-off. You will need to have a secure location, such as the mailbox of one of the facilitation team members.

Offer the survey to everyone on staff. If you select only certain individuals, you can be sure the word will get around, and there may be suspicion about why the others weren't included. This is not a good way to start building trust.

Tell participants they can skip questions that they are uncomfortable with. Ask them to be candid but also professional, and give them a specified length of time to return the surveys. A week should be long enough.

Ask Open-Ended Questions

You may also wish to include open-ended questions after the scaled questions. If doing so, remember to provide a carefully defined framework for participants to use for their responses. Pure open response is too difficult to analyze. In an attempt to define common concerns, specific sentence stems or criteria will assist in keeping the response and subsequent analysis controlled and manageable. Here are two examples from Patrick McKenna and David Maister (2002) to choose from:

1. What three accomplishments are you proud of that we have achieved as a staff?

2. What three things should we have accomplished by now but haven't?

Include the Trust Glass

Include a copy of the Trust Glass (page 10), and ask respondents to:

- Mark an *X* where they think the overall level of trust is for the staff

- Draw an arrow to mark where their personal level of trust is as a staff member

Score the Survey

With an electronic scoring program like TurningPoint (www.turningtechnologies.com), all the survey takers come to a meeting and receive a remote device of their own. They look at the question on the screen and then press a button to enter an answer to each question. This system has several advantages:

- It is anonymous.

- It is fast—everyone completes the survey at the same time.

- Everyone sees the data at the same time, so there can be no suspicion of "fudging" the results.

- It saves the data in both database and graphic formats for future use.

If you're not using electronic scoring, a computer program or spreadsheet will make the scoring faster, but an old-fashioned hand tally will work just as well.

Refer to table 2.2 (page 52), which contains the same rubric we used earlier, and reflect on the score. Consider how it affirms your overall thoughts concerning the level of trust within the current situation.

Table 2.2: Trust Level Indicators

Score	Level	Indicator
0–09	-1	Distrust
10–19	0	No Trust
20–29	+1	Early Trust
30–39	+2	Developing Trust
40–50	+3	Mature Trust

Read the Results

The facilitation team's next step is to study the results from the survey along with the open-ended responses. While the intent of the survey is to provide an overall indicator of trust, it is important to recognize that each individual question can provide a specific reference, or "window" into the specifics of some of the concerns. When generalizing the finding, do not overlook the critical elements contained within the individual questions. They may actually help to identify the focus of a further investigation.

Things to think about include:

- What sticks out—are there obvious consistencies in response?
- What confirms the expectations of the facilitation team?
- What "surprises" are there in the data?
- How do these responses reflect the findings of the administrative feedback process?
- Where would you place the overall level of trust on the Trust Scale?

Share the Results

Decide how you want to share the results. Ideally, the facilitation team members would be the ones to do this. It is critical that the staff see a written copy of the results as soon as possible. Use their exact comments wherever you can.

The facilitation team should present its summary first. Invite comments from the staff and ask for their conclusions. What next steps do they see from this information? It can be helpful while this is occurring for the facilitation team to just listen and record comments on a flip chart. Let staff members talk, even if it takes a while to get a conversation going. This is sensitive information about their relationships. It may be a surprise to some—and it may be a relief for others that someone finally asked these questions. It will definitely be a topic for conversation. Some may still need to review and discuss within a smaller or more private context. Consider the instructional methods listed earlier in addition to other small to large group practices.

The Staff Trust Survey can be administered each year to track changes, growth, and new information.

> ## What Now?
>
> Because this important strategy of information gathering has taken time to complete, you will want to give the staff and the facilitation team some time to think about the results. If there is something tangible and concrete that can be changed, acting on it will prove the sincerity of your intention to listen to opinions.
>
> While some actions will become obvious from the feedback, take your time in deciding on major changes. You will need more staff input to prioritize and agree on an action plan. Developing and publicly posting an action plan with possible timelines will be the evidence of intent and will provide an implementation record for all to monitor.

Give Permission to Have Some Fun

Groups of employees who laugh together are more productive than those who are more serious. They also enjoy their jobs more when their supervisors have a good sense of humour.

—LaughLab

Use caution with this strategy, and respect the limits of your school's culture. In a culture of distrust, any attempt to have fun or be funny can be received with suspicion or anger at worst or mild enthusiasm at best. A fear of conflict is common among educators. This can manifest itself in a stifled, tight atmosphere in both teacher-teacher and teacher-principal relationships. Any formal attempt to open the opportunity for humor and laughter must be authentic and carefully introduced to communicate mutual respect.

Developing a stronger sense of camaraderie is a surefire way to build trust between employees. If a distrustful feeling has built up over time, people may be afraid of laughing for fear of being embarrassed, reprimanded, or ridiculed. What staff members need in a culture of distrust is simply permission to lighten up. (This strategy will be expanded in chapters 3 and 4.) Whatever you do here will set the tone for what is to come.

Although the best form of humor is spontaneous, in a distrusting environment permission to laugh needs to be formally extended and then nurtured. Having a good laugh together can be the catalyst for loosening up enough to talk about key issues. Staff members need to know that while they will be sure to disagree on issues at times, they can still be cordial and maybe even enjoy their fellow colleagues. Having some fun can help ease vulnerability and build relationships. Fun is an often-undervalued piece of the trust solution.

"Like all living things, your group is constantly changing and evolving. A periodic self-evaluation can help the group grow in the right direction."

—Patrick McKenna and David Maister

Any formal attempt to open the opportunity for humor and laughter must be authentic and carefully introduced to communicate mutual respect.

Fun at Work

Which attitude do you think fits your attitude to fun at work? Which one is most prevalent among your staff?

1. Fun *or* work

2. Work then fun

3. Fun then work

4. Work and no fun

5. Fun *and* work

I hope it's the last one. Finding the right balance between fun and work is the big challenge.

Activity

Arrange Lighthearted Social Activities

Someone needs to set the tone and maybe even give permission for laughter by modeling safe, nonhurtful humor. This starts with the principal and other facilitation team members and extends to include the whole staff. Fun might be mandated or structured at first, for example, by bringing in a motivational speaker. Hopefully, it will become more spontaneous over time. The facilitation team has to make decisions about which of the following suggested activities would be best received by the majority of the staff. Timing is critical. Consider them individually, and plan what and where you want to start. If you can get people smiling, you have been successful. If they end up laughing—you are real winners!

Everyone has a unique fun temperament or "funprint." Don't expect everyone to have the same sense of humor or find the same activities to be fun. You will need to plan for different personalities to get them laughing in order to break the ice and encourage people to get to know each other better.

Staff members need to know each other's names to build relationships. This includes all staff members, not just the ones they work with in their division, grade, or department. Here are some suggestions:

- Make name tags to be worn at meetings.

- Have the school photographer take two different staff group photos—an official one where everyone looks very professional and a second one just for fun using props and costumes representing their hobbies or sports or personality. Post copies of the second one in the staff room, work room, and so on, with all the names identified. This will give people a place to go to learn names.

You can also organize social activities at a neutral location or home so everyone can come. You may want to include spouses, partners, and their children too. Here are some ideas: potluck dinners, cook-offs, bake-offs, barbeques in a park, bowling nights, TGIF at a local pub, fall fairs, baby or wedding showers, and birthday celebrations.

Do the Unexpected at Meetings

Take a chance and try something different and unexpected to get people's attention and bring a smile to their faces. Serve refreshments. Take some time arranging the room and setting the professional atmosphere and theme for the meeting. Put some music on as people are getting coffee and mingling. And always start meetings with a positive item, piece of information, or amusing anecdote.

Activity

Start meetings with a positive item, piece of information, or amusing anecdote.

Give Recognition for Outstanding Effort

Activity

Taking the time to recognize contributions at a meeting creates happiness and pride in the group. This can be done verbally or accompanied with a hand-written card or a token.

Invite the staff to take the initiative here. Ask them to present awards to each other. Present an award each month to a new person. The awards can be serious or silly. Here is a story that schools have used.

The Starfish Award is based on a story about a man gathering starfish on a beach. There are many variations now circulating of this widely told tale, which is loosely based on an idea in a short story by Loren Eiseley called "The Star Thrower" (1979). Once the story is introduced to the staff, suggest that they begin giving a monthly award to a staff member who made a positive difference in some way to another staff member. The person who receives the award has the honor of giving it to someone else at the next staff meeting. Attach an actual or toy starfish to the award. It's always fun for the staff to see who gets the award.

> One day a woman was walking along the shore. As she looked down the beach she saw a human figure moving like a dancer. As she got closer, she saw that it was a young man. The young man wasn't dancing, but instead was reaching down to the shore, picking up something, and gently throwing it into the ocean.
>
> As she got closer she called out, "Good morning! What are you doing?" The young man paused, looked up and replied, "Throwing starfish in the ocean. The sun is up and the tide is going out. And if I don't throw them in, they'll die."
>
> "But young man, don't you realize that there are miles and miles of beach and starfish all along it? You can't possibly make a difference!"
>
> The young man listened politely then bent down, picked up another starfish, threw it into the sea past the breaking waves, and said, "It made a difference for that one."

Assemble the Pieces of the Puzzle

Activity

The purpose of this activity is to highlight the contributions people can make to the school if they participate and share their ideas in a group. Conversely, it quickly shows what can happen if people withhold their pieces of the puzzle—their ideas, thoughts, and feelings.

Use a ready-made children's puzzle with large pieces. For a small staff, distribute the pieces so that everyone has one, two, or three pieces. For a large group, have an inner circle that does the activity and an outer circle that observes what happens. You could also have several puzzles being put together at the same time by several groups.

The only rule is that people cannot take pieces from each other. Give only that one instruction and step aside. Eventually people will start to put the puzzle together. It's more challenging—more like real life—if they don't have the picture of the finished puzzle to follow. You could even leave a few pieces out.

The debriefing after the activity is critical. Here are some guiding questions:

- "How did the process go?"
- "What signs of collaboration did you see?"
- "How does this model the way we work together and trust each other as a staff?"
- "Are there missing pieces? Does the puzzle still work?"
- "Was it fun?"
- "What do the pieces represent?"
- "Did all people freely share their pieces? What does this represent on our staff?"
- "What did they learn from this activity?"

A variation on this activity is to use a blank puzzle (see www.compozapuzzle.com). Give each person a photocopy of a puzzle piece, so they can practice their artwork. The photocopy should indicate the top, bottom, left, and right of the piece so that none of the pieces will be upside down when they are all assembled.

Use a theme for the puzzle that is fun yet not too threatening, such as "things that make you happy" or "your hobbies or interests." People could initial the piece or sign their name. Then start the activity by asking participants to piece together their personalized pieces. The finished puzzle can be turned over and taped together for mounting or display.

Hold a Parking Lot Meeting

Here is an example of a truly unusual story that is attributed to Roland Barth. He told about leaving a staff meeting and observing the "real" staff meeting occurring out in the parking lot. He said that we need to figure out how to get the parking lot conversations back into the school—in other words, to create an environment where educators could talk openly with one another.

How about asking the caretaker to set up chairs and a flip chart out in the staff parking lot, and then asking everyone to meet there instead of the staff room? The effect will be both dramatic and memorable.

If parking lots are not feasible for you, try a hallway or somewhere other than the usual staff meeting location. You could even book a room at the local diner or restaurant and have a surprise meeting there.

Add a Rumor Mill

Share rumors at meetings to get them out in the open as discussable topics. If they're true, people will know that, and if they're false, you can quash them before they do any damage. Doing the unexpected surely will break old patterns of behavior. Try it and see what happens. New surroundings can be a breath of fresh air to a stale group atmosphere.

Celebrate Successes and Failures

Activity

We have suggested ways to celebrate and recognize individual effort. It is also important to celebrate the accomplishments of groups in both academic and nonacademic areas. Celebrations are a way of saying thank you in public and showing appreciation for hard work. Even small accomplishments need to be recognized.

It is also critical in a low-trust culture to acknowledge setbacks as well as successes. For example, factories that discover a flaw in their systems and continue working in the same way do so at their own peril. Toyota Motor Corporation is aware of this and tries to catch the defects right when they happen. In addition to relying on its unique corporate culture of respect and *kaizen* ("continuous improvement"), Toyota is adamant about product quality—doing things right from the beginning. If a Toyota employee makes or detects any defect, he or she pulls the "andon cord," a cord that runs the entire length of the production line and alerts the team leader. If the team leader cannot solve the problem with the employee, the entire production line is stopped. This behavioral norm is expected and celebrated at Toyota.

"Don't worry about failure. Worry about chances you miss when you didn't even try."
—Source Unknown

Failures need to be seen as learning experiences that happen naturally whenever we try something new. Mistakes are to be expected. The same principle holds true in education. But even when mistakes are made, celebrate the intent of the effort, and people will continue to try.

Tell Jokes

Activity

Some people may think you are asking them to become joke tellers when you raise the topic of laughter. You will need to reassure them that they can be very funny and have a lot of fun without telling jokes. Some people are good at telling jokes and others aren't. Laugh with people, never at them or at their expense. The only person you can safely laugh at is yourself.

Avoid jokes that are racial, political, or otherwise harassing. Be inclusive of your humor. Jokes should be appropriate, helpful, and constructive. Weed out any jokes or comments that are hurtful and destructive. You may need to reconsider your comments if you use sarcasm regularly, as it can be hurtful too, even when it's funny.

Laugh with people, never at them or at their expense. The only person you can safely laugh at is yourself.

What Now?

Take your work seriously, but never yourself.

—Margot Fonteyn

The most important benefit of laughter turns out to be the positive social interaction it brings—the glue that binds a diverse group of individuals together. Humor improves trust and morale, eases communication, and strengthens teamwork and relationships. It goes deep into the attitudes people bring to work and how they treat each other.

Humor and laughter are not a panacea. But when they are combined with genuine appreciation and praise, they can help teachers become more productive, trusting, loyal, and willing to work collaboratively. Trust and loyalty are not created by a paycheck; they are nurtured by strong relationships with colleagues and a caring, supportive leadership team. When introduced with a harsh tone or a mean comment, the whole opportunity for improving morale and having some fun is lost.

One afternoon, in the cafeteria of a large high school, I was all set to start a Laughing Matters! workshop with the staff. The principal came to the microphone. I thought she was going to introduce me and kick off the session. Instead, she chose to reprimand a few teachers who were still standing at the refreshment table—even calling them by name—and telling them to sit down.

Those few unfortunate words spoken at the microphone sucked all the energy out of the room. It was clear to me that they were not used to laughing in that school.

Some of the teachers said that the session was valuable, but clearly the tone had already been set by the principal—no laughing here, not even at a Laughing Matters! workshop.

Agree on Norms of Acceptable Conduct

A basis for every championship team, in every endeavor, is having hard-and-fast, non-negotiable "ground rules" that everyone agrees to abide by.

—Patrick McKenna and David Maister

Norms are a short set of behaviors that everyone agrees to try to abide by. Norms define how meetings will be run and what kind of behavior is expected and acceptable. They:

- Separate what will and will not be tolerated
- Are constructive and assume positive intentions
- Are explicit rules of conduct for adult conversations

In staff development literature, there are several synonyms for *norms*—*protocols*, *contracts*, *working agreements*, and *ground rules* are the most common. It doesn't matter which term is chosen as long as the staff agrees on it and gets the process going, so that there is a written document that addresses how business will be conducted.

While the literature often suggests setting norms earlier in a group's development, norms set too early often fail because staff members need time to build some commitment to each other. By this time in the trust-building process, the group should be ready to agree on collaboratively established norms that will guide their professional behavior and for which each member will be held accountable. This strategy can help significantly to build trust among group members.

Agreed-upon behaviors possess many benefits, including the following:

- Reduced fear and tension in tough discussions of sensitive issues
- Increased participation and more honest participation
- A shared sense of ownership
- Increased comfort levels, fairness, and mutual respect
- A shift in ownership of the discussion to the group, not the leader
- Better decisions and clearer agreements

Every group has established norms of behavior that have developed over time, whether they realize them or not. Some of those norms may be counterproductive to the well-being of the group. Formalizing positive norms by making them explicit ensures that peer influence and even pressure will help to improve the group environment, and it will also help ensure that each member is treated fairly in the future.

If the staff has difficulty getting along, this step may take considerable time to complete. Be sure to include all staff members—extroverts and introverts It is also critical that the facilitation team work through this strategy for themselves before taking it to the whole staff.

Some groups aren't aware of the unwritten rules they follow that determine acceptable and unacceptable behavior. Once they are in place, people know what the acceptable behaviors are. Many activities can be used to create norms for a group. Two are included here.

Identify Highs and Lows

Activity

To start the discussion, it is helpful to identify functioning norms that exist in high-trusting groups as compared to low-trusting groups. Here is the procedure:

1. Explain to participants they are going to participate in a process that identifies, sorts, and prioritizes norms that they will follow in their meetings from now on.

2. Set up two chart stands or posters, and label one *Low Trust* and the other *High Trust*.

3. Starting with the Low Trust chart, ask people to call out any behaviors these groups would exhibit in meetings that would ensure continuation of the low trust level. They may even recall their own low-trust experiences. Record these on the chart. Strive for five to ten ideas. Examples include the following:

    - Teachers mark papers or read newspapers during meetings.
    - No one says anything.
    - People talk over people, and no one can hear the comments.

- They come late and disturb the train of thought.

- Sarcasm is acceptable—even when it is hurtful.

- Notes are passed around, but the comments are never said out loud.

4. Move to the High Trust chart, and repeat the process.

These steps should take about ten minutes.

Activity

Use Sticky Notes

Members of the facilitation team, along with the group leader, could share the facilitation of this activity.

1. Distribute sticky notes and pens or pencils to staff members. You will need enough to give five notes to each person. If anonymity is important in your group, give everyone the same kind of pen or pencil to start with.

2. Describe the value of agreeing on group norms.

3. Define and describe a behavior-specific norm, that is, what a person does that is observable. For example, asking people to "be fully present" may sound good, but it has many possible meanings. Compare that statement to this one: "We agree that we will focus on the business of the meeting only. This means people will not opt out by bringing newspapers to read or tests to mark." The latter statement identifies specific behaviors that are either followed or not.

4. On a poster or chart, share some categories to consider. For example:
   - Mutual respect
   - Agenda input, frequency, and format of meetings
   - Attendance and punctuality
   - No "parking lot conversations"—say it here!
   - Decision making and dealing with conflict
   - Use of appropriate humor, laughter, and fun
   - What happens when the norms are broken
   - Creativity, risk taking, and sharing new ideas

5. Share some examples of behavior-specific norms from other groups to "prime the pump." For example:

   We agree that . . .
   - If you have something to say, you need to speak up and say it.
   - We will start and end on time—maybe even end early sometimes.
   - Fun and humor are important as long as they are constructive.
   - If someone violates one of our norms, we will take responsibility to gently remind that person of our norms and ask for a change in behavior.

6. Ask each person to think about the five most important commitments they need to make to the others regarding behaviors at meetings that will build trust. (Allow at least five minutes for this.) Then ask that each separate norm be written on a separate sticky note. Encourage them to use observable, behavioral language.

7. When they have written out their sticky notes, ask them to rank them from one to five, with 1 being the most important to the success of the group and five the least.

8. Collect all the sticky notes, mix them up, and read them randomly. If it is a small group:

    a. Read each one out loud, and start to create categories with input from the group.

    b. Stick them on a flip chart with similar ideas grouped together.

    c. When all of the sticky notes have been read and grouped, ask participants to write norms that reflect the ideas in each category.

    d. Write the finished list on a new flip chart, and sit back to reflect on the final product.

    e. Give people a week or so to continue to reflect and refine the norms to what they think is the "essential list."

    f. When they are all in agreement and can say that they will support the norms on the list, they should each sign the chart and date it.

    g. Give each person a printed copy of the final norms.

9. If it's a large group (over twenty):

    a. Collect all the sticky notes, and make five groups ranked from one to five.

    b. Start with everyone's number-one ranked norm.

    c. Read each one out loud, and start to create categories with input from the group.

    d. Stick them on a flip chart with similar ideas grouped and posted together. Then either use a steering committee to eliminate duplicates in each set or divide them up into groups and hand them out to groups in the room to eliminate duplicates.

    e. Then go on to the number-two ranked norms and follow through with this pattern.

    f. Write the finished list on a new flip chart, and sit back to reflect on the final product.

    g. Give people a week or so to continue to reflect and refine the norms to what they think is the "essential list."

    h. When they are all in agreement and can say that they will support the norms on the list, they should each sign the chart and date it.

    i. Each person should be given a printed copy of the final norms.

10. Try these phrases to make sure you have clarity and involvement:

- Let's get a reaction from everyone in the group.
- Let me repeat what I think I heard you say.
- Has everyone had a chance to express an opinion?
- Can you live with this decision and support it in public?
- Do you want to ponder this more and come back to it?

It is important that everyone's ideas are heard and discussed, but don't let it become a long and complicated process. Share the norms you have arrived at with newcomers, and help them understand the purpose and process behind them. Some schools print their norms in their staff handbooks.

Share the Responsibility

If your teammate isn't doing what you think he/she should it's up to you to speak up. . . . When teams try to rally around aggressive change or bold initiatives, they need to be prepared to address the problem when a team member doesn't live up to the agreement. Success does not depend on perfect compliance with new expectations, but on teammates who hold crucial conversations with one another when others appear to be reverting to old patterns.

—Kerry Patterson, Joseph Grenny, David Maxfield, Ron McMillan, & Al Switzler

Group members need to take responsibility for monitoring and policing their own behavior instead of looking to the group leader as the enforcer. A system of mutual accountability needs to develop. Over the next few months, quickly review the posted list of norms at the beginning of each meeting so everyone has a refresher.

Acknowledge breaches and enforce the norms during meetings. Participants can "call a time out" to discuss violations of norms. This is done in a gentle spirit, remembering that we are all human and that occasionally honest mistakes will be made. Phrase the statement like this: "Help me to understand how your actions [be specific about what pattern of behavior you observed] followed our norms." Continue to bring the discussion back to the agreed-upon norms rather than focusing solely on the person.

Use a process observer (someone whose task it is to listen, observe the process, and alert the group if they get off task) to tally participation and give feedback to the group on its progress toward new norms at the end of each meeting. Do a quick check at the end of each meeting to reflect on whether or not the process honored the established norms. Focus on the positive, and ask for comments about the good job group members are doing following their own norms.

Whose Norms Are These?

There could be a temptation to take the norms established by one group and apply them to other groups. I caution against this. Each group needs to develop norms to suit its particular situation. The facilitation team needs different norms than the science department members. Some schools even develop staff room norms.

What Now?

Norms are never carved in stone; they need periodic review and updating. This could involve additions, deletions, or revised wording.

Norms are especially important to follow in times of distrust and conflict, because they clarify expectations and build relationships. They become part of the group memory and conscience.

Established collaborative norms will make it much easier for staff members to get to know each other and share personal stories as relationships grow.

Share Personal Stories

When team members reveal aspects of their personal lives to their peers, they learn to get comfortable being open with them about other things. They begin to let down their guard about their strengths, weaknesses, opinions and ideas.

—Patrick Lencioni

This strategy builds on growing mutual trust now that permission has been extended for some fun and laughter and norms have been agreed on for group behavior.

How much do you really know about each other? Do you have to wait for a retirement speech or a eulogy to find out about your colleagues' life stories? Who is caring for an older parent, who has teenagers at home? Who is taking night school courses? As teams, we need to get to know each other better for trust to start to take root.

People may now be willing to open up and share some stories that can break the power of distrust. This activity is designed to help people disclose and share some personal information in a safe environment. It is important that everyone's voice be heard and that people understand each others' stories.

Patrick Lencioni's definition of trust emphasizes the importance of this strategy:

Trust is about vulnerability. Team members who trust one another learn to be comfortable being open, even exposed, to one another around their failures, weaknesses, even fears. Vulnerability-based trust is predicated on the simple and practical idea that people who aren't afraid to admit the truths about themselves are not going to engage in the kind of political behavior that wastes everyone's time and energy and more important, makes the accomplishment of results an unlikely scenario. (2002, p. 14)

All people have stories waiting for the right time to be told. Suzanne Bailey taught me that there are secret stories (below the surface), sacred stories (rituals and legends over time), and cover stories (stories told instead of the truth). Leaders need to nurture an environment in which staff members feel safe enough to begin telling some of their secret stories. People shouldn't feel pressured to reveal everything about themselves; some secrets may be too personal or tender to share in a professional context. The goal here is for people to reveal more of themselves in order to become more human to each other.

Activity

Lencioni's Personal Histories

According to Lencioni (2002), this is a low-risk activity that helps people who feel vulnerable with each other get to know each other better. He says:

> My colleagues and I have done [this activity] with virtually every team we work with, and I have to admit, I'm always worried that it's not going to work. And every time, it does . . . I always find that people are shocked about what they didn't know about their peers. (p. 19)

Everyone in the group must be involved. Don't let people opt out for any reason. The formal leaders must participate as well as everyone else.

At the meeting, go around the room and have every member of the team explain three things:

1. Where they grew up
2. How many siblings they have and where they fall in the birth order
3. The most difficult or important challenge of their childhood (not their *inner* childhood, just the most important challenge of being a kid!)

You could develop different questions from the ones mentioned above. Aim for ones that aren't too private and personal. Don't make the questions trivial, such as What's your favorite movie? as there would be no vulnerability involved. For example:

- The best team you were ever part of and why
- Something no one knows about you—but should
- Why you became an educator
- Why you choose to continue to be an educator
- What you learned about the "working world" from your first job

Here are some facilitation tips:

- Be prepared for the sensitive nature of this activity, and tell people upfront that it is "touchy-feely." Tell them they don't have to reveal their deepest, darkest secrets.
- Sometimes they will say they can't think of anything. That's okay.

- Listen carefully to every person. Sometimes people will go deeper than you expected. Thank them and slow down and invite the group to go on when they are ready.

- To bring closure, ask people what they learned about one another that they didn't know before.

If you have a large group, the challenge is how to have everyone hear all the stories. It would take too long to do this in one sitting. An alternative is to break people into smaller, task-specific groups and go around the circle with fewer people. This way, people who work closely together get to learn more about each other. The principal and assistant principal and anyone else without a group could go first, so everyone hears them, or they could form a small group themselves. The activity could be repeated with random groups to reach more listeners later. It may spawn conversation starters in the lunchroom and beyond over time. Lencioni (2002) writes:

> By going through the Personal Histories activity, team members come to understand one another at a more fundamental level; they learn how they became the people they are today. As a result, there is a far greater likelihood that empathy and understanding will trump judgment and accusation when it comes to interpreting questionable behavior. (p. 21)

The Shoebox

Activity

To add a tangible quality to the personal activities, ask people to bring three artifacts or photos that represent their answers to the questions you've chosen. They can bring these artifacts or photos (if they fit) in a shoebox. By adding this dimension, more intrigue is created, as people open their boxes and share their stories.

Invite them to decorate the shoebox and see what happens. A little creativity reveals a lot about personalities.

What Now?

The outcomes of this strategy will be powerful and memorable. It sets the stage for people to open up about their feelings about the school and put real issues on the table—instead of out in the parking lot. Stephen King writes in *Different Seasons* (1982):

> The most important things are the hardest things to say. They are the things you get ashamed of, because words diminish them—words shrink things that seemed limitless when they were in your head to no more than living size when they're brought out. The most important things lie too close to wherever your secret heart is buried, like landmarks to a treasure your enemies would love to steal away. And you make revelations that cost you dearly only to have people look at you in a funny way, not understanding what you've said at all, or why you thought it was so important that you almost cried while you were saying it. That's the worst, I think. When the secret stays locked within not for want of a teller, but for want of an understanding ear. (p. 293)

Put the Real Issues "On the Table"

Some core issues may already be known to most people and discussed openly in public. Sensitive issues that are undiscussable are under the table. Although it may be difficult, core issues that people may be afraid to talk about need to be surfaced in order to be discussed and resolved.

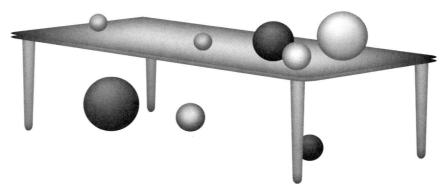

Do not start into this strategy unless you are fully committed to following through and dealing with the issues that come out of it—even if they are about you. If you can, combine it with Move From Issues to Actions (page 70), doing both in one day. Once the information is gathered and issues are proactively identified in a public forum, there will be more commitment to working together, and this in itself will build trust and restore relationships.

These activities act like steam vents to release built-up pressure and prevent explosions. There may be anger, there may even be confrontation, but encourage people to behave in a professional way. Confrontation doesn't have to mean fighting; it means speaking up in a positive way about the issues. Doing this effectively is a skill that will take practice and time.

Emphasize to the group that you all need to help each other move forward. No one person can or should take responsibility for the changes the group identifies as necessary. Everybody needs to be actively involved to make the strategy successful. Explain that this is going to be the way you want to do business from now on; that this is not a "one-time event," but the first of many opportunities to share and discuss issues and directions together. The issues raised in this strategy will form the basis for the next strategy, Move From Issues to Actions (page 70).

The activities used by the facilitation team for this strategy focus on the following:

- Going offsite
- Opening up
- Starting with hopes and concerns
- Introducing "on the table or under the table?"
- Writing specific problem statements

> Confrontation doesn't have to mean fighting; it means speaking up in a positive way about the issues. Doing this effectively is a skill that will take practice and time.

Go Offsite

There is tremendous benefit to be gained from changing the usual meeting location to somewhere neutral and fresh. Staff rooms evoke feelings and memories of past meetings and discussions. Try a local banquet hall or golf club. Swap meeting spaces with another school.

It is even more powerful to take the staff to a more secluded location and plan an overnight "advance" or getaway. (Calling it a retreat can have a backward-sounding connotation.) Social activities can be part of the agenda. Getting people away for a day or two can give them the energy to work on the real issues.

Open Up

Activity

Refer the staff back to Roland Barth's article, in which he defines a *nondiscussable* as:

> an issue of sufficient import that it commands our attention but it is so incendiary that we cannot discuss it in polite society . . . School improvement is impossible when we give "nondiscussables" such extraordinary power over us. (2006, p. 1)

These nondiscussables (or undiscussables) are like the proverbial elephant (or, if you're Canadian—the moose) in the room that everyone can see but no one talks about. So don't be surprised to find that people can be very shy and even fearful about discussing even issues that might have simple solutions. Many such issues, if talked about early, can lead to swift changes. On the other hand, some issues, once raised, will be unsolvable or beyond the authority of the school, as shown in table 2.3.

Table 2.3: Consequences of Ignoring the Undiscussables

Degree of Severity	The "Undiscussable"	Consequence
Most serious	The assistant principal is not competent in sufficiently disciplining violent students.	Staff members don't feel safe in the school or in their classrooms.
	A mentor gossiped negatively about a recent classroom visit in the staff room, and the teacher she observed heard about it through the rumor mill.	The partnership falls apart, and the mentor loses the trust of other staff.
	The facilitation team was delegated a task by the principal. She did it herself after they had done the work.	Facilitation team members won't get involved in a task again but won't tell the principal why.
Least serious	Some teachers use the photocopier and don't record it, so the principal has said, "No more photocopying."	Everyone loses out. Staff members are angry that everyone is reprimanded instead of those who deserve it.

Introduce the analogy of the table by talking about how we use the expressions "under the table," "off the table," and "on the table" to describe the acceptability of talking about certain topics. Explain to the staff that in this activity, they will be dealing with all of those categories.

Start With Hopes and Concerns

Allow people some reflection time to read and then answer questions like the ones that follow. Also, allowing staff to write their responses privately will make it easier for them to start talking about them.

- "What would high levels of trust look, feel, and sound like in the school?"
- "Let's capitalize on what we do well and focus on being more trusting. What do we want to do more of?"
- "What are our hopes and concerns for this strategy?"
- "Whose interests are being served by the way things are?"
- "What is at stake to gain or lose?"

Introduce "On the Table or Under the Table?"

Stephen M. R. Covey talks about holding a type of meeting in which the leaders can listen but not respond. Before the meeting, distribute questions such as the following to the whole group in writing or at a staff meeting:

- "What do we gain and what do we lose by keeping our issues under the table?"
- "Is the fear of talking about our fears so great we cannot deal with it?"
- "People talk over people, and no one can hear the comments."
- "How can we create the conditions needed to put our issues on the table and discuss them?"

Let the staff members own the following activity and do it as a whole group.

1. Prepare a poster or chart with a graphic like table 2.3 (page 67).
2. Post and quickly review the norms of acceptable behavior the staff have agreed on.
3. Post a sign that says "Pretend you are in the parking lot" to get a chuckle, and remind them that you want the important discussion to take place here and now, not there and later.
4. Share a few of these conflict strategies if they aren't part of your norms:
   - Listen with your heart and your head.
   - Listen until you experience the other side.
   - Always treat people with respect.
   - Disagree with dignity.
   - Criticize ideas and not people.

5. Pass out sufficient quantities of 3" x 3" square sticky notes in two colors, one for issues already on the table and another for issues still under the table that need to be addressed.

6. Ask for specific examples of the situation, event, or behavior and the feeling it evokes.

7. Invite people to write one issue per sticky note, and then place the sticky notes on the poster, either on the table or under it. (The sticky notes can be given out ahead of time with instructions to write and post them when the participants have thought about it. They may want an opportunity to post them privately.)

8. Collect the sticky notes, and have participants sort them into categories either at or after the meeting in preparation for the next one. (Just make sure that you're not in sole custody of them at any point: if you take them away and sort them in private, there may be suspicion that some comments have been removed.)

9. When the categories are agreed upon, write them right on the poster.

10. Make a last call for anything that isn't on the poster.

11. When all the issues have surfaced, step back and give the group time to reflect on the process and its results.

Write Specific Problem Statements

Anne Conzemius and Jan O'Neill, authors and consultants who founded Quality Leadership by Design in 1998 to focus on improving K–12 education, advise us to "be patient and learn as much about the problem as you can before attempting to define the problem too narrowly. The time you spend up front in the definition and identification phase could save you huge amounts of time later on in the process" (2002, p. 197).

They suggest writing simple and concise problem statements from the issue categories. These statements should:

- Be objective and factual—not imply a solution
- Identify key characteristics of the problem, such as—
  - Where and when it is and is not observed
  - The extent of the impact it is having on student—or staff—learning
  - Observable evidence of its existence
- Be relatively short
- Identify the problem at its deepest level of manifestation
- Identify for whom it is a problem and when

Here are two examples of problem statements:

This is the third month that our open-supply room has been raided and emptied. It was just replenished, and two days later there's nothing left—again! We want the open-supply room to work so we don't have to go back to the system of each teacher ordering their own supplies and wasting money buying too much.

The teacher regularly came to school late and gave no reason for it. During examination days, she took days off to have home improvements made and called in sick. The department head had politely asked her why she was doing these things, but he knew her responses were lies. But he didn't confront the lies because he valued a friendly team in his department.

What Now?

Writing problem statements is a powerful exercise if people genuinely get involved. When people discover the courage to speak up, it is an emotional experience, and that can be a relief for everyone.

Everyone will need to reflect on the results before developing action plans. Once you have done that, you are ready to start making action plans for concrete change.

Move From Issues to Actions

This final strategy includes activities for consolidating and agreeing on specific, tangible actions for moving out of distrust and into the early stages of trust. To increase the chances of implementation, and for maximum buy-in for these activities, you will need to have everybody in the room. Avoid spending too much time here (paralysis by analysis), but aim for enough commitment to get going.

In many cases, small but strategic changes can be a tipping point and have incredible impact. At times, the change may feel overwhelming. Once the issues are on the table, and you have become serious about taking action, some people may even choose to leave the staff. Or, you may choose to leave and let new leadership take over the reins. This is of course a pivotal decision. Seek the advice of trusted others before you make this step. Whether or not you, or other staff members, decide to leave, the staff must work through a process of action planning to be able to see improvement. The activities in this culminating strategy will help you:

- Avoid agreeing too quickly
- Move from issues to actions
- Evaluate whether to use outside help

Activity

Avoid Agreeing Too Quickly

Perhaps the most potentially dangerous habit in collaboration is the tendency to hold back our real thoughts and feelings and go along with the crowd. This leads people to the false impression that there is agreement when there isn't. This desire not to "rock the boat" can sabotage the sincere efforts of any group. Often, the end result is that tremendous amounts of effort and money are spent, only to find out much too late that nobody wanted to do it anyway.

The mistakes that led to the disintegration of the Space Shuttle *Columbia* in 2003 are an example of this type of thinking. Reports say that NASA's culture of denial kept safety staff and some engineers largely silent when they knew there was a problem with the O-rings during the months leading up to the accident.

Sometimes when people know what the issues are, they don't want to go the extra mile and find the time and energy to take action. You must push through this inertia, fear, and discomfort.

The Abilene Paradox

Written by Jerry Harvey, an expert in organizational dynamics, "The Abilene Paradox" is based on a family situation with which all of us can identify. Visit **go.solution-tree.com/leadership** to download and print this story. It can also be done as a role play with four voices.

The Abilene Paradox

That July afternoon in Coleman, Texas (population 5,607), was particularly hot—104 degrees according to the Walgreen's Rexall thermometer. In addition, the wind was blowing fine-grained West Texas topsoil through the house. But the afternoon was still tolerable—even potentially enjoyable. A fan was stirring the air on the back porch; there was cold lemonade; and finally, there was entertainment. Dominoes. Perfect for the conditions. The game requires little more physical exertion than an occasional mumbled comment, "Shuffle 'em," and an unhurried movement of the arm to place the tiles in their appropriate positions on the table. All in all, it had the makings of an agreeable Sunday afternoon in Coleman. That is, until my father-in-law suddenly said, "Let's get in the car and go to Abilene and have dinner at the cafeteria."

I thought, "What, go to Abilene? Fifty-three miles? In this dust storm and heat? And in an un-air-conditioned 1958 Buick?"

But my wife chimed in with, "Sounds like a great idea. I'd like to go. How about you, Jerry?" Since my own preferences were obviously out of step with the rest, I replied, "Sounds good to me," and added, "I just hope your mother wants to go."

"Of course I want to go," said my mother-in-law. "I haven't been to Abilene in a long time."

So into the car and off to Abilene we went. My predictions were fulfilled. The heat was brutal. Perspiration had cemented a fine layer of dust to our skin by the time we arrived. The cafeteria's food could serve as a first-rate prop in an antacid commercial.

Some four hours and 106 miles later, we returned to Coleman, hot and exhausted. We silently sat in front of the fan for a long time. Then, to be sociable and to break the silence, I dishonestly said, "It was a great trip, wasn't it?"

No one spoke.

Finally, my mother-in-law said, with some irritation, "Well, to tell the truth, I really didn't enjoy it much and would rather have stayed here. I just went along because the three of you were so enthusiastic about going. I wouldn't have gone if you all hadn't pressured me into it."

I couldn't believe it. "What do you mean 'you all'?" I said. "Don't put me in the "you all" group. I was delighted to be doing what we were doing. I didn't want to go. I only went to satisfy the rest of you. You're the culprits."

My wife looked shocked. "Don't call me a culprit. You and Daddy and Mama were the ones who wanted to go. I just went along to keep you happy. I would have had to be crazy to want to go out in heat like that."

Her father entered the conversation with one word: "Shee-it." He then expanded on what was already absolutely clear: "Listen, I never wanted to go to Abilene. I just thought you might be bored. You visit so seldom I wanted to be sure you enjoyed it. I would have preferred to play another game of dominoes and eat the leftovers in the icebox."

After the outburst of recrimination, we all sat back in silence. Here we were. Four reasonably sensible people who—of our own volition—had just taken a 106-mile trip across a godforsaken desert in furnace-like heat and a dust storm to eat unpalatable food at a hole-in-the-wall cafeteria in Abilene, when none of us had really wanted to go. To be concise, we'd done just the opposite of what we wanted to do. The whole situation simply didn't make sense.

From *The Abilene Paradox and Other Meditations on Management*, by Jerry Harvey. Copyright © 1988 by the American Psychological Association. Reproduced with permission. The use of APA information does not imply endorsement by the APA.

When performed as a role play, the character who plays Jerry reads the scenario, and three other people take the parts of his wife, mother-in-law, and father-in-law. Acting it out usually gets some laughs and also gives you a chance to personalize the story to your locale. After reading or role playing the story, focus on these discussion questions:

1. Can you think of specific examples when you "went to Abilene" against your will?

2. What reasons are there for collusion in "The Abilene Paradox"?

3. How can we avoid it?

4. What could you do if you realized you were somewhere "along the way to Abilene" in your planning? Would you have the courage of your convictions to speak up?

Consider these reflections from the author:

Since that day in Coleman, I have observed, consulted with, and been part of more than one organization that has been caught in the same situation. As a result, the organizations have either taken side trips or, occasionally, terminal "journeys to Abilene," when Dallas or Houston or Tokyo was where they really wanted to go. And for most of those organizations, the negative consequences of such trips, measured in terms of both human misery and economic loss, have been much greater than for our little Abilene group.

I now call the tendency for groups to embark on excursions that no group member wants "the Abilene Paradox." Stated simply, when organizations blunder into the Abilene Paradox, they take actions in contradiction to what they really want to do and therefore defeat the very purposes they are trying to achieve. Business theorists typically believe that managing conflict is one of the greatest challenges faced by any organization, but a corollary of the Abilene Paradox states that the inability to manage agreement may be the major source of organization dysfunction. (Harvey, 1988, pp. 12–13)

Use this story as a reminder each time a decision is made by asking: "Is this another wasted trip to Abilene, or do we really have commitment that this is a decision we will support?"

Complete the Action Plan

Activity

On a large piece of chart paper, write "Put the Real Issues on the Table." If you have a wall large enough, you could post them on individual posters, so they can be rearranged or combined.

Think of the issues as a job jar at home in which jobs have been piling up and need to be taken out and prioritized into short- and long-term actions. Conzemius and O'Neill suggest a practical mindset for this that they call "levels of fix." Every issue can potentially be addressed at one of these three levels:

Level 1 Fix: Solve the immediate problem.

These are necessities . . . that require immediate action to prevent further damage.

For example: Not enough teachers are on yard duty before school, and it is unsafe for children. Those who aren't following the schedule need to do so.

Level 2 Fix: Improve the process that created the problem.

These should be the minimal goals of most teams—to improve the process so that the problems or gaps [issues] identified by the team will not happen again.

For example: We need a new process to make up the yard duty schedule so that teachers can sign up for the time slot they prefer.

Level 3 Fix: Improve or redesign the system that created the process that led to the problem.

These are ideal because improving a system usually has a far-reaching impact. But they also require extensive effort and input, not to mention authority, so they may be impractical in many cases.

For example: The teachers' contract is unclear about minutes of yard duty. This needs to be included in the next round of discussions. (Conzemius & O'Neill, 2002, p. 190)

Sort your problem statements into levels 1, 2, or 3. Start with the smallest things you can do to have the greatest impact, and prioritize them within each group. A show of hands might work if there is enough trust to do this. Everyone has already agreed that each issue is important. You are just sorting them by level now.

You will need to get a commitment from staff regarding the issues. Are these the right ones to be working on? You don't need 100 percent agreement—you can decide together what percentage is enough. At least an 80 percent level in strong commitment would mean more chance of success. Very successful teams have members who disagree with each other but commit to a decision once it is made.

The reproducible Commitment Continuum (page 211) is an easy method for showing commitment levels.

Look first for the small steps in Level 1 issues that can be early wins for the staff—a manageable project that everyone agrees on that can be accomplished and a win for the staff. Make it the number-one action.

For each issue you will need to agree on the following:

- Which staff members can adopt this issue and lead the solution?
- What exactly are they charged with doing?
- When should this be done?
- What are the suggested components of this step?
- Do they need any resources or information?
- How often do we need to hear back from them?
- How will we know when it's a success and we can celebrate?
- Are any of these actions another "Trip to Abilene"?
- How will these actions impact student or staff learning?

Staff members need to be crystal clear about what they have decided on when they leave this meeting.

Write up each as a reference document for the team that volunteers to implement that plan. Remember, you are not developing the whole plan—just the parameters to get the people started.

Try to involve more staff members than just the administration and the facilitation team. Look for leaders to emerge to share the workload here. Try to have support staff and union representatives join an implementation team whenever possible.

At a group I facilitated, a frustrated person said, as we were trying to agree on a plan of action, "Are you in the boat or not in the boat with us?" That question led to the group pulling together two rows of ten chairs in the formation of a long canoe or dragon boat. One by one, they decided to get "in the boat" and take a seat indicating that they were "on board" with the decision. It got down to two left standing outside, on dry land. One said he would tie a dinghy to the main boat and come along but on the outside for the time being. The other said he wouldn't get "in the boat" but he wished them all well.

Consider Using Outside Help

If progress is not being made or the group is mired in deep, protracted conflict after experiencing these strategies, you should consider asking for formal outside help. The trust violations in the past may have been so severe that trust has been eliminated. Sometimes there is just a shell of a culture left in place. One person described this kind of culture as a "collection of classrooms held together by a common parking lot."

You don't want to negate all the work the staff has done up until this point and go back to zero again. But you can reach out to a number of people and groups for help.

- Invite a third-party facilitator or mediator from your school board or community to help you. Sometimes a fresh set of eyes and ears can offer a new perspective. If this is a trusted person, he or she can offer immeasurable help.

- Use your mentors. Consider calling the local principals' or teachers' organization, union, or a trusted advisor in your local school board to talk over the situation confidentially. What advice can they offer?

Decide to Stay or Leave

If you have tried to make a distrusting situation improve and seem to be getting nowhere, you have two choices: stay the course and keep going, or decide to quit and move on.

At the conclusion of trust workshops, I have been asked what people should do if they work with or for people who are untrustworthy. If it is your supervisor or colleagues, you have to face reality and assess your options. Here are some suggestions to deal with this tough situation.

First of all, take a good look at yourself, and see if you are perhaps making assumptions that are not entirely true. Maybe there has been a misunderstanding in which you played a role. Gracefully put your concerns to the person or people you feel are untrustworthy—in private, not in public. Be as specific as you can. Try to work out an agreement about specific behaviors that would work toward building a trusting relationship. This may take a long time and will require patience. If you get a chance to work together with the person you feel is untrustworthy, you may both start to learn more about each other and build a stronger relationship.

If that doesn't work, you will have to decide whether it is time to change jobs. It may be better for your wellness and mental health to move to a new job than to accept the current situation. Try to find a trusted supervisor for advice and help in transferring to a new position.

Quitting while you're not ahead may actually be good for your health. However, if that is your ultimate choice, be up-front with the situation and leave in an honorable way, with dignity.

Be prepared for some staff to make the decision to leave because they don't agree with what's happening. Some people complain but then won't do

"Be careful of your thoughts, for your thoughts become your words. Be careful of your words, for your words become your deeds. Be careful of your deeds, for your deeds become your habits. Be careful of your habits, for your habits become your character. Be careful of your character, for your character becomes your destiny."

—Source Unknown

anything when the path is clear to make change. They are not ready or open to change. It may be a good thing for everyone if the unhappy people move on. Try not to take it personally.

In some cases, the issues really aren't trust issues at all. People can be lazy, incompetent, defiant, or just plain unprofessional and resistant to change of any kind. Power struggles are hard to win.

Keep in mind, too, that distrust is extremely resistant to change. Sometimes the low levels of trust are ignored for too long, until it is impossible to recover from them. In the corporate world, this condition often leads to bankruptcy or serious downsizing. In education, the option of shutting down and starting over is rarely a viable one.

I encourage you to persevere and keep going in all but the direst of situations. Optimism is a key factor in a trust-rebuilding process.

Now it's time to move on to the second phase—building early trust. This is the focus of the next chapter, which will help you lay the groundwork for the possibility of mature trust in the future. Building trust is a continuous process of growth and relationship building.

Key Messages

1. It is reassuring to know there are strategies that can build trust from a situation where little or no trust exists.

2. Focus on student and staff learning as the overall purpose of dealing with distrust.

3. Skip over personal strategies at your own peril. The causes for distrust may lie within your values and behavior.

4. Deal with the barriers to trust, especially fear and betrayal.

5. Involve the union representative in a leadership role.

6. Surveys will give you useful data. The results of the survey Staff Feedback About Leader (page 209) are as important as the results for levels of trust staff members have in themselves.

7. An effective facilitation team of teacher leaders is needed to work with the principal and bridge the gap between staff and administration.

8. Distrusting groups need permission to have some fun, but be cautious in how you introduce it.

9. Trust is built through relationships and learning more about ourselves and others.

10. The help of an outsider (principal or consultant) may be needed for objectivity.

Questions

1. Do you agree that the personal strategies are as important as the interpersonal ones?

2. What did you learn about yourself from the personal strategies?

3. Can you add other activities from your experience that would work with these strategies?

4. How did you find the concept and the process of establishing a facilitation team of teacher leaders? What were the reactions?

5. Do you find people are talking more positively with each other and building new relationships?

6. When your group norms are in place, how do you plan to make sure they stick?

7. Do you feel the real issues are being put on the table for discussion? Is there more work to be done?

Further Resources

Jones, J. E., & Bearley, W. (1996). *360° Feedback: Strategies, Tactics and Techniques for Developing Leaders*. Amherst, MA: Human Resources Development Press.

360 Degree Leader Assessment and *Full Peer and Employee Assessment*. These are completed by a wide range of staff via email to a website. A detailed report is provided from the responses. Visit www.maximumimpact.com/360 for more information.

Walk the Talk: Resources for Personal and Professional Success. Visit www.walkthetalk.com for more information.

VIPs

Take time and reflect on the Very Important Points you feel were made in this chapter. What resonated with you the most?

CHAPTER 3

The Courage to Begin Building Trust

Schools are not buildings, curriculums, and machines. Schools are relationships and interactions among people.

—David R. Johnson and Frank P. Johnson

All of us have experienced the awkward silence of being asked in a group of strangers to comment on an idea, start a discussion, or ask a question. No one wants to be the first to speak, either because we don't trust ourselves to say something relevant or because we don't trust one another to be positive and encouraging. Even in groups where distrust isn't an issue, we fear negative judgment.

This chapter is intended for groups or schools that already have a sense of early trust and schools or groups that are new and therefore have no relationship history.

Regardless of the situation, building trust is easier than dealing with distrust. To groups that have faced their level of distrust and worked through the issues—congratulations! For brand new schools, the strategies that follow will help them create their history in a positive way.

All schools in this early stage of trust need perseverance and courage to keep going. Gains will be small and may seem negligible at first, but

Central to the strategies are conversations—talking together and listening for meaning. People need an opportunity to put critical issues out in the open—on the table—and to address the barriers of fear and betrayal.

collectively they will start to make a difference over time. Cheer each other on, and don't give up.

The chapter explores the research on trust: its complexity, stages, and dimensions. The practical strategies that follow, in chapter 4, focus on building the capacity for both early personal and interpersonal trust.

But this stage of early trust is not the ultimate goal—we must not lose sight of a higher level of optimal trust, one where schools rarely find themselves. That is the mission of chapter 5—to paint a vision of success for high-performing teams with mature levels of trust. But for now, let's focus on trust at its earliest stages.

The Nature of Trust

Much of the original research about trust was based on romantic relationships. Recently, more attention has been focused on trust in the workplace. In either case, trust is a complex concept that is difficult to capture in one definition.

Before looking at more formal definitions, try to develop a personal definition by completing one or both of the following sentences:

- If a young child asked me: "What is trust?" I would say . . .
- If a teenager asked me: "Is it risky to trust someone else?" I would say . . .

It isn't easy, is it? Here are a few definitions to start with. Which ones most appeal to you? Why? What is one key word in each definition that goes to the heart of the meaning?

- Trust is a state involving confident, positive expectations about another's motives with respect to oneself in situations involving risk. (Lewicki & Bunker, 1996, p. 117)
- Trust is an individual's belief in, and willingness to act on the basis of, the words, actions, and decisions of another. Distrust is not merely the absence of trust, but is an active negative expectation regarding another. (Lewicki & Wiethoff, 2000, p. 87)
- Trust means that one can expect that the word or promise of another individual, whether verbal or written, can be relied upon. It determines a reputation as trustworthy or not. (Rotter, 1967, p. 653)
- Trust is a glue that holds things together as well as a lubricant that reduces friction and facilitates smooth operations. (Tschannen-Moran, 2004, p. 38)
- Trust is reciprocal—you have to give it to get it—and it's built incrementally, step-by-step over time. (Reina & Reina, 2006, p. 13)
- Trust exists when we make ourselves vulnerable to others whose subsequent behavior we cannot control. (Kouzes & Posner, 1987, p. 146)
- Trust is the safe feeling you have when you let someone else know your inner feelings and private information and believe that he or she will not share this with others indiscriminately. (Fortune, 2007)

In a cross-discipline study of trust, Rousseau, Sitkin, Burt, & Camerer (1998) concluded that scholars fundamentally agree on the core meaning of trust. Compare it to your definition. They suggest the following as a widely held definition of trust:

> Trust is a psychological state (not a behavior or a choice) comprising the intention to accept vulnerability based upon positive expectations of the intentions or behavior of another. (p. 395)

They isolated two conditions that must exist for trust to arise:

1. Risk creates an opportunity for trust, which leads to risk taking. Trust would not be needed if actions could be undertaken with complete certainty and no risk.

2. Interdependence is needed where the interests of one party cannot be achieved without reliance upon another. (p. 395)

The Complexity of Trust in Schools

Within a school, the variety of reciprocal relationships makes it challenging to analyze the barriers to trust and to plan steps to build it. The history of past levels of trust in the building is another factor. The prior staffs' experiences with the credibility of previous administrator teams will definitely have an impact on the type of welcome any new administrator receives.

Trust is formed within individuals themselves (as self-trust), between pairs of staff members, or within groups (as interpersonal or relational trust).

When talking about trust in a school, you need to be specific about which relationships you mean. High trust in one relationship isn't always reflected in others. It is situational and fragile. As Bryk & Schneider (2002) point out, trust relationships within a school resemble a fine web of interconnected strands:

> An interrelated set of mutual dependencies are embedded within the social exchanges in any school community. Regardless of how much formal power any given role has in a school community, all participants remain dependent on others to achieve desired outcomes and feel empowered by their efforts. (p. 41)

Many educators might assume that it is the relationships between administrators and teachers that are the most fraught with trust issues. In fact, teachers' own trust for each other demands just as much attention in the trust-building process:

> Teachers' relationships with each other can often be more challenging than those between teachers and their bosses. Unfortunately, many schools are organized in ways that discourage trust building. Teachers are isolated from each other and have little time to discuss different views. The researchers also identified procedural blocks in districts where teaching jobs get filled based on seniority and credentials rather than professionalism or where incompetent teachers are protected by such rules. (Gordon, 2002, p. 2)

Stages of Trust Development

Trust cannot be captured by a single, "static" definition of its key elements and attributes. Trust is viewed as a dynamic phenomenon that takes on a different character in early, developing and "mature" stages of a relationship.

—Roy Lewicki and Barbara Bunker

In chapter 1 we began discussing trust using the metaphor of a partially filled glass. However, the development of trust through distinct stages is more complex than this image implies. In figure 3.1 you can see the way trust grows over time.

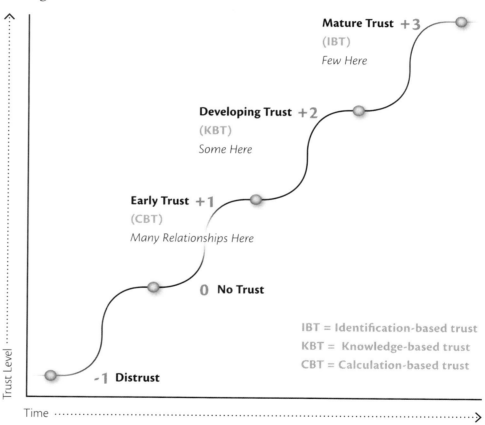

Figure 3.1: Stages of Trust Development

Adapted from Roy J. Lewicki's Trust Development. Used with permission of Roy J. Lewicki.

In 2006, Roy Lewicki, Edward Tomlinson, and Nicole Gillespie published an article called "Models of Interpersonal Trust Development." In it, they describe the difference between psychological and behavioral approaches to trust development. (This book largely uses the psychological approach to trust, which they call a "transformational model.") They assert that "there are different types of trust and that the nature of trust itself transforms over time" (p. 1006) in interpersonal relationships.

Visit **go.solution-tree .com/leadership** to download and print the Stages of Trust Development.

Lewicki, Tomlinson, and Gillespie note that individuals may approach initial encounters with distrust (or negative trust) for three reasons:

1. Cultural or psychological factors that bias an individual toward initial distrust

2. Untrustworthy reputation information about another, suggesting that distrust is appropriate

3. Context and situational factors that warrant such an early judgment

Most trust relationships find themselves at the early stage, some move on to the developing stage, and a few make it to the highest level of mature trust. As Roy Lewicki and Barbara Bunker (1996) write:

> The three stages of trust are linked in a sequential iteration in which the achievement of trust at one level enables the development of trust at the next level. . . . Our model of transitional stages in trust development creates the necessary groundwork to specify how trust declines and how it may be repaired. (p. 119)

Trust is not static and changes over time. It can improve and grow through stages as the diagram shows, but it can also dissolve, either slowly or rapidly. It may even come back later on. Every relationship has a different trust wave pattern of ups and downs. As people get to know each other and take more risks, in either a personal or professional context, they move through stages to mature levels of trust. The dynamics of the relationship change at each stage, and the stakes become greater as time goes on.

New leaders sometimes assume that people know and trust each other when, in fact, they may not even know each others' names. These leaders may jump in and impose tasks requiring far more honesty and risk than staff are ready for. It is critical to slow down and take the time to build a strong foundation for the future, especially as newcomers to existing groups. Make an honest self-assessment, establish your trustworthiness, and then apply these principles to groups and teams on a larger scale.

Early Trust: Stage One

When people meet for the first time and begin to work together, even as fellow employees, they spend some time in this beginning stage of trust. If there is any meaningful work to be done together and the results are successful, the relationship then moves to the next stage. Many relationships may remain at this level, although some trust is definitely better than no trust. Lewicki and Bunker named this *calculation-based trust* (CBT) because it is "a . . . calculation . . . of the outcomes resulting from creating and sustaining a relationship relative to the costs of maintaining it or severing it" (2006, p. 1007).

Participants at this stage of trust development feel that the relationship is both fragile and vulnerable. They constantly weigh the costs and benefits of staying in it, and the growth of trust is slow. They may fear disclosing too much too fast. Early trust is ensured and strengthened not only by the possible rewards of being trusted, but also by the threat of a reputation being hurt by ending it.

For a variety of reasons, some relationships never develop past CBT:

- The relationship at work just doesn't require it.

- It's a "one time" relationship.

- There are too many rules.

- They don't like each other enough.

- Something happens to cause less trust or even distrust.

Lewicki and Bunker liken this stage to the game of Chutes and Ladders (or Snakes and Ladders). Players roll dice to move their game piece forward from square to square to the top of the board and victory. If they land on a ladder, their progress is rapid; if they land on a chute (or snake), they slip back, perhaps even to the beginning. Relationships in the early trust stage are uncertain in the same way.

Developing Trust: Stage Two

In relationships with repeated interactions over time, there can be growth into the next phase. Lewicki and Bunker call this stage *knowledge-based trust* (or KBT): "Trust grows with a positive relationship history and increased knowledge and predictability of the other, and further when parties come to develop an emotional bond and shared values" (2006, p. 994). Now the question one asks is not so much, How much do I trust this person? but, In what areas and in what ways do I trust?

For example, if one person in a relationship has always been on time for meetings and is late one day, the other member of the team would be inclined to forgive the transgression, because over time the transgressor's behavior has been both predictable and respectful. He trusts that this occurrence is the exception because of the historical pattern up to that point. In a new relationship, lateness to a meeting might trigger a whole different set of concerns.

The stage of developing trust often involves compromises, with fairly mature people interacting. They have respect for each other, but they want to avoid the possibility of ugly confrontations, so they communicate politely—but not empathically. The creative possibilities are not fully opened up.

Lewicki and Bunker liken this stage of the process to gardening, with its experimenting, fertilizing, weeding out, and deadheading. Each year, the gardeners learn more about what will grow best in which part of the garden and what the soil is like and begin to try new types of plants, flowers, and arrangements with wild expectation of the vivid results as they grow. Some parts of the garden bring surprises with unexpected new growth. Maintenance is constantly needed to cut back overgrown areas and plan new parts of the garden.

High-Performing Trust: Stage Three

Very few relationships make it to this final stage, which Lewicki and Bunker (2006) called *identification-based trust* (or IBT). This stage is characterized by feelings of personal attachment and identification with other people's desires and intentions. The paucity of workplaces and schools actually working at this level makes it more difficult to imagine the vision we can attain. In these trust relationships, people experience total empathy and begin to think, feel, and respond like their other team members. They understand each other so well that they can act on one another's behalf. High-trust produces synergy and creativity. Although high-performing trust is rare, it is our goal!

Lewicki and Bunker call this stage "a leap of faith, grounded in the conviction that the partner can be relied upon to be responsive to one's needs in a caring manner, now and in the future" (2006, p. 1011).

An apt metaphor for mature trust is a symphony orchestra. The individual musicians are highly skilled with their own instruments. Some are versatile and even play several instruments. They meet to rehearse and dialogue regularly, perfecting one common piece of music in preparation for a performance. The conductor, a trained musician, has an overview of everyone's music and listens to each musician play. Leading only with rhythmic body language and the movements of a baton—the conductor is the only member of the team who makes no sound—he encourages each section of the orchestra. The result is truly magnificent when it works well, with many different instruments being played in harmony by a high-trusting team of professionals.

A fable about the chicken and the pig is commonly used to illustrate the need for people who are committed to a company, project, or investment. Both the chicken and the pig are necessary for making a breakfast of bacon and eggs. The chicken is "involved" (by providing the eggs), but the pig is "committed" (by providing the ham). In high-performing trust, it's definitely time for commitment—although the price to be paid isn't as high.

> An apt metaphor for mature trust is a symphony orchestra. . . . The result is truly magnificent when it works well, with many different instruments being played in harmony by a high-trusting team of professionals.

Linking the Stages of Trust With School Culture

The way people treat each other and go about their business at school is commonly referred to as the school's working "culture." School culture is not a new concept, but it has significant relevance when talking about the high levels of trust required to build collaborative teams and schools. Traditionally, educators have worked in cultures of isolation and individualism.

Balkanized cultures may have a slightly higher level of trust, but only within small groups, for example first grade teachers or physical education teachers. For teachers to change the norm and choose to work collaboratively requires a high degree of trust—and new skills.

Five Types of School Culture

Louise Stoll and Dean Fink (1996) describe the following five types of school culture:

1. Moving—In this culture, the staff
   - Boost students' progress and achievement.
   - Work together to respond to changing context and keep developing.
   - Know where they are going and have the will and skill to get there.

2. Cruising—In this culture, the school
   - Appears to possess many qualities of school effectiveness.
   - Is usually in a more affluent area.
   - Has students who achieve in spite of the teaching quality.
   - Has staff who tend to disregard the minority who are struggling.
   - Does not prepare all students for a changing world.

3. Strolling—In this culture, the staff
   - Is neither particularly effective or ineffective—it's "in-between."
   - Moves at an inadequate rate to cope with pace of change.
   - Has ill-defined and sometimes conflicting aims that inhibit improvement.

4. Struggling—In this culture, the staff
   - Is ineffective and they know it.
   - Expend considerable energy to improve.
   - Are unproductive ("thrashing about") but willing to try anything.
   - Will ultimately succeed.

5. Sinking—In this culture, the staff
   - Are ineffective—isolated with patterns of blame and self-reliance.
   - Are unable or unwilling to change.
   - Blame the parents if they are in a low income area.
   - Need dramatic action and significant support. (Stoll & Fink, 1996, pp. 6–7)

These five cultures are pictured in figure 3.2.

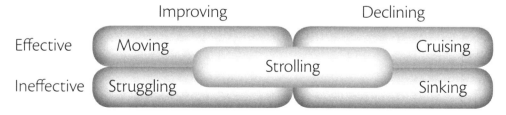

Figure 3.2: Five types of school culture

Cruising schools are particularly complacent and resent outsiders suggesting they could improve. They represent the greatest challenge in building trust. I remember the anger and resistance I received when I worked with a school that was "cruising": I had only two hours with them one afternoon and had planned an activity in which they would identify what was working, what needed improvement, and what they could do to help themselves after we talked about learning communities. It became apparent in my preactivity comments that they felt they were just fine and didn't need me or any other outside staff developer. Granted they had a point, in that they deserved to be more involved in the planning and use of time in these rare "PD Day" afternoons. Because it was a magnet school, the students' test scores were well above the rest, and the staff was proud of this. But I got the feeling that some of them didn't seem willing to worry about the few students who were not doing well, even though it would have been easy to identify and intervene with this group of kids. I wondered how they would feel if their own sons or daughters were in this ignored group.

Linking the Stages of Trust to Stages of Team Development

The stages of trust can also be linked to Bruce Tuckman's classic four-stage developmental sequence. Tuckman, an educational psychologist, described these stages in 1965 after studying the behavior of small groups. He observed that groups need to go through each of these stages to achieve high performance. Understanding them can improve both the chance of building trust and the amount of time it takes to do so. As described in Smith (2005), his model provides a predictable sequence and helps us make sense of what happens in groups and teams:

1. **Forming**—Orientation, dependence and testing of boundaries and behaviors, gathering information about each other, avoiding conflict

2. **Storming**—Real issues start to surface, with inevitable conflict and polarization around interpersonal skills. At this stage, groups either revert back to the more comfortable "forming" stage or move through this conflict and begin to do the hard work needed for improvement.

3. **Norming**—Arguments die down, cohesiveness builds, standards and roles develop with more intimacy and appreciation of each other.

4. **Performing**—Trusting enough to be interdependent, flexible, functional; group energy and morale are high.

   [In 1977, Tuckman refined the model by adding a fifth stage, "adjourning," in conjunction with Mary Ann Jensen.]

5. **Adjourning**—Dissolution, termination of roles, completion of the task. This stage can either be one of pride of accomplishments and being part of the group or it can be stressful if the ending is unplanned or unexpected. (It is sometimes called "de-forming and mourning.") (p. 3)

In my experience, an understanding of these stages helps groups push beyond the storming phase for more productive teamwork in the performing stage. New members can often challenge a group as it moves back to the storming and norming stages.

The reproducible graphic Stages of Trust and Team Development and School Culture (page 212) represents a combination of Tuckman's stages of team development and Stoll and Fink's types of school culture with the stages of trust.

Visit **go.solution-tree.com/ leadership** to download and print this graphic.

Our Willingness to Trust

It is better to suffer wrong than to do it, and happier to be sometimes cheated than not to trust.

—Samuel Johnson

The stage of trust we experience (early, developing, or mature) in a personal or professional relationship rests on our predisposition with regard to trust. A person might be so basically distrusting that it would be very hard for him or her to ever experience deep relational trust.

Erik Erikson, the famed psychoanalyst, developed eight psychosocial stages of human development throughout the life span. The first stage, Trust vs. Mistrust, occurs from approximately birth to one year:

> Mothers create a sense of trust in their children by that kind of administration which in its quality combines sensitive care of the baby's individual needs and a firm sense of personal trustworthiness within the trusted framework of their culture's life style. This forms the basis of the child for a sense of identity which will later combine a sense of being "all right," of being oneself, and of becoming what other people trust one will become. (Erikson, 1963, p. 249)

If trust is not formed at this stage and mistrust takes over, the child can become withdrawn, suspicious and mistrusting as an adult.

Children are therefore born neither trusting nor untrusting and need to learn for themselves if the world is safe or unsafe. They watch and learn from experience and the behavior of their parents, family members, and other caregivers and adults. Adults who lived through traumatic situations as children, such as divorce, child abuse, or bullying, may have their trust in others shaken or even destroyed, and they may carry this feeling into adult life.

Issues of trust, then, begin very early in human development and recur throughout life when we encounter new or stressful situations (Hoy & Kupersmith, 1984). We can't assume that our colleagues' trust will be automatic, nor should we feel personally responsible if people don't immediately trust us.

In his book *Bringing Out the Winner in Your Child* (1996), John Croyle tells the story of a father who promised to go on a Boy Scout camping trip with his twelve-year-old son. On the day of the campout, the son was ready to load their gear in the car the moment his dad arrived home from work early, so they could meet the others at 5:00 p.m. But Dad didn't arrive till 7 p.m. He told the boy not to worry—they would leave early in the morning and catch

We can't assume that our colleagues' trust will be automatic, nor should we feel personally responsible if people don't immediately trust us.

up with everyone. Early on Saturday the boy loaded the car—sleeping bag, cooking stove, pup tent, supplies—but Dad woke up late, complaining of a bad back. He was sorry, he just couldn't make it. Deeply disappointed, the boy unloaded the gear. A half hour later, the boy saw his dad throw his golf clubs in the trunk and drive off.

Consider the effect this early betrayal of trust must have had on that young boy.

Think of your inclination to trust or not in terms of the level of water in the Trust Glass, which we picture again in figure 3.3.

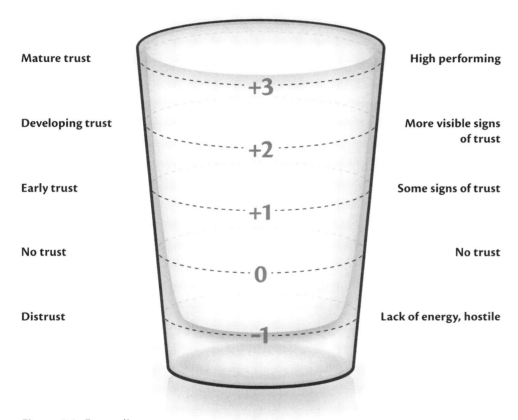

Figure 3.3: From distrust to mature trust

Reflect on life experiences where you trusted someone either too little or too much in your estimation. Do you think that overall you tend to be a high-trusting or low-trusting person? Rotter (1980) points out that high trusters are "more willing than low trusters to give people the benefit of the doubt." The high truster says, 'I will trust this person until I have clear evidence that he or she cannot be trusted'" (p. 102). Megan Tschannen-Moran (2004) writes that people with a disposition to trust:

- Are more likely to see the good points and overlook the flaws.
- Tend to be more trustworthy.
- Seem to be happier and more popular.
- Are less likely to lie, cheat, and steal. (pp. 47–48)

On the other hand, according to Rotter, a low truster says:

> "I will not trust this person until there is clear evidence that he or she can be trusted." It is hard for a low truster to feel safe or to become vulnerable. It may be true that high-trusters are fooled more often by crooks, but low trusters are probably fooled just as often by distrusting honest people; they thereby forfeit the benefits that trusting others might bring. (Rotter, 1980, p. 36)

People have low levels of trust for many reasons, including the following:

- They have been put down or bullied.
- They have experienced emotional neglect or abuse.
- They have been through a bitter end to a relationship or the traumatic loss of a friend or parent.
- They have lived in an unpredictable and volatile environment.
- They have low self-esteem and feel victimized.
- They are critical and skeptical—personality types that want facts, not feelings.

The seeds of distrust may have been sown years before. People believe that they have been hurt too much in the past and refuse to be hurt again now or in the future. The walls they build around them are meant to protect them from being hurt ever again or having to face the problem.

The level of trust people carry in their lives as part of their core personality will differ depending on the situation, time, and place. For example, one teacher may come to school totally trusting the principal and staff regardless of her past experiences. Another enters with caution, and a third arrives totally distrusting her colleagues and the administration because of the deep emotional damage she experienced as a young girl. All three teachers enter the same door of the school. The task is to get to know these three different teachers and help them become trusting and positive team members.

A Note on Trust and Intelligence

According to clinical psychologist Julian Rotter, one of the most prominent researchers on the trust phenomenon (as cited in Kouzes and Posner, 1987), there is no relationship between individuals' trust levels and their scores on scholastic aptitude tests.

Reciprocal Trust

This story was told to me by Susan Chisholm about a time when she was a new leader in an alternative school, and had arranged an in-service session for staff using True Colors, a personality type instrument:

> One teacher was openly skeptical about its value. She didn't know me well enough to automatically trust my judgment about its worth, but she did offer me her conditional trust and participated in the session in a professional way.

She gave me the benefit of the doubt. Years later we talked about that day, and she spoke about the value of the ideas she learned in that workshop. Not only had she gained some insight into her approach to teaching and learning, but she had also discovered the positive results of taking a risk. (Chisholm, personal communication)

The Trust Glass could just as easily portray the reciprocal nature of trust *between* members of groups. At one level, individuals bring a basic level of trust based on their background and life experience. At this second level, people then interact with others in pairs, groups, or teams and build reciprocal trust.

The level of reciprocal trust can move up and down depending on what happens, the nature of the group's task, and how long the relationships have been in place.

At times in life it is appropriate to be skeptical and cautious, and at other times trusting someone else without question must happen swiftly. For example, in an emergency such as a car accident or flood, strangers often move into immediate action to help each other.

The Phenomenon of Swift Trust

In certain situations, people experience a leap of faith and move quickly to the next level of trust. According to Lewicki et al. (2006), this swift trust may occur with a stranger who is instantly liked. Myerson, Weick, & Kramer (1996) also discuss "how teams of individuals can come together quickly and successfully to work on highly complex, skilled interactions in temporary groups and teams, such as surgical teams, disaster rescue teams, and airline cockpit crews" (p. 1000).

In a school setting, swift trust may occur during a crisis, when people put aside their differences and work together with police and ambulance attendants to assist an injured child or respond to a violent situation.

We need to trust appropriately and size up different situations while recognizing that we each have a certain predisposition according to our personal trust scale. Some distrust is healthy in certain situations:

Some authors argue that high-trust creates a "blindness" that can allow the truster to be exploited and taken advantage of and that a certain amount of 'prudent paranoia' is appropriate in a relationship. There is an emerging role for distrust in creating organizational change and healthy intra-organizational competition. Too much trust can be damaging also, as "over-generalized" trust may set the stage for highly trusted yet under-monitored employees to either exploit trust relationships . . . to engage in crimes against the organization. . . . The best conditions exist when there is a healthy dose of both trust and distrust. (Lewicki et al., 2006, p. 1016)

Never trusting and always trusting are both inappropriate.

The optimal level of reciprocal trust may differ depending on the situation, time, and place. For example, a team of grade one teachers may trust each other to plan curriculum and lessons together and share the workload, but only a few feel trusting enough to share their personal lives.

Blind trust can prevent us from seeing what is really happening. Con artists and scammers make a lot of money preying on overly trusting people. They rely on the fact that many people will miss obvious signs of deception and won't be able to tell that they are being lied to. An article in the Toronto *Star* (Lawton, 1998), about a book on scams by Chuck Whitlock described how readily trusting people open their wallets:

> Whitlock started this one himself with a speech at a convention on business opportunities. The message in his talk on how to avoid becoming a victim of business opportunity fraud was take your time and do your homework before investing. Afterward, Whitlock donned a disguising wig, moustache and horn-rimmed glasses and stood in front of a sign that said: "Platinum 1000: The light bulb that never burns out. Buy a franchise today!"
>
> Ten people who had just listened to the cautionary speech actually signed the distributing contracts and wrote $1000 dollar checks on the spot. (p. A12)

According to Lawton (1998), Whitlock offers four rules to live by: 1) trust your gut, 2) do your homework, 3) don't succumb to pressure tactics, and 4) if it sounds too good to be true, it probably is.

While overtrusters experience the difficulties described by Whitlock and need to draw a firm boundary, undertrusters may simply need some time. Once, I met with a teacher in my office to discuss his yearly PD plan. I was asking a few questions about his goals and vision for the year, but his response revealed how uncomfortable he was sharing his learning plans. We completed the paperwork in an impersonal way, and the task was finished. I know now that I was engaging him in a discussion involving more trust than he was willing to give to me at the time. As I got to know him better, I could see he was a kind and conscientious teacher—even creative—with his students. He indeed was committed to professional development. He did start to talk about his dreams and vision with me over the coming months in more relaxed settings than my office. It took time for him to see that I really was interested in his plans and that I might even be able to help him. I realized at the time that perhaps it wasn't as simple as his "never trusting administrators." No one had ever taken the time to build a relationship with him to the point that he felt trusting enough to talk about his professional life.

When we have enough risk-taking experiences to reflect on and analyze what worked or didn't work for us, and as we experiment to find the appropriate level of trust to extend to people, we have accumulated what Stephen M. R. Covey would call "smart trust." He combined both the propensity to trust with the analysis that needs to take place and came up with the four-zone Smart Trust Matrix (see figure 3.4, page 93).

- **Zone 1** (High Propensity to Trust, Low Analysis) is blind trust. Covey calls it "the Pollyanna approach." This is where the gullible and naive suckers discussed in Scam School are found.

- **Zone 2** (High Propensity to Trust, High Analysis) is the Smart Trust zone that "elevates instinct and intuition to the realm of good judgment" (Covey, 2006, p. 290).

- **Zone 3** (Low Propensity to Trust, Low Analysis) is the no trust zone of indecision. Covey says this zone is characterized by "indecision, insecurity, protectiveness, apprehension, tentativeness and immobilization" (p. 291).

- **Zone 4** (Low Propensity to Trust, High Analysis) is the distrust zone of suspicion. People here don't trust anyone much except themselves. This would be the zone of the TV show *X Files,* with its motto "Trust No One."

Surprisingly, Covey points out that Zone 4 is one of the highest-risk zones. Here, with little interaction that involves trusting others, and with collaboration seen as undesirable, we miss opportunities. Not trusting people is often the greatest risk of all.

Covey cautions that Zone 2, with the lowest risk and highest return, doesn't necessarily mean you extend trust to someone: "You may decide to extend limited or no trust at all . . . but the approach itself will almost always build trust" (2006, p. 293).

Figure 3.4: Four quadrants of trust, according to Covey's Smart Trust Matrix

From *The Speed of Trust* (2006), by Stephen M. R. Covey. New York: Free Press. Used with permission of the author.

The Two Sides of Credibility

Most researchers on trustworthiness agree that credibility is its foundational dimension and that credibility has two sides: who we *are*—our character, and what we *can do*—our competence. Each is important in building and maintaining trusting relationships.

Think of colleagues whom you know to be trustworthy. What makes them so? Is it their character or their competence that you are impressed with—or is it both?

Character: Who We Are

Here are the dimensions of trustworthiness that collectively make up our character:

- Integrity and honesty
- Consistency and reliability
- Maturity
- Respect and support
- Willingness to admit mistakes
- Fairness, ethics, equity, and justice
- Ability to take risks and be vulnerable
- Benevolence, caring, and compassion
- Putting students first

Note that risk is necessary for trustworthiness. If there is no risk, there is no need to trust. Why? Because risk creates a feeling of vulnerability, David Johnson and Frank Johnson say that "trust is a perception that a choice can lead to gains or losses, that whether you will gain or lose depends on the behavior of the other person, that the loss will be greater than the gain, and that the person will likely behave so that you will gain rather than lose" (1997, p. 130).

This gain/loss calculus is illustrated in the example that follows. A teacher new to the school approaches a more senior teacher in the same department and asks if they could co-operatively plan two new units in the semester's curriculum. The senior teacher realizes she can gain the trust and cooperation of the new teacher, but there is a risk that the curriculum won't be ready in time if their collaboration doesn't work out. She decides that beginning to gain the trust in the short term with the new teacher is worth the risk. She also imagines it will be more fun doing it this way and looks forward to her new relationship with the younger teacher—and to the ways it will benefit their students.

Benevolence—or a sense of caring, personal regard, and compassion—takes on more significance as relationships get deeper and last longer, while ability and integrity seem to factor in earlier. Educators talk about benevolence as a major factor in feeling safe enough to teach, especially at a school where violence is an ongoing issue. Knowing that the principal and other staff members are looking out for them or "have their back" builds a feeling of trustworthiness among the staff members.

Character vs. Reputation

Abraham Lincoln was very concerned with character, but he was also aware of the importance of having a good reputation. He explained the difference this way: "Character is like a tree and reputation like its shadow. The shadow is what we think of it; the tree is the real thing."

Put another way, your reputation is what people think of you. Your character is what you actually are.

In a world preoccupied with image, it's easy to worry too much about our reputation and too little about our character. Building a reputation is largely a public-relations project; building character requires us to focus on our values and actions. Noble rhetoric and good intentions aren't enough— what's needed is moral strength based on ethical principles. Character is revealed by actions, not words, especially when there's a gap between what we want to do and what we should do and when doing the right thing costs more than we want to pay.

Our character is revealed by how we deal with pressures and temptations. But it's also disclosed by everyday actions, including what we say and do when we think no one is looking and we won't get caught.

The way we treat people who we may think have little to offer us (such as housekeepers, waiters, and secretaries) reveals more about our character than how we treat people we think are important. People who are honest, kind, and fair only when there's something to gain shouldn't be confused with people of real character who demonstrate these qualities habitually, under all circumstances.

Competence: What We Can Do

Let's turn our attention next from "who we are" to "what we can do" or our perceived competency or capability. Here are some of its dimensions:

- Prior training and experience
- Knowledge of the current job
- Willingness to learn in a new job
- Technical ability, expertise, and skills
- Efficiency with use of technology, information sharing, and time management
- Interdependence—being a team player and learning with and from others
- Positive track record for producing results

Educators talk about benevolence as a major factor in feeling safe enough to teach, especially at a school where violence is an ongoing issue.

"Character is not a fancy coat we put on for show. It's who we really are."

—Michael Josephson

Why We Need Both

Belief that another person is competent to perform what is needed on the job is key to building trust. Often as educators we are thrown into a new job without much prior training, and we rise to the occasion and do what we need to do to get started. Once in the job, we continue to develop our competency as we learn from our own experiences and from working with others. We become competent through hard work and positive attitude. However, if we have proof that someone is unable to successfully complete an assigned task or do a critical part of their job, our trust in them decreases, and we see them as untrustworthy.

At the same time, belief in the general good character of an individual can also affect trust levels. While you can quickly learn to be competent at most tasks in education, character doesn't change so fast. Self-awareness of the trustworthiness of our character is a first step that can lead to actions that show others that we are trying to change.

Honest people who continue to be incompetent in their work are not trustworthy. Competence without character doesn't inspire trust, either. Just as a doctor who has a warm bedside manner but cannot perform a medical procedure expertly will not inspire trust, educators need both character and competence to earn the trust of others.

Trust, Respect, and Popularity

A principal once said to me that, above all, he wanted to be "RTL." He went on to explain that this meant **r**espected, **t**rusted, and **l**iked. He felt that all three of these values were important to his success as a leader. Although his statement had merit, I doubted that things were as simple as his slogan suggested. I realized that fact when I became a principal and had to make a decision that was the right one but that would make me unpopular with the staff, at least in the short term.

How closely associated and necessary are these three aspects of a leader? If you are trusted, is respect automatic? If you are liked, is trust automatic? Team members may see each other as trustworthy, but they may not respect their decisions. It helps if groups put these distinctions on the table and clarify their thoughts and beliefs about them.

Mutual respect is often included in the character side of trustworthiness. In fact, the words *trust* and *mutual respect* often go hand in hand in a discussion about trust. McKenna and Maister (2002) make an important distinction between the two terms:

> Trust and mutual respect are not necessarily synonymous. Mutual respect is an added dimension that can be as important as trust, particularly in the early stages of group work before personal trust has time to develop. . . . You can have respect for someone that you do not necessarily like—and you can work effectively with them. On the other hand, you can also trust someone whom

Just as a doctor who has a warm bedside manner but cannot perform a medical procedure expertly will not inspire trust, educators need both character and competence to earn the trust of others.

you do not necessarily "respect." . . . One of the best ways for two people to develop trust is to do "real work" together. (p. 161)

Tschannen-Moran (2004) distinguishes between trust and affection:

Trust is not the same as liking a person. It is possible to like someone you do not trust and trust someone you do not especially like. Because caring is an element of trust and we tend to like those from whom we feel benevolence or goodwill, it may be more likely that you will trust those you like and like those you trust. But affection is not necessary for trust to develop. (p. 22)

Credibility is also the basis on which we judge the trustworthiness of our leaders (including teacher leaders). Think of a leader or manager that you judge to be trustworthy. What roles do character and competence each play in your judgment about that person?

In *The Leadership Challenge* (2002), James Kouzes and Barry Posner report that those who believe their manager is credible are far more likely to:

- Be proud to tell others they're part of the organization.

- Feel a strong sense of team spirit.

- See their own personal values as consistent with those of the organization.

- Feel attached and committed to the organization.

- Have a sense of ownership of the organization.

On the other hand, when people perceive their managers to have low credibility, they're significantly more likely to:

- Produce only if they're being watched carefully.

- Be motivated primarily by money.

- Say good things about the organization publicly but criticize it privately.

- Consider looking for another job if the organization experiences problems.

- Feel unsupported and unappreciated. (pp. 33–34)

Kouzes and Posner administered a questionnaire to over 75,000 people in which they asked respondents to select seven qualities that they "most look for and admire in a leader, someone whose direction they would *willingly* follow" (p. 24). Only these four qualities received more than half of the votes:

1. Honest—having integrity and character. People do not want to be lied to or deceived.

2. Forward-looking—having a sense of direction. People want leaders who have a vision of success, take dreams seriously, and have ways to achieve them.

3. Competent—having a track record and an ability to get things done. Leaders do not need to know how to do every task in the workplace, but they must have relevant experience to draw on.

4. Inspiring—having an enthusiastic, energetic, and positive attitude. When the going gets tough, leaders keep everyone going and cheer them on. (p. 27–31)

All four of these top qualities are dimensions of trustworthiness. Thus, credibility relates both to who people are (character), as shown in 1 and 4 and what people do (competence), as shown in 2 and 3.

Violations of Credibility

In order to build trust, we must determine which side of credibility (character or competence) is the cause of low trust in a particular relationship and then decide if and how it can be improved. Trust that is lost as the result of a violation of character is far more difficult to regain than a loss based on a violation of competence.

For example, I may trust a famously temperamental chef to cook me a wonderful meal (competence), but that doesn't mean that I would trust him to be respectful to my friends when he meets them (character).

What Would You Do?

A newly appointed assistant principal joins the staff. Her first task is to design the yearly teaching timetable for the staff, an assignment for which she has little experience. Consider her options. Does she admit her inexperience and solicit staff advice and help, or does she go it alone because she believes that the staff expects her to be able to do it? What are the trust risks for each choice in terms of competence and character? How does being trustworthy differ from being trusted in this situation?

School Trust and Student Achievement

The social encounters of schooling are more intimate than typically found in associative relationships within most modern institutions.

—Anthony Bryk and Barbara Schneider

In their study of the Chicago elementary school system (1991–1997), Bryk and Schneider (2002) researched why some Chicago schools improved student achievement, while others did not. Resoundingly, they found that schools with strong relational levels of trust—teacher to teacher, teacher to leader, and teacher to parent—were much more likely to make academic gains (specifically measured by standardized mathematics and reading test scores) than schools without strong levels of trust. In fact, if the low level of trust continued over time, they concluded, there was virtually no chance of the school improving student achievement. See figures 3.5, 3.6, and 3.7 (pages 99–100) for the dramatic results.

The top ten schools in the study also tended to have the following characteristics:

- Fewer than 350 students (this study included only elementary schools)
- A stable student population that allowed for good relationships between parents and school professionals to develop over time

On the other hand, Bryk and Schneider found that racially isolated and predominately minority schools with high levels of poverty were much less likely to demonstrate improved academic productivity. In large part, the obstacles to improvement had to do with a lack of relational trust caused by racial or ethnic tensions, among other elements. Teachers in these schools had little trust in one another, their principal, or the parental community.

Significantly, although the characteristics of the student body and community may be beyond the control of the staff, the authors emphasize that the single most important factor influencing school improvement and academic achievement that can be changed and improved is the degree to which staff members trust and respect one another.

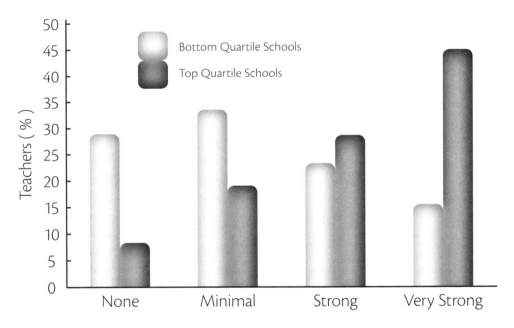

Figure 3.5: Teacher-teacher trust

From Bryk, Anthony S., and Barbara Schneider, Figure 6.2 of "Comparing Responses in Top and Bottom Quartile Schools on Teacher-Teacher Trust (1997 Survey)." In *Trust in Schools: A Core Resource for Improvement.* © 2002 Russell Sage Foundation, 112 East 64th Street, New York, NY 10021. Reprinted with permission.

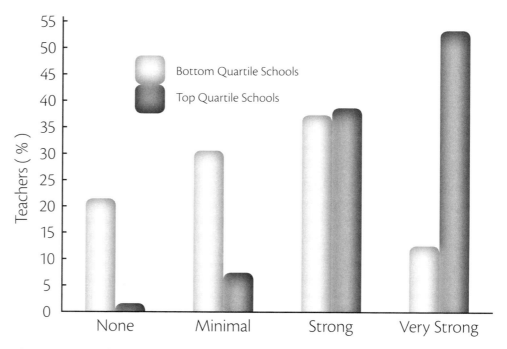

Figure 3.6: Teacher-principal trust

From Bryk, Anthony S., and Barbara Schneider, Figure 6.3 of "Comparing Responses in Top and Bottom Quartile Schools on Teacher-Teacher Trust (1997 Survey)." In *Trust in Schools: A Core Resource for Improvement.* © 2002 Russell Sage Foundation, 112 East 64th Street, New York, NY 10021. Reprinted with permission.

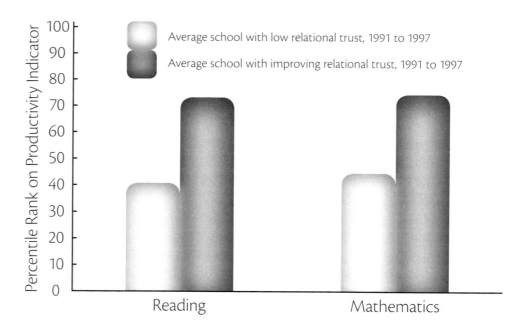

Figure 3.7: Effect on reading and math scores

From Bryk, Anthony S., and Barbara Schneider, Figure 6.12 of "Comparing Responses in Top and Bottom Quartile Schools on Teacher-Teacher Trust (1997 Survey)." In Trust in Schools: A Core Resource for Improvement. © 2002 Russell Sage Foundation, 112 East 64th Street, New York, NY 10021. Reprinted with permission.

Benefits of Trust for Schools

Trust-building doesn't come with overnight successes or quick fixes. It takes many years to see significant change. Keep in mind these benefits as you build trust:

- Collaboration instead of competition among staff, students, and administrators
- Synergy, innovation, and experimentation in classrooms
- Higher energy levels and self-esteem
- Buy-in, true implementation
- Risk-taking, lasting change, and increased confidence
- Willingness to challenge the status quo
- Conflicts aired and surfaced earlier
- Happiness, endurance, and tolerance
- Feelings of safety and security
- Increased capacity and personal growth

Most importantly, strong statistical evidence links all of these benefits to improvements in student achievement. In their ten-year study of Chicago elementary schools, Bryk and Schneider found the following:

> Schools reporting strong positive trust levels in 1994 were *three times* more likely to be categorized eventually as improving in reading and mathematics than those with weak trust reports. By 1997, schools with strong positive trust reports had a *one in two* chance of being in the improving group. In contrast, the likelihood of improving for schools with very weak trust reports was only *one in seven*. Perhaps most telling of all, schools with weak trust reports in both 1994 and 1997 *had virtually no chance* of showing improvement in either reading or mathematics [emphasis added]. (2002, p. 111)

> Our analyses document a strong statistical link between *improvements in relational trust and gains in academic productivity.* [italics in original] . . . Short of a large-scale social experiment with specific interventions aimed at building relational trust in schools, it is hard to envision a stronger evidence base documenting the significance of relational trust as a resource for school improvement. (p. 113)

Six Assumptions About Trusting Schools

The following six assumptions are key to the success of building and sustaining trust. We will identify and briefly describe them here, then expand on each as we discuss subsequent strategies.

1. **Shared leadership earns trust**. In traditional hierarchies, power flows up and blame flows down through the ranks. Instead of the power and control associated with authoritarian leadership and supervision, sharing leadership and governance will empower the staff and win over their trust. The involvement of the union repre-

sentative will be vital to any success. This requires flat lining the hierarchy in a school that inhibits change and risk taking through the delegation of significant tasks. The principal needs to focus on those jobs that only a principal can do. A clear process needs to be established to determine which decisions will be collaborative and which ones can be trusted to one person or a few people.

As Smith (1987) notes:

> A collaborative school requires a higher caliber of leadership than does a bureaucratic school. Principals of collaborative schools have often discovered that power shared is power gained. Teachers' respect for them grows. (p. 6)

2. **Change and improvement are part of learning.** People react to change in a variety of ways. Some resist change at all costs. Others follow the majority once they are convinced of the merits. A few step out in front as leaders of the change. Regardless of the reaction to change, it is part of learning and growth. It is inevitable. People will resist change if it comes without consultation and involvement, especially if it comes without their choice, or as a mandate. Knowledge of the process of change and skill with its implementation will build trust, as solutions to problems are put in place and new ways of doing business are required.

3. **Teamwork is essential.** While there will always be independent work, more productive work in learning organizations takes place when staff work interdependently, in pairs or small groups. No one person can do all the work that needs to be done. Even a bad team is usually better than no team. It can take more time, but the end result is usually better when there is more than one person facing a job. Trust is the foundation of teamwork and needs to be in place in order to get real work accomplished. Many staff members—even administrators—will need to learn the skills of working together as they move away from isolation to teamwork.

4. **Resistance and conflict are inevitable.** Some people just don't like to change, especially if they didn't choose it. Most resistance stems from broken promises in the past or fear of what is being done to them externally. Older staff members can feel worn out from too many changes. Take all resistance seriously and deal with it.

The term *community* often conjures images of a culture of consensus, shared values, and good spirits. But author Betty Achinstein tells us that community and conflict form an unexpected marriage. She writes, "Collaboration and consensus—critical elements that build community—actually generate conflict. Not only did the teacher professional communities experience multiple conflicts, but also the core norms and practices of collaboration that define teacher communities promoted conflicts" (Achinstein, 2002, p. 40).

5. **Action planning needs to be collaborative.** Instead of a leader standing up at a staff meeting and telling others what his or her

"It is not a great step to take power out at the top and put it at the bottom. It is still power. To build achieving organizations, you must replace power with responsibility."

—Peter Drucker

"We must first get teachers to understand and accept the limitations of what they can do if they continue to work alone."

—Ron Edmonds

vision is, a collective dialogue needs to take place with the whole staff to earn their trust and commitment.

Action planning involves five separate yet ultimately connected discussions:

    a. Shared vision—a discussion of hopes and dreams for the future

    b. Mission: the purpose of the school including values and beliefs

    c. Assessment of current status

    d. Short- and long-term actions that would achieve the vision of success

    e. Decisions regarding what needs to stop or slow down to focus on actions, and measuring success along the way at regular intervals

It is not enough for educators to only talk about what to do anymore. Much time has been wasted talking about what we should do. Schools either get caught up in a "paralysis by analysis" or by overplanning that never seems to result in real implementation. The difficult parts lie in both knowing *how* to do what needs to be done and then actually *doing it*. This "knowing-doing gap" has to be closed. With a collaborative action planning process, you can move ahead with small but strategic acts toward a vision that everyone is excited about.

6. **High-quality staff development needs to be the reality, not the vision.** What happens in the name of professional learning in schools is often a shameful waste of time. Large group "sit and git" sessions are all too common. But this kind of mandatory staff development is a barrier to trust formation. More ownership and commitment result when there is staff input and collaboration into the planning of learning opportunities.

Real professional learning happens each and every day in a "moving" school. It isn't always a large group event. Some of the best staff learning happens in small groups—almost invisibly—during the school day as best practices and ideas are shared. Each staff member needs to have his or her own growth plan linked to the vision of the school. Many collaborative forms of learning are necessary, such as coaching, mentoring, grade teams, and study groups. High-quality adult learning principles need to become a reality.

The research base around building trust in schools gives us a clear understanding of the challenges we face when working through its stages. By this time you should be experiencing "more ladders, and fewer snakes." Much of your success will be due to consistent, honest messages about the process of building trust and subsequent, real conversations, as people begin to speak up and say what they really think and feel. Making trust a discussable topic will be refreshing in itself.

"Collaboration and consensus—critical elements that build community—actually generate conflict."
—Betty Achinstein

"We constantly talk about the importance of student achievement, of teachers' staff development and professional growth of principals as if they occur on different planets during different epochs. In a community of learners, learning is endemic and mutually visible."
—Roland Barth

The strategies and activities in chapter 4 will provide ideas for your facilitation team to discuss and adapt to suit your school as you move from early trust to developing trust.

Don't stop here. Keep going—it only gets better. If you feel complacent and focus less intensely on trust, it's so easy to quickly slip back into a state of low trust or even distrust.

Key Messages

1. Trust is a state, not a behavior or choice.

2. Everyone has a history of trust that he or she brings to work each day. Some people are low trusters, others are high-trusters.

3. Schools have numerous, overlapping circles of trust. The larger the staff, the greater the number of circles and therefore more complexity.

4. Trust grows over time through distinct stages. Most schools remain at early trust levels at best. Some move on to developing stages, and a few achieve the highest level of mature trust.

5. Credibility is the foundational dimension of trust. It has two sides: competence and character. Both sides need attention.

6. Research has proven the direct correlation between levels of trust at school and student achievement.

7. Six conclusions we can draw about trusting schools are:

   a. Shared leadership earns trust.

   b. Change and improvement are part of learning.

   c. Teamwork is essential to staff and student learning.

   d. Resistance and conflict are inevitable.

   e. Action planning toward an exciting vision needs to be collaborative.

   f. High-quality staff development needs to be the reality, not the vision.

> "In a learning community, people construct meanings and structures that extend personal, interpersonal, and organizational capacity in support of professional improvement in teaching and learning."
>
> —Coral Mitchell and Larry Sackney

Questions

1. How important do you think trust, respect, and popularity are? Rank their importance to you as a team member or as a leader. If you had to drop one of these values, which one would it be?

2. Are you a high truster or a low truster by nature?

3. What other analogies can you think of that suit the stages of trust?

4. Read these sayings, and decide where they fit on the Trust Scale. Do any of these apply to your life?

   Neither a borrower nor a lender be.—Shakespeare

   Trust, but verify.—Ronald Reagan

Fool me once, shame on you. Fool me twice, shame on me.
—Chinese proverb

Once bitten, twice shy.—Anonymous American proverb

It's better to have loved and lost than never to have loved at all.
—Alfred Lord Tennyson

Love all, trust a few.—William Shakespeare

Trust no one, tell your secrets to nobody and no one will ever betray you.—Bigvai Volcy

It is impossible to go through life without trust: that is to be imprisoned in the worst cell of all, oneself.—Graham Greene

Trust No One—The X-Files

5. Which one of these definitions of trust applies most to you and your workplace? Why?

6. Would the definition change if the relationship had lasted a long time?

7. Which part of credibility do you think is more important—character or competence?

    ·   When would character without competence inspire trust?

    ·   When would competence without character inspire trust?

    ·   Which is more important to you as an educator?

Further Resources

Bellman, G. (1992). *Getting Things Done When You Are Not in Charge.* New York: Simon and Schuster.

Bridges, W. (2004). *Transitions: Making Sense of Life's Changes.* Cambridge, MA: Da Capo Press.

Brown Easton, L. (2004). *Powerful Designs for Professional Learning.* Oxford, OH: National Staff Development Council.

Killion, J. (2008). *Assessing Impact: Evaluating Staff Development.* Thousand Oaks, CA: Corwin Press.

Sparks, D. (2002). *Designing Powerful Professional Development for Teachers and Principals.* Oxford, OH: National Staff Development Council.

Sparks, D. (2005). *Leading for Results: Transforming Teaching, Learning, and Relationships in Schools.* Thousand Oaks, CA: Corwin Press.

Stephenson, S. (2001). When Your Heart Is in Your Dreams. *Register, 3*(3), 28–31.

Stephenson, S. (2003) Saying "NO" to the Unimportant. *Register, 5*(2), 21–24.

Stone, D., Patton, B., & Heen, S. (1999). *Difficult Conversations: How to Discuss What Matters Most.* New York: Penguin Books.

Strand, P., Christensen, J., & Halper, A. (2006). *Schools of Fish! Welcome Back to the Reason You Became an Educator.* Burnsville, MN: Charthouse International Learning Corporation.

Tschannen-Moran, R., & Tschannen-Moran, M. (2005). *Strengths-Based Focus Improves School Climate.* Accessed at www.celebrateschools.com/strengths-improve-climate.pdf on February 2, 2009.

VIPs

Take time and reflect on the very important points you feel were made in this chapter. What resonated with you the most?

CHAPTER 4

Medium-Risk Strategies to Develop Trust

If there is a bridge of trust between you and me that's only a two-ton bridge and I try to drive ten tons of truth over it, I'll break the bridge. Our relationship has fallen apart. But if I work on the relationship between you and me and build up that trust until the bridge can hold a ten-ton truck, then I can drive ten tons of truth across it.

—Ian Jones

The practical strategies that follow are designed to continue building the capacity for both early personal and interpersonal trust. Central to these strategies are conversations—talking together and listening for meaning. People need an opportunity to put critical issues out in the open—on the table—and to address the barriers of fear and betrayal. Leaders need to sincerely share control and power with their followers. Staff can then begin to work collaboratively to achieve the goal of improved staff and student learning.

These strategies are based on the three categories in the recursive model for building learning communities proposed by Coral Mitchell and Larry Sackney (2000):

1. Personal capacity strategies

2. Interpersonal capacity strategies (including affective and cognitive capacities)

3. Organizational capacity strategies

They write, "Growth in each category is built upon prior growth in itself and other categories, and builds a foundation for subsequent growth" (p. 12).

At certain times one category can take precedence over the others; at other times all three categories will merge or "nest" together and act as one. Mitchell and Sackney explain that "capacity builds not in a smooth, linear flow but in eddies and swells as well as in dips and depressions when no learning appears to be going on" (p. 12).

There are four personal capacity strategies and eight interpersonal strategies included in this chapter.

Personal Capacity Strategies

Building personal capacity has to do with the active and reflective construction of knowledge. It begins with a confrontation with the values, assumptions, belief systems, and practices that individuals embrace. . . . This knowledge empowers them to begin a search for new knowledge and to reconstruct their personal narrative.

—Coral Mitchell and Larry Sackney

Building personal capacity involves a search, beginning with inward reflection and moving to reflective conversations with trusted or "critical" friends and networks when it feels safe enough. Mitchell and Sackney identify the following stages of growth:

1. Denial

2. Rationalization

3. Questioning

4. Acceptance

5. Growth

They also discuss two different kinds of insight provided by a search for learning opportunities. One kind is internal, in which the individual recognizes an uncomfortable personal truth. The other is external, in which the individual experiences a sense of discovery—a eureka moment—that can add to his repertoire of personal competencies.

Balance is the key. Too much focus on the internal can cause a sense of inadequacy and self-doubt; too many eureka moments can result in a feeling of being overwhelmed and incapable of assimilating the knowledge.

In frank language, Mitchell and Sackney (2000) call the signals that can help identify the value of these searches the "Aha/Oh Shit! Syndrome." Learning that evokes an "Aha!" suggests the search is working—that the person has added something new to his or her repertoire of competencies. But when the opportunity causes someone to utter the popular profanity, then the internal search is not working, and the person has encountered an uncomfortable personal obstacle. Both insights need to be in balance. Too many "Ahas" lead to information overload and unassimilated professional knowledge, and too many of the other type "can lead to psychological risk and a conflicted professional identity. We believe that a healthy blend of these two kinds of insight is essential for extending personal capacity in an environment of psychological safety" (p. 29).

Let's look now at the following personal capacity strategies:

1. Focus on your own happiness.

2. Continue your feedback search.

3. Trust yourself.

4. Walk your talk.

Focus on Your Own Happiness

Psychologists have found that, compared to those who view the world with suspicion and disrespect, trusting people are more likely to be happy and psychologically adjusted. We like trusting people and seek them out as friends. We listen to people we trust and accept their influence.

—James Kouzes and Barry Posner

You may be wondering why happiness is included here as a strategy. The reason is that, without a positive attitude and environment, trust cannot thrive. Educators often put everyone else first in their desire to please, and their own health may suffer. They lose touch with themselves and their mental, physical, and emotional needs and can become stressed and burned out. Having a sense of humor, being fun to be with, and having a sense of camaraderie with colleagues are not often considered in school life. We are usually too busy to think of these important but not urgent factors. You don't have to be giddy or superficially funny or tell jokes. But your ability to stay positive in your job—most of the time—builds self-trust as well as others' trust in you.

The Power of Positive Psychology

Counselors and psychiatrists have traditionally focused on what can be called negative psychology. The number of research studies on depression far outweigh the number focusing on well-being or happiness. When building trust, it is important to focus on our own happiness level as well as that of the group.

"We either make ourselves happy or miserable. The amount of work is the same."

—Carlos Castaneda

It is impossible to hold both a positive and a negative thought at the same time. When you feel the negative thoughts creeping in, experiment with consciously replacing these with more positive ones and see what happens. It's hard to trust someone who is negative all the time. Happier people help to build relationships through their attitude. They increase team morale and focus on solutions instead of just problems. Optimism breeds trust as well as more fun and a joyful life.

This suggests that if you want to increase your happiness level, the first step is realizing that where and with whom you work are within your control. Sometimes it means talking with different people in the staff room, getting involved in school teams or clubs with the students, or changing your old attitude about "us" and "them" into "we." Becoming involved in school improvement on a collaborative team or study group gives participants the chance to voice opinions and disagree with dignity. Sometimes, if all else fails, in order to find a happier environment you need to look for a new school or a new school district—or even a job in another field—where the staff feel more involved and you will be happy.

The perspective on morale offered by Ken Leithwood in *Teacher Working Conditions That Matter* (2006) relates to the concept of happiness. He says morale is "a generalized and relatively enduring state of mind. Good morale is typically associated with hopeful attitudes, an optimistic view toward one's colleagues, and enthusiasm for one's work, whereas low morale is associated with cynicism, feelings of despair, and lack of enthusiasm" (p. 38).

Where would you place the staff of your school as a whole on the happiness scale? Has it always been this way? What were the critical turning points that led to change?

Tips for Staying Positive

Here are some suggestions for increasing your happiness level:

- Take control of your attitude.
- Rediscover your inner child.
- Search out funny entertainment.
- Go fun places with fun people.
- Carpe diem—seize the day. Live each day like it's your last.
- Slow down, be present, and pay attention to what's happening in the moment.
- Find some quiet time to meditate or clear your mind each day.
- Appreciate people for who they are. Don't try to change them.
- Forgive yourself and others. Let past hurts go. Let it be.
- Experience gratitude for what you have.

The language we choose to use can affect our attitude. I heard about a minister in Kansas City, Missouri, Will Bowen, who was inspired to give out

"I am convinced that life is 10 percent what happens to me and 90 percent how I react to it."

—Charles Swindoll

purple rubber bracelets to everyone in his congregation. These bracelets, which have on them the word *SPIRIT,* were to remind people of the hazards of complaining. He says, "Negative talk produces negative thoughts; negative thoughts produce negative results. To live a happy and prosperous life, you have to stop complaining for twenty-one days." He explained that after you put on the bracelet, each time you hear yourself complaining, switch the bracelet to the other hand and start the twenty-one days again. This has been so successful that his church has mailed five million purple *SPIRIT* bracelets all over the world and continues to do so at a rate of 25,000 per week.

Sense of Humor

Activity

Each of us has a unique sense of humor that needs regular nurturing and nudging. This is like our "funprint"—as unique as our fingerprints. Educators have often told me that they are much different people outside of school or when they are on vacation. They somehow feel that they need to hide their sense of humor at work. What a shame that is. Let your sense of humor hang out at work, too!

Telling jokes isn't the same as having a sense of humor. You can be very funny without ever telling jokes. Caution is urged if you are a joke teller, though. Be careful not to offend anyone. The rule of thumb is: Laugh with people, never at them. Be sensitive and aware of the effect your humor has on others.

Reflect on these questions:

- What did you used to laugh at when you were young?
- How would you describe your sense of humor? What tickles your funny bone?
- Where did you get your sense of humor? Was it nurtured or repressed by your family?
- How would someone who knows you well describe your sense of humor?
- What gets in the way of your being more humorous?
- Have you lost your sense of humor?
- Did you ever have one?
- What do your colleagues find funny? How do they show their sense of humor at work?
- Are you suffering from the "YALE Complex" (You Aren't Laughing Enough)?

How Much Fun Am I to Be With?

Activity

In the film *School of Rock,* Joan Cusack plays a principal who at one point in the plot is being asked by Jack Black, playing a substitute teacher, to approve an extraordinary field trip. She begins to confide in him, saying:

I wasn't always like this, you know. I wasn't always wound this tight. There was a time when I was fun. I was funny. I was. But you can't be funny and be the principal of a prep school. No you cannot, because when it comes to these kids, their parents have no sense of humor. No, and if anything goes wrong, it's my head in the smasher. These parents will come down on me like a nuclear bomb. I can't make a mistake. I've got to be perfect and that pressure has turned me into something that I never wanted to be. (Rudin & Linklater, 2003)

If you can, view this segment of the film in a group setting, and reflect on these questions:

"Most folks are as happy as they make up their minds to be."

—Abraham Lincoln

- What would you say to the principal if you were in the car with her?
- Have you ever felt the same way—that you can't be funny and do your job, whatever it is?
- How many people do you think have turned into something they never wanted to be?

What Now?

Think about what strikes a chord with you the most from this first personal capacity strategy on happiness. What are the connections between trust and happiness for you? How would you treat yourself and others differently to have more fun?

Continue Your Feedback Search

Now is the time to review the activities in the Ask for Feedback strategy (page 31). You may want to repeat some of those activities and surveys, or you may want to continue the dialogue you started. Review what your key learnings were from that feedback.

If you didn't do those activities, consider how you will reach out and get some information about yourself now. This is risky, but you need to have this information to know what to change and what to keep the same.

A new feedback activity is included later in this section using the Johari Window (page 113). This is also a useful activity for groups to consider when comparing themselves to other groups. But for now, focus on yourself.

Activity

Our Needs Are at the Core

In her book *Understanding Yourself and Others: An Introduction to Temperament* (2000), Linda Berens uses the analogy of the tree trunk to talk about our personalities. What we see of the tree trunk is the bark, but other, crucial aspects of it are hidden from view. As with our personalities, our needs are deep inside of us, surrounded by our values and talents; it is our behavior that people see from the outside. See page 213 for a reproducible graphic.

Visit **go.solution-tree .com/leadership** to download and print this graphic.

As the cross-section of the tree shows, "Our psychological core needs and values must be met in order to grow and develop our natural talents and behaviors" (Berens, 2000, p. 6).

Your Disposition to Trust

The Trust Glass is repeated in figure 4.1. Consider your own personal disposition to trust using the questions that follow.

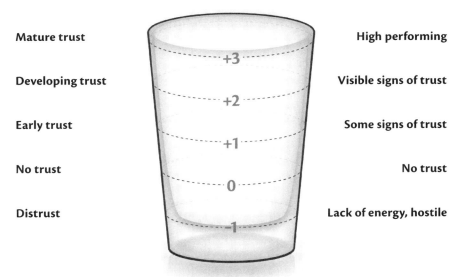

Figure 4.1: Levels of personal trust

1. Decide where on the scale your level of self-trust is—how much you trust yourself. What causes can you pinpoint for this?

2. Are you satisfied with this or would you like to change—to move up or down the scale?

3. Think back to earlier times in your life—your teens, twenties, thirties, and so on. Has the level changed over your life or remained at the same place?

4. How trusting are you in relationships with other people? For example, think of specific people you work most closely with or your immediate supervisor.

"I am afraid to tell you who I am because, / If I tell you who I am, / You may not like who I am / And that's all that I have."

—John Powell

The Johari Window

The Johari Window was developed in the 1950s by two American psychologists, Joseph Luft and Harry Ingham, while they were researching group dynamics. (*Johari* is derived from Joe and Harry.) It is a useful tool for disclosure and feedback for self-awareness, as well as team development and trust building.

Shown as a four-region (or panes-of-glass) model, each region contains information about a person. Figure 4.2 (page 114) shows the usual representation of the Johari Window model, with each quadrant the same size.

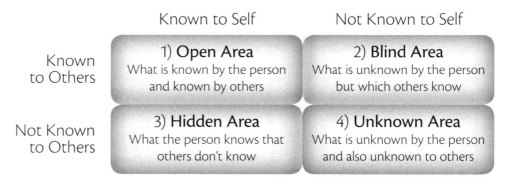

Figure 4.2: The Johari Window

From Luft, Joseph, *Group Processes: An Introduction to Group Dynamics,* 3rd Edition. © 1984. Reprinted with permission of The McGraw-Hill Companies.

When you consider the groups you interact with, the goal should always be to develop the open area for each person, including yourself, up to their comfort level. The more people know about each other, the more productive they will be. This builds better communication and increases trust.

The regions or quadrants are different sizes, depending on what is known or not known about a person (by themselves or by others). For example, in a team with early trust, the size of region one will be smaller at the outset, until they build a deeper relationship. The overall aim of this and many other strategies in this book is to help people get to know each other in order to build trust. In this way, region one gets bigger and regions two and three shrink. Blind spots are reduced in size, as more hidden areas become revealed through risk taking.

The Johari Window in figure 4.3 represents a person who is known well by others and discloses information freely about himself or herself. High-performing teams tend to have a similar culture of openness.

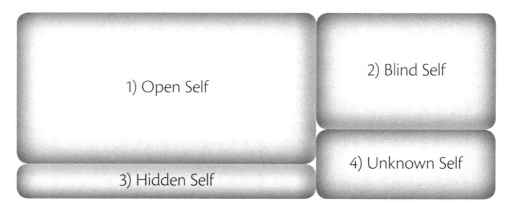

Figure 4.3: A Johari Window reflecting openness

A reproducible page with a Johari exercise window can be found on page 214, or you can visit **go.solution-tree.com/leadership** to download this exercise.

Talk With Critical Friends

Continue this process of self-discovery. Reach out and ask for feedback about region two from others you respect. Often the questions you take the time to craft are more important than the answers.

A "critical friend" can help you with this type of feedback. Mitchell and Sackney (2000) describe this type of friend as:

> an individual with whom one feels comfortable and safe enough to engage in reflective conversation. It is an individual with whom one can share the embarrassments as well as the successes of professional practice. It's an individual who will challenge one's perceptions of reality in a spirit of trust, mutual respect, and deep personal regard. We admit that such friends are rare, but we have found such people when we have looked for them and when we have been willing to hear them. (p. 22)

You may want to develop a small group or network of critical friends that can meet together to support each other.

The single most important way to build trust is to be trustworthy! Trust grows out of trustworthiness as our colleagues see it modeled over time. Second, be trusting. If you trust others, they will see you as trustworthy because they believe that it is part of your value system. Finally, be open. Ask for feedback and reflect on reactions in an honest and positive way. Over time, your colleagues will trust that you value their input and ideas.

> The single most important way to build trust is to be trustworthy.

People You Trust

Activity

1. Think of two or three people whom you trust the most in your professional life.

2. Then think of two or three people you trust in your personal life.

3. Describe the qualities or dimensions of trust each person has that have made you want to include him or her on your list. Was there an incident that solidified this trust, or did it build slowly over time?

4. If a symbol or metaphor for these relationships becomes apparent, record or draw it with your notes.

5. Have you ever told these people you trust them this much?

6. Who do you think would include you on their trust lists?

Self-Assessments

If you haven't had the opportunity to complete a self-assessment instrument, this may be the time to consider using one provided by companies that focus on individual, team, organizational, and leadership effectiveness (see Further Resources, page 175).

There is an inherent bias with self-assessments, as people tend to answer only from their knowledge about themselves (region one of the Johari Window). To get a more complete picture, it may be enlightening to ask one or more people who know you well to answer the assessment, not about themselves but about *you* and then to look for gaps between your and their impressions (region 2). All of these tools have strengths and limitations. Be as honest as you can to get the most useful results.

Once you have the feedback, consider how you can use it to shift gears into situations you least prefer. Try working from your weakest preferences now and again to develop them. For example, if you are a practical, hands-on learner, try an abstract problem for a change. Or, if you are more introverted, move into a more extraverted situation like a party or family gathering and see how it feels. We all have to work with all kinds of people. Adaptability and flexibility with other personalities and working styles are key to your success.

What Now?

Taking the time to step back and assess how you're doing every six months or so, especially when you feel that things are not right, will help you decide if you need to do things differently. Feedback can give you a much-needed wake-up call and help you change your behavior.

Trust Yourself

It's our attitude at the beginning of a difficult task which, more than anything else, will affect its successful outcome.

—William James

This personal capacity strategy for confronting distrust involves consolidating what you have learned from the previous two strategies. The Pain-to-Power Chart (page 29) will be a key resource here, in addition to the results of your personal reflection and the feedback from staff.

This strategy invites you to devote some important reflection time to develop your own trust touchstones or personal rules. These touchstones will become your guide for moving on to the interpersonal strategies in the latter part of this chapter.

The Importance of Self-Trust and Credibility

"And this above all, to thine own self be true, and it shall follow as the day the night—thou can'st not then be false to any man."

—William Shakespeare

Many leaders fall into the trap of believing that they have to know everything, do everything perfectly, and please everybody. While we all have individual strengths, we cannot possibly be good at everything. But leadership requires more than specific skills, and we often forget about the wealth of experience and intuition inside us that guides us as leaders. A lack of self-trust can make others think we aren't trustworthy. This trust in ourselves is often the most difficult type of trust to build.

One easy way to develop self-trust is to show up each day, fully present and aware. Living in the present and not feeling guilty about what we could or should be doing gives us the confidence to be able to handle whatever happens. How high is your level of self-trust?

Mary Jane Ryan tells us in her book *Trusting Yourself* (2004), "Self-trust is a virtue, like patience." She says it is a combination of three emotional and spiritual qualities:

- Self-awareness, the accurate assessment of who we are and what we care about

- Self-acceptance, the embracing of who we are in all our complexity, and

- Self-reliance, the ability to use what we know about ourselves to get the results we want in our lives without constant worry about the approval or disapproval of others (p. 8)

Self-trust does not mean being conceited or narcissistic. Instead, it can help us relax, go with the flow of each day more calmly, and be happier living in our own skin.

The Role of Positive Affirmations

Activity

If you expect the worst and get the worst, you suffer twice.

If you expect the best and get the worst, you only suffer once.

—Anonymous

The messages we whisper to ourselves dramatically affect our attitude. It would be easy when getting negative feedback to beat ourselves up with negative self-talk. Here are a few examples:

- "I always knew I was unpopular."

- "I never can do anything right in this job."

- "I shouldn't have taken this position after all."

- "It's all my fault."

We need to move away from self-blame and toward more positive affirmations and beliefs about our ability, skills, and behaviors. Here are some examples of positive self-talk:

- "It will be a challenge, but I am up to it."

- "Together we can do anything."

- "I am here for a purpose."

- "A new day has begun."

Loretta LaRoche, an educator and humorist, suggests that we get out of bed and greet the day by saying, "Ta-dah! I'm back!" Here are her Eight Steps to Effective Affirmations:

1. Make your affirmations short, clear and specific.

2. Phrase them in the present tense. You want them to start taking effect today.

3. Put them in very positive terms. Avoid words based on wish fulfillment, fear or negativity.

4. Don't make affirmations about changing other people. Direct the attention toward changing yourself.

5. Write your affirmations when you're in a receptive state, perhaps after meditating or taking a nice long walk.

6. Keep your affirmations in handy places. Take them with you. Repeat them often. Keep in mind how long it took to create negative thoughts.

7. Change or rewrite your affirmations as you see fit. You may change your mind about a specific goal or need.

8. Have FUN with them. Don't make them a job. (1996, pp. 24–25)

Self-Doubt and Self-Trust

Stephen M. R. Covey, co-founder and CEO of CoveyLink Worldwide, led the strategy that made the book *The 7 Habits of Highly Effective People*, written by his father, Stephen R. Covey, into one of the most important business books of the last century.

Covey links self-trust to his principle of credibility, which has competence and character as its two main components. Two of the questions he poses are: Do I trust myself, and Am I someone others can trust? Covey says:

> What's the net result of repeated failure to make and keep commitments to ourselves? It hacks away at our self-confidence. Not only do we lose trust in our ability to make and keep commitments, we fail to project the personal strength of character that inspires trust. . . . The good news in all of this is that every time we do make and keep a commitment to ourselves or set and achieve a meaningful goal, we become more credible. The more we do it, the more confidence we have that we *can* do it, that we *will* do it. The more we trust ourselves. (2006, pp. 45–46)

Sometimes we are faced with multiple changes at the same time. One at a time, our experience and credibility would provide enough self-trust to effectively deal with them all, but when they arrive together, our self-trust can be tested to its limits. When I was promoted from assistant principal to principal, I began to doubt myself. I was also moving from a high school to an elementary school, a brand new one at that. While I had always relished big challenges in the past, this time I thought it might be too much for me. My anxiety was affecting my ability to plan for this new school and hire the staff that would make it a success. One of the steps I took was to tape large sheets of chart paper on the wall in my bedroom. I wrote several affirmations in large letters on the charts, so that each night when I went to sleep, these were the last messages I gave myself. Each morning I started the day reading them. While "giving birth" to this new school was very difficult, I had assembled a great team around me. The affirmation I remember needing the most was: "Together, with this great team we have, there is nothing we can't do for the kids in this school!" I realized that I needed to trust both myself and the team I had assembled.

The process of formulating trust touchstones (personal rules or commitments) will strengthen your self-trust and become useful, especially at difficult times. Follow the instructions to create your touchstones using the reproducible My Trust Touchstones (page 215), or visit **go.solution-tree. com/leadership** to download and print this activity.

Trusting Others

What are the practical steps you can take to trust others? Remember that it usually isn't an all-or-nothing situation but involves degrees of trust in different situations—even with the same person.

What are the acceptable behaviors, forgivable behaviors, and uncondonable behaviors you can identify with regard to trusting other people?

For example: "I need to trust people more—until they give me a reason to distrust them."

Regaining the Trust of Others

What are the practical steps you can take if others have lost trust in you?

While you cannot force someone to trust you, what can you do to gain their confidence in your character and competence? Can you ease their sense of vulnerability when they are around you? What new actions can you plan to take when distrust happens again? Have you taken responsibility for the part you played in the problem?

For example: "I need to slow down and be more approachable during the day so people can talk to me about what's on their minds."

> "The most fertile ground for personal growth is often found in the most painful of experiences: betrayal."
>
> —Beth Hedva

Trusting Yourself

Do you need to trust yourself more in order to make it easier to trust others? What do you want to remember most about your trust level with yourself?

For example: "Instead of hiding what I know needs to be said, I will speak up." "While I will listen to the advice of others, I will trust my own judgment more often." "I will give up hope of having a perfect past and live in the present."

Kouzes and Posner (1987) write:

> In the final analysis, only you can decide whether to take the risk of trusting others and whether the risks are worth taking. In a sense, this means that to have others trust you, you must actively take some initiative and not simply wait for others to make the first move. The opening gambit always involves risk. Leaders always find the risk worth taking. Sowing seeds of trust with people creates the fields of collaboration necessary to get extraordinary things done in organizations. (p. 160)

Apologies Count the Most

As reported by Ohio State University, it seems that apologizing is the one single behavior that can make tremendous gains in repairing lost trust. Roy Lewicki and Edward Tomlinson, as reported in Grabmeier (2004), conducted research with forty-five business students at the graduate level. Their results

> "One's philosophy is not best expressed in words; it is expressed in the choices one makes. In the long run, we shape our lives and we shape ourselves. The process never ends until we die. And, the choices we make are ultimately our own responsibility."
>
> —Eleanor Roosevelt

showed that victims were far more willing to consider reconciliation when a client gave an explicit apology as opposed to simply trying to placate the victim. Moreover, these apologies were most effective when, instead of blaming outside forces, the client took personal blame for the situation. Are apologies something you do naturally? Is it difficult for you to find the right words at the right time? How many ways can you say, "I'm sorry for what I did"? Should you add this to your trust touchstones?

What Now?

It's time to apply your trust touchstones and personal insights around self-trust and use them in working with others. Understanding yourself is one aspect of emotional intelligence. The other aspect is understanding others and their feelings.

Walk Your Talk

Opportunity is missed by most people because it's dressed in overalls and looks like work.

—Thomas Edison

To build personal capacity and increase the trust others have for you, you need to become conscious of your actions. Intending or planning to do something is the easy part. Actually following through and doing it takes more courage and determination. Walking your talk will increase both self-trust and interpersonal trust.

People you work with will be watching to see if you practice what you preach. They look for consistency and predictability over days and weeks. There is an acronym that fits here—DWYSYWD—"do what you say you will do." Commitments must be kept, and your word must mean something. The corollary is, don't promise to do something you are unable or incapable of doing in the first place.

This strategy involves writing your personal growth plan based on your touchstones, and then, most importantly, putting it into action.

Three considerations need to be understood before you begin your personal growth plan:

1. The difference between management and leadership
2. Shared leadership as a two-way street
3. The difficulty of transitions in behavior

The Difference Between Management and Leadership

Leadership is an action, not a position.

—Donald McGannon

Stephen Covey Sr. tells a story that illustrates the distinction between management and leadership. As the story goes, a man works feverishly to clear a field of high grass with a long knife. He is really making progress and covering a lot of ground when he suddenly realizes he is working in the wrong field altogether. He was doing things right but not doing the right things.

It is true that both management and leadership are necessary for trust to be developed in a school. Leadership, however, is more than managing or supervising. Trust resides in leadership, with its emphasis on interpersonal relationships. We may be very efficient and orderly and get things done, but not at all effective or working on the right problems.

Management is a focus on:

- Efficiency and productivity
- Doing things right
- Programs
- Rules and logistics
- Things first versus people

Leadership is a focus on:

- Effectiveness and relationships
- Doing the right things
- Inspiring the overall vision
- People first versus things

It is important to clarify the difference between management and leadership so you can focus on both as you prepare a personal growth plan.

Shared Leadership as a Two-Way Street

Richard DuFour, Rebecca DuFour, and Robert Eaker make a further distinction between traditional schools and leadership in a learning community:

> In traditional schools, administrators are viewed as being in leadership positions, while teachers and staff are viewed as implementers or followers.

> In professional learning communities, administrators are viewed as leaders of leaders. Teachers are viewed as transformational leaders. (2002, p. 23)

Everyone in the school has a vital role in a shared leadership structure. The "formal" leaders need to share the control by empowering the staff and delegating meaningful responsibilities. Simultaneously, staff members need to look for opportunities to step up, choose to get involved, and offer help and advice. This includes specifically inviting the union representative to participate.

Mitchell and Sackney offer this advice about shared leadership: "We do not believe (nor does the literature confirm) that a shift in governance automatically translates into improved professional practice or improved student achievement" (2000, p. xiii). More important is the quality of learning for staff and students. As trust grows, more people will take the risk and step forward to get involved and openly help each other. The explicit strategies in

"Formal" leaders need to share control by empowering the staff and delegating meaningful responsibilities. Simultaneously, staff members need to look for opportunities to step up.

the following interpersonal capacity section will reduce vulnerability and increase risk taking.

The Difficulty of Transitions in Behavior

Change is the visible shift in an external situation. It happens in real time. However, just managing the change itself doesn't affect the human side of change. The success of coping with any change lies in dealing with transitions. Transitions are internal and happen more slowly—in "heart and soul time." William Bridges (1980) states that it is not change itself that people resist but "the losses and endings that they experienced and the *transition* that they are resisting" (p. 24). According to Bridges, there are three transition phases, called *endings, neutral zones,* and *new beginnings*—and all are equally upsetting. Endings happen when people say goodbye and try to let go of the way things used to be. Schools don't do endings very well. It is important to officially mark the ending and celebrate the past in order to move on. As the old saying goes, "You can't steal second base with your foot on first." Being able to succinctly describe the change and explain the rationale for it will help with the ending. Steps need to be planned to help people let go of old practices with dignity and respect.

The neutral zone represents the period between an ending and a new beginning. If there is a positive vision of the end product, people have something tangible to aim for. We sometimes try to rush this neutral zone and push for visible changes or retreat back to a more comfortable time. It takes time to make this transition and start something new. In this neutral zone we find the energy and creativity to move ahead.

The new beginning will start on a broken front for the members of the staff, as each person finds his or her own way there. Table 4.1 outlines some of the common feelings in each phase.

Table 4.1: Feelings Associated With Transition Phases

Endings	Neutral zone	New beginnings
Stressful	Being lost	Relief
Caring	Panicky	New energy
Angry	Disoriented	Competence
Difficult	Confused	Understanding
Mournful	Devalued	Hope
Sensing loss	Overreacting	Joy and fun

Even when a group of people experiences the same change, each member of that group will move through the transitions in his or her own time and manner. It is common for the initiators of the change to move through the neutral zone faster. With an awareness of this model, staff members can talk about their feelings and coach each other through the phases.

Covey's Thirteen Behaviors That Build or Restore Trust

In *The Speed of Trust,* Stephen M. R. Covey (2006) expands on the two sides of credibility—character and competence—as seen in the following behaviors. As you read through them, think of how they apply to your own personal growth plan.

The Character Side of Trust

1. Talk straight. Be honest and upfront, and give the whole truth.

2. Demonstrate respect. Be fair, kind, and caring, and ask questions of those who disagree.

3. Create transparency. Be open, real, and genuine. Let them know more rather than less.

4. Right wrongs. Admit mistakes and apologize. If you mess up, fess up.

5. Show loyalty. Give credit abundantly to others where it is due. Catch people doing things right. Don't engage in backstabbing.

The Competence Side of Trust

6. Deliver results. Focus on action, and convert cynics fast. Follow up, and do what you say you will. Don't make promises you can't deliver.

7. Get better. Take risks. Regard continuous improvement as a given.

8. Confront reality. Deal with it even if it's hurtful. Take the tough issues head on.

9. Clarify expectations. Develop clear timelines and models of what you are envisioning.

10. Practice accountability. Taking responsibility applies to everyone.

Behaviors Entailing Both Character and Competence

11. Listen first. Listen to understand the issues and feelings before jumping in. Listen to yourself, too!

12. Keep commitments. If you say you will do something—do it. Be honest if you can't do it or don't have time. The quickest way to build trust is to be trustworthy.

13. Extend trust. Especially as a leader, extend trust beyond what you think is reasonable. This is the most challenging behavior and one of the best ways to build trust in a distrusting situation.

(Covey, 2006)

Your Personal Growth Plan

Work through the following steps as you develop and commit your personal growth plan to paper. You may want to consider your personal

> "All changes, even the most longed for, have their melancholy; for what we leave behind us is a part of ourselves; we must die to one life before we can enter another."
>
> —Anatole France

> "When you make a commitment, you build hope.
>
> When you keep a commitment, you build trust."
>
> —Roger Merrill

Activity

and family life as well as your professional plans as it's almost impossible to separate them.

Step one. Think ahead a year or two and describe your vision of success. These are your hopes and dreams for a better tomorrow. What would it feel, sound, and look like? How would the situation be better than today? What difference would higher levels of trust play in the scenario?

Step two. Review your My Trust Touchstones (page 215). These are the personal rules or core beliefs that guide you. Some people think of these as small stones that you carry with you for courage and inspiration.

Step three. From the touchstones, can you see a credo or motto that would represent your purpose or mission in life?

Step four. Take stock of where you are now. From the previous activities, you have several sources of information about yourself, such as the following:

- The Pain-to-Power Chart (page 29)
- Reflection on Covey's two sides of credibility and dimensions of trust (page 94)
- The Johari Window activity (page 113)
- Feedback from colleagues and critical friends (page 115)
- Positive affirmations (page 117)

Think of any other information you have about yourself that would help. What mysteries are you still exploring?

Compare where you are now after step four to your vision from step one. How can you close the gap between these two? What are the priorities? Identify two to three actions that you will commit to doing that you feel will make the most difference. You cannot do fifteen things well, so be selective. Where would be the best place to start?

Part of deciding where to focus your energies and spend your time involves sorting out what you are going to have to let go of. This skill is perhaps least polished among educators, who spend so many hours above and beyond what the public is aware of. Remember, it isn't a question of doing more things faster but doing the right things well, of doing what's important rather than simply what's urgent. What do you need to do less of, or not do at all?

Actually putting into words that you cannot do something is not easy for some people. (If you tend to be a people pleaser, refer to an article I wrote called "Saying 'No' to the Unimportant.")

Have your personal growth plan witnessed by a critical friend. Talk it over. Decide on the time frame around these commitments and report back to your colleagues on your success and reflections.

Now it's time to put this into action. Start doing things differently. See how it feels as you take your dreams seriously. Give yourself a timeline, such as a month or so, and then reflect on your progress regularly. Celebrate your successes—no matter how small they are! As Margaret Wheatley writes:

Visit **go.solution-tree.com/ leadership** to download and print this article.

I've found that I can only change how I act if I stay aware of my beliefs and assumptions. Thoughts always reveal themselves in behavior. As humans, we often contradict ourselves—we say one thing and do another. We state who we are, but act contrary to that. We say we are open-minded, but then judge someone for their appearance. We say we're a team, but then gossip about a colleague. If we want to change our behavior, we need to notice our actions, and see if we can uncover the belief that led to that response. (2002, p. 18)

A Caution About Sharing Your Vision

You don't have to share your vision with the whole staff. If you do this in a low-trust setting, it can seem as if your vision is more important and others don't have one worth talking about. They will be less likely to open up about their hopes and dreams. Share your vision later, at a time when everyone else is talking about vision in the action planning process.

Specific Ways to Build Your Personal Capacity

Here are some specific learning strategies to use as you continue to explore your personal capacity and "walk your talk":

- Small study groups or networks
- Professional reading
- Professional portfolio or journal as a basis for discussion
- Daily walkabouts to chat with others in the building
- Committee work on a worthwhile project
- Mentoring, peer coaching, and peer observation

These methods require higher levels of trust than most people are accustomed to. They will work if there is a working relationship and if the participants have chosen to learn with each other. It may be too early for some people who feel more vulnerable having another person in "their space." In some relationships, it's wiser to wait until significant trust has been developed. This level of readiness will vary from person to person.

Action Research

This is a process of disciplined research leading to significant actions that improve situations personally, interpersonally, or as a school organization. It involves many of the methods already listed. In actual fact, the work you have been doing here with the strategies for building trust is true action research—for example, the concept of using a facilitation team to work with the principal is action research.

Keep your trust touchstones visible as you continue to build your personal capacity for trust.

Walk It, Talk It, and Stop It

When you see something untrustworthy happening, step up and try to stop it. For instance, if you see behavior that you cannot condone, you must do something. June Callwood, a journalist and activist from Toronto, always said, "If any of you happens to see an injustice, you are no longer a spectator, you are a participant and you have an obligation to do something."

For example, if you overhear people maliciously gossiping about a friend of yours, you can step in and tell them, "This is a friend of mine you are gossiping about. I'd appreciate it if you stopped." You must take into consideration your physical safety, but acting on your values by speaking up and saying something may change a situation for the better.

The Lesson of the Five Balls

Suzanne's Diary for Nicholas (Patterson, 2001) provides a final message for the personal capacity early trust phase. Imagine life is a game in which you are juggling five balls. The balls are called *work, family, health, friends,* and *integrity*. And you're keeping all of them in the air. But one day you finally come to understand that work is a rubber ball. If you drop it, it will bounce back. The other four balls-family, health, friends, and integrity-are made of glass. If you drop one of these, it will be irrevocably scuffed, nicked, or even shattered. And once you truly understand this lesson of the five balls, you will have the beginnings of balance in your life.

Two Special Messages

Do not think that you are the best and that you can do everything all by yourself—only teamwork brings the best results.

—Hans-Ulrich Schaer

Before we introduce the medium-risk interpersonal capacity strategies, read these special messages for building your trust capacity for leaders new to a school and leaders opening a new school.

Leaders New to a School

As the new person "on the block," you need to be aware that as soon as the staff gets the news that the current leader is leaving and that you are the one who is coming, the questions will start flying and apprehension and feelings of vulnerability will grow. Staff will dig and gossip to find out any information about you. What they find out may be true, or it may be exaggerated or even blatantly wrong. Your reputation will precede you.

Plan your entry into the school with sensitivity to the fears people may have. Don't feel that you need to forcefully create changes and assert your authority immediately. The newcomer mantra should be, "I will *not* include mission, vision, values, and goals as the first steps in my entry plan! I *will* get to know the people and culture and level of trust first. Then we can plan the

"People with integrity inspire others and change lives, not usually in dramatic ways, but with quiet, unassuming honesty and trustworthiness. They lead by example."

—Dana Telford and Adrian Gostick

future together." Yes, you will want to put structures in place for everyone's involvement in decision making, but these philosophical discussions require higher trust levels. Linda Lambert describes the entrance of many newcomers in the following way:

> It is not surprising that schools do not maintain their improvements. New principals and superintendents often come to a school or district with their own agendas. Or they respond to a charge from the superintendent to "turn this school around," "get us back on an even keel," "undo what the incumbent did," or "move us into the future." Such sweeping mandates ignore the history, passions and qualities of an incumbent staff, choosing instead to import reforms that are generic and popular.

> Less often do administrators hear, "This is a good school that is getting better. Structures are in place to continue the work. Teacher and parent leadership is strong. We need a principal who can co-lead this school in the direction it is already going." (1998, p. 17)

Learn the name (and spelling and pronunciation) of each and every staff member as quickly as you can, and that means everyone—custodians, secretaries, lunchroom ladies, and teachers. If you aren't good at this, get some help and make a sincere effort. Get a photo or an old yearbook and put names to faces. Use a floor plan and write names on it. This effort will have huge rewards.

While some leaders may be new to a school, many are new to the profession itself. For many reasons, principals and assistant principals are being appointed with only a few years of teaching experience. It is not uncommon for teachers with fewer than five years of experience to be promoted to an administrative role. Young teachers also take on department chair roles and other in-school leadership roles. Suspicion and skepticism will be high among the rank and file staff toward these young leaders. It will take a long time to gain the trust of more senior staff. Every step you take will be analyzed. The most important thing an inexperienced leader can do is to openly acknowledge this fact and invite cooperation by asking questions and respecting those with more years of experience. Novice administrators need patience for trust to develop—they need to go slow at first to go fast later on.

Your predecessor's legacy will have set the stage for you to follow. Get to know and then build on the structures that already exist in the school. Use the expertise that is there. Go slowly; you may have to wait awhile before introducing anything new.

Ask a lot of questions. Here are some examples you could use:

- "How are things done around here, and why are they done that way?"
- "How else could they be done?"
- "What is most important to you about this school's culture?"
- "What strengths do you bring to this school?"

- "What successes have you had with students?"
- "How may I help you this year?"

Your role is to keep these meetings brief; listen and make notes. Be organized. You won't get a second chance. Plan on talking to everyone eventually. When you hear an idea that you can implement without stepping on anyone's toes, do it. Small changes after these meetings will show you are listening and serious about actions that will help students learn and teachers teach.

As you work through your interviews, develop a map of the team structure and social relationship patterns currently in place.

Review chapter 2, especially the strategies for soliciting feedback. It would be inappropriate to do a survey as soon as you come to a school, but you could be looking for suitable members for the facilitation team and getting to know the union rep and support staff. Of course, getting to know the teachers in leadership roles is particularly important. They won't all be supporters, but they do have leadership responsibilities and need to be respected for that alone.

The staff members need to hear about your background and beliefs in order to start a relationship with you. You could put something in writing in a newsletter or speak at a staff meeting. Remember to be brief. There will be lots of time for you to talk more about yourself, but first you need to listen to the staff. It's all about them. The most visible message you communicate will be your actions, not your words. Will they feel safe to have you as their leader?

Entering a High-Trust Culture

If you have inherited a "moving" school, it would be demoralizing for the staff to arbitrarily impose new structures and replace what is already working. "Going back to zero" is all-too-common an experience with school staffs who experience a leadership revolving door. They will not take you or your leadership seriously if you don't honor their expertise. The worst thing you can do is to ignore the teams and collaborative structures that are functioning and try to do everything by yourself.

Honor the work that your predecessor did with the staff. Watch what you say, even casually, about him or her. Unflattering judgments will rankle his or her allies and drive a wedge between you and them.

Test out the waters carefully with low-trust interactions. If they go well, you can move quite quickly to more high-risk activities.

Entering a Low-Trust Culture

If you are entering this type of culture, focus on relationships above all else. Consider the research and strategies in chapters 1 and 2, and proceed very carefully. Plan in close consultation with the other leaders.

Try to understand the reasons for their lack of trust. As Megan Tschannen-Moran says, "It is important to recognize that those individuals come by their wariness honestly. Rather than taking their suspicion personally, it will be important for you to be patient and persistent in earning their trust" (2004, p. 58). No leader, especially an outsider, can lead without trust.

Above all, resist the temptation to criticize their way of doing things and to introduce your new ways without their commitment. Geoffrey Bellman puts it this way:

> We do a great job spouting off about how things ought to be and the big changes that are needed. In the process, we often succeed in alienating many people who worked very hard to bring the organization to where it is today.
>
> While we are spouting, do we recognize that we will need the help of these silently resentful people who are listening to us? Do we recognize how our proposals sound to them? Do we care? . . . For years they have found part of their personal meaning in how they have approached their work—and here we come with something new. (1992, p. 51)

I once had an experience that made me vividly realize my importance in the ongoing history of the school. Early in my career as an administrator and newly assigned to a school, I was putting up my nameplate above the door of my office when I noticed that there were numerous pieces of tape and glue under the last person's nameplate. In that moment I realized how many people had had this office before me, and I knew that I had to make my time count for something. I started by asking myself this question: How can I, as an assistant principal, win over the trust of the students and also the staff—who had been there many more years than I had and might be there long after I had gone?

If your school has one or more assistant principals, you need to work with them as a team right from the start. Spoil them with attention and time. Take time to review the administrative tasks to see how they could be divided to best use each other's talents. Don't make an assistant person into a "bench jockey." Let them try new ideas. That may mean making mistakes. Use your judgment about whether they need or want your help, and whether it is appropriate to give it.

Talk with each other every day, all day—whenever you can. Find times for mutual reflection and feedback and times to laugh and maybe cry together.

Leaders Opening New Schools

Opening a new school is a wonderful privilege for anyone. It usually involves working at one job while at the same time doing double-duty and planning for the new school. Decisions need to be made about the physical school design, equipment, furniture, resources, and technology and impact that each of these will have on the staff you hire. Here are some tips for opening a brand-new school:

1. The interview process is critical. Use a team approach to make the best decisions. If you can make it possible for a teacher to be part of each interview team (if only in a listening role), the fit of the new hires will be better. Craft your questions carefully, and make

sure they focus on trust, conflict, and teamwork. Ask for specific examples. Check all references carefully.

2. In some situations, teachers may be transferred to the new school without an interview. Even though there is no veto power here, meet with each person and talk with them in lieu of a formal interview.

3. It is very easy to get caught up in the management issues and ignore the leadership issues—the people themselves. Meeting with parents and students who will be coming to the school will create lasting bonds.

4. Involve the teachers, students, and parents in all decisions they have time for, including school colors, school uniforms, and mascot. Ask them what resources and supplies they want. Ask them to make three lists: critical, important, and desirable. Try to get everyone's critical items first.

You are building an identity in these first few months and years. If you can, plan offsite meetings, even overnight retreats to do some team-building and make decisions.

Don't take it personally if, at the end of the first year, some staff members decide to leave. You will have to hire new staff and start again with some new folks, but it is part of any new venture. Respect their decisions to find a place where they feel they can teach the best. The real staff will emerge after this first year is over and people settle in. These first few years will set the tone for the life of the school.

You may want to access an article I wrote, called "When Your Heart Is in Your Dreams," when I was the founding principal of a new school in the Toronto District School Board.

Visit **go.solution-tree.com/ leadership** to download and print this article.

What Now?

Working through the personal strategies will be worth the effort, no matter how difficult they were for you. Ignore them at your peril. It's now time to move on to considering the whole staff and your interactions with them.

Interpersonal Capacity Strategies

What makes schools successful has less to do with budgets than building a certain kind of climate, less to do with innovations than with values and relationships.

—Learning in America: Schools That Work (video)

The next six strategies shift from building personal capacity to building interpersonal capacity—from the individual to the group. As Mitchell and Sackney point out, this can be "a heavily contested process of negotiation among different people with different knowledge bases, different histories, different hopes and aspirations, different personal styles and emotions, and different desires and needs" (2000, p. 45).

Interpersonal capacity strategies one through three address the affective domain (the "heart"). Appealing to logic and research is important, but it is not enough. Education is a people business that involves feelings as well as thoughts. Interpersonal capacity strategies four through six address the cognitive domain (the "head").

1. Share stories and start conversations.

2. Encourage dialogue about change.

3. Lighten up and play more.

4. Create the future through action planning.

5. Collaborate through teams.

6. Make decisions together.

As Ken Leithwood says in *Teacher Working Conditions That Matter* (2006):

The most direct effects of teachers' thoughts and feelings on student learning come from teachers' schoolwide and classroom-based practices. Teachers' thoughts and feelings also give rise to their decisions about whether to continue working in their current school, seek employment in another school, or leave the profession altogether. (p. 8)

Affective Interpersonal Trust: Speaking to the Heart

People may not remember exactly what you did, or what you said, but they will always remember how you made them feel.
—Source unknown

To attend to the affective or feeling side of trust in order to facilitate change, the school climate must make everyone feel valued and welcome. Building caring relationships is especially important to people who are either new to the profession itself or new to a particular school. Change is a process packed with many emotions. Emotion provides the energy needed to overcome the barriers of fear, betrayal, and cynicism and can enable educators to work together to increase trust and thereby raise student achievement levels.

These three interpersonal capacity strategies involve telling memorable stories, having conversations about the personal nature of conflict, and remembering that schools are by nature meant to be joyful places.

In 1980, a young Canadian named Terry Fox decided to run a marathon across Canada to raise money for cancer research. He himself had been diagnosed with the disease and had lost a leg to it. At the start of his journey, there was little or no public interest in him, but by the time he was forced to quit his quest because of a recurrence of the cancer, the whole country had been moved by his courage and grit.

I was teaching an eleventh grade human relationships class at the time, and we were all inconsolable as we watched the coverage of him being placed in the van that would take him to get medical care. When he died later that year just one month short of his twenty-third birthday, we shelved the regular curriculum and talked about his life story and how one person can make a difference in the lives of many. Sometimes the human story—the heart—must take center stage even when the head—in this case the lesson plan—says otherwise.

Two Reminders

First, the facilitation team must continue to take a leadership and facilitation role in the overall trust-building process. If you don't have a functional facilitation team, now is the time to create one (page 43). Remember that the union representative needs to be approached to be as much a part of the team as anybody else.

Before any strategy is used with the whole staff, the facilitation team must first discuss and plan its use. You may want to rotate some members off the facilitation team and bring in a few new members to establish a natural turnover pattern. If some of the initial cynics and resistors are now at all willing, encourage them to join. Because the role of the facilitation team is critically important to the success of this process, the staff must trust it. As Hulley and Dier (2005) write:

> If a relationship is built that is based on trust and trustworthiness, the staff will view the team as a helpful and supportive partner on the school improvement journey. If, on the other hand, members of the design team are perceived as having power over the rest of the staff, the likelihood of a good outcome will be diminished. (p. 177)

Second, keep the norms you have developed "front and center" as you consider the next group of strategies. If you haven't developed norms yet, go back to chapter 2 and put this essential step in place. You will want to consider if any staff members feel marginalized or left out of the process. All should feel welcome as they participate in the strategies. Behavior needs to be monitored so that no one feels ignored or not taken seriously. Sometimes more dominant staff members talk over and interrupt the quieter or more introverted people. If this pattern continues unchecked, these marginalized staff members will withdraw or even become saboteurs.

Start Conversations and Share Stories

I believe we can change the world if we start listening to one another again. Simple, honest, human conversation. Not mediation, negotiation, problem-solving, debate at public meetings. Simple, truthful conversation where we have a chance to speak, we each feel heard, and we each listen well.

—Margaret Wheatley

There is no interpersonal strategy more important for developing trust than starting conversations, inviting stories, and being interested enough to listen to each other.

"Only with trust do people allow others into their minds and hearts. Only with trust do people have a reason to engage in learning with another person or group of persons. This is as true for teachers as it is for students."

—Coral Mitchell and Larry Sackney

For this strategy I have drawn on Margaret Wheatley's book *Turning to One Another: Simple Conversations to Restore Hope to the Future* (2002). This book's message about the lost art of conversation was revelatory for me. It reminded me of all those hours at the cottage spent talking around the dinner table, or out on the dock, or around a roaring campfire.

Telling the stories that make up a school's history serves two purposes: it invites conversation, and it also bonds staff members together. Making these forms of dialogue acceptable and expected will give people the courage to start their own conversations about what they feel is important. It can open the door to the creativity needed for future challenges.

Of course, the whole staff doesn't need to be present for all conversations. People who trust each other will start having great private conversations on their own. But there should be a time for conversation as part of all meetings.

The Art of Conversation

Wheatley shares her own stories of the many places in the world where she has been part of groups talking together about what worries them, a problem they see that needs fixing, or a dream they have to make the world a better place. It takes courage to open up the conversation and patience to listen with curiosity. She writes, "All change, even very large and powerful change, begins when a few people start talking with one another about something they care about" (2002, p. 9).

This means listening to everyone—even to people we wouldn't normally listen to. Fear of what people will think, fear of their reactions, and fear of their anger keep many of us quiet. Her belief is that when you know someone's story, you aren't afraid of them anymore. In Wheatley's words:

> We need to be able to talk with those we have named "enemy." Fear of each other also keeps us apart. Most of us have lists of people we fear. We can't imagine talking to them, and if we did, we know it would only create more anger. We can't imagine what we would learn from them, or what might be possible if we spoke to those we fear most. (Wheatley, 2002, p. 5)

Having conversations like these can take us to a place we rarely go—the heart of the matter.

Start With Margaret Wheatley

Ask the staff to arrange themselves so that they are sitting in a circle with everyone within eyesight. If the group is large, have individuals sit in smaller groups around tables or pull some chairs into a circle.

Put the quotations you have just read from Margaret Wheatley's book on a chart or slide so that they can be shared with the staff. These quotations in themselves will invite conversation.

Listening respectfully and following the group's established norms of behavior will make deeper conversations possible. Discuss these behaviors if they are not already part of your norms:

Telling the stories that make up a school's history invites conversation and also bonds staff members together.

Activity

Visit **go.solution-tree .com/leadership** to download and print Wheatley's quotations.

- We acknowledge one another as equals.
- We try to stay curious about each other.
- We recognize that we need each other's help to become better listeners.
- We slow down so we have time to think and reflect.
- We remember that conversation is the natural way humans think together.
- We expect it to be messy at times. (Wheatley, 2002, p. 29)

Having the voices of all those in the room heard leads to their entering the space of here and now. This "grounding" increases the possibility of more sharing as the meeting progresses and the future unfolds. As Wheatley says, it is also healing:

> Why is being heard so healing? I don't know the full answer to that question but I do know that it has something to do with the fact that listening creates relationship. Listening moves us closer, helps us become more whole, more healthy, more holy. Not listening causes fragmentation and fragmentation always causes more suffering. (2002, p. 89)

Storytelling

The power of narrative cannot be underestimated. Humans organize their knowledge through storytelling. Stories make us feel a sense of commonality in that we all have them to tell. Many are told in hallways and parking lots. These activities invite the stories into the meeting room for all to hear and learn from.

Activity

What's in My Name?

The theme song from the hit TV series *Cheers* included the sing-along line: "You want to go where everybody knows your name."

This is a higher-risk activity than the activities like the Shoebox (page 65). Ask people to share the history of how they got their first name. This may sound simple, but it often reveals information never before shared within a group and is an important step in building enough trust to share other important thoughts. If possible, do this as a whole group. If the staff is too large for this, break up into smaller groups. The activity could be repeated at several meetings until everyone has heard about each person's name.

Here are some prompts you could use:

- "What is your first name?"
- "How did you get it?"
- "Do you have second or third names?"
- "Are you named after someone else? Who?"
- "Is it a short form for a longer name?"
- "Do you have any nicknames?"
- "Do you like your first name?"

"Trust may sometimes be forged in moments of great drama; it is more likely to be formed by small, moment-to-moment encounters."

—Source Unknown

- "Were you ever teased about it?"
- "Are you known to others by a name that isn't your first name?"

If you want to make people listen even more carefully, give everyone a blindfold. Listening to someone when you cannot see them heightens the experience. Talk about how this felt to the participants after everyone has finished.

School History Map

Activity

This activity invites the telling of stories—built up over the years—about people who were part of the school culture who got the big picture. It deepens the understanding of a place to learn about its history. David Bohm, the physicist and philosopher, is credited as the source of this activity.

It is very useful for new staff members and administrators to hear the wealth of stories. They can then see how they fit into the school's history. The "knowers" tell the "don't knowers." In some older schools, you can invite staff members who have taught or worked there since it opened who can contribute some information.

Here is a brief but attention-getting introduction written as advance notice by a facilitation team for an overnight retreat: "It's informal, informative, maybe even surprising and entertaining. What type of story? I can't tell a story! I hate this pressure! I'm not funny! Whoa! Stop! Relax! We want this to be as painless as possible, so it doesn't have to be rehearsed, or funny, or long."

Using a roll of butcher paper, shelf paper, or the back of an old roll of wallpaper, make a timeline of the decades since the school opened—for example, the 50s, 60s, 70s, 80s, 90s, 00s—and a space for recent stories. Different strands could be identified across the paper such as:

- Educational policy eras
- Events that took place
- Key people or groups
- Physical changes to the building

Attach the paper to the wall with artist's tape (which won't peel paint off the wall) or tacks. Have some old yearbooks, artifacts, photo albums, newspaper clippings, and so on available that will jog memories. You'll also need colored pens and large sticky notes.

Allow two to three hours. Divide the staff into random groups or by the era they started at the school. Tell them that their task is to write down on the sticky notes provided any stories that they can recall and the year (or decade) in which the story occurred. They then place the sticky note on the butcher paper in the appropriate area.

Here are some prompts that may get people's memories activated:

- A time that they were most proud of the school
- A time when they were most sorry

- Changes, endings, and new beginnings
- Key staff members coming and going
- Historic events that shaped the school
- An encounter-with-a-student story
- The class "from hell"
- Their worst or best lesson
- A random act of kindness
- Reunions and graduations
- Marking the year 2000
- Clothing, music, and hairstyles that were popular
- Traditions like annual school trips or events

Then capture the stories with titles right on the strip of paper or on sticky notes stuck securely on the chart.

The debriefing of this activity is very important. Ask participants for their reflections about the lessons learned and the overall themes, patterns, or trends. Invite comments, especially from newcomers. Be prepared for emotional stories, too.

Participants should talk about the activity's meaning for each person afterward. What predictions and recommendations can they suggest for what the future holds?

These stories told in front of the group may lessen the negative gossip in the hallways and in email messages. Some stories are repeated over and over—listen carefully to those.

Alan Wilkins says that the stories that are told in companies can affect performance. He concluded the following:

> Some kinds of stories were powerful ways to motivate, teach and spread enthusiasm, loyalty and commitment; others served an equally powerful purpose: to perpetuate cynicism, distrust and disbelief. . . . They reveal underlying beliefs or doubts people feel but are unwilling to confess to you directly. So take the time to lean in and listen close. Care about stories you hear and treat them as the crucial company heartbeats they are. (as quoted in Peters & Austin, 1985, pp. 327–328)

In a higher-trust culture, the stories told will be more hopeful and inspirational, and often more humorous, too. They are symbolic of the lives of the people who have lived in the school and the philosophy they share. Good stories tell the listeners that their school is different from all others and is special in many ways.

What will your future stories be? How will you remember them the next time future staff members sit down to do this?

I learned this activity from Suzanne Bailey. You may also want to consult the article "Visualizing Your School's History" in *Tools for Schools*, *9*(4), May/ June 2006, published by the National Staff Development Council, and Jan

Stories told in front of the group may lessen the negative gossip in the hallways and in email messages.

O'Neill's "Capturing an Organization's History," in *Educational Leadership*, April 2000.

What Now?

Becoming comfortable with recalling and telling stories is worthwhile in itself, but it also is an especially useful activity during the action planning process that follows.

Encourage Dialogue About Change, Conflict, and Resistance

A learning community is forged in the fires of conflicting beliefs as much as it is shaped in the shadows of shared norms.

—Coral Mitchell and Larry Sackney

This strategy is a continuation of the previous conversation strategy, with a focus on three intertwined concepts: change, conflict, and resistance. These are often included as topics in leadership courses, but they are rarely introduced to all staff members for discussion.

Think about the level of resistance in your school and how this strategy would be most successful. Even if things seem to be improving, it is critical to put these issues on the table for discussion. They are integral to the norms of behavior and form the basis for future strategies.

Change Is a Process

We believe that effective leadership for change is characterized by commitment, tenacity, optimism, and strong, respectful relationships. Moral purpose and hope provide a solid foundation for the efforts of leaders in the change process.

—Wayne Hulley and Linda Dier

When a manufacturing business wants to make a big change, it usually shuts down to retool the production line. In education, we don't have that luxury. Some say change in education is like changing a tire while the car is still moving.

School improvement and change have a lot of similarities to home improvement. Suppose you are dissatisfied with something in your home and decide that it needs to be changed. You usually start with an image of the finished project. You decide what you need to replace, what you can keep, what you need to throw out, and what can be recycled. The job itself creates mess and a sense of dislocation. Costs are always more than budgeted for. Most importantly, relationships are sometimes tested to the limit as tempers get short and energy wanes. (Think of trying to wallpaper a bathroom with your significant other!) But in the end, with a little luck and planning, you feel pride in the finished project. Then you sit back and think of your next one!

Reactions to Change

People have a variety of reactions to change. It helps to talk about them during the change process. Of course, people are far less enthusiastic about doing this when they feel they are being manipulated or forced to change.

On any staff there will usually be the following groups:

- Innovators—eager to try new ideas and take risks
- Leaders—open to change but examine things before deciding
- Early majority—cautious and deliberate about deciding to change, and follow the leaders if they respect them
- Late majority—skeptical of new ideas, set in their ways, but can be won over by peer pressure and trust
- Resistors—suspicious, opposed to the idea and can openly block or sabotage

Think about where you and your colleagues fit into these adopter types. Recognize that all are appropriate and to be expected—even resistors.

Sometimes the innovators get too far ahead of the majority of the staff and are viewed with suspicion for their real motives. Are you that type of innovator?

While visiting a hospital one day, I was drawn to look at a mural that had been created by the patients in an adult day treatment program. The mural was of a long, winding road with a big bend in the middle. Before the bend was a stream of words: *pain, anxiety, guilt, fear, tears, anger,* and *confusion*. Then came the phrase *turning point*, with these words after it: *hope, love, understanding, caring, happiness, peace,* and finally *strength*.

Accepting and Expecting Conflict as Inevitable

Conflict is seen as a challenge to be met rather than a condition to be avoided.

—Coral Mitchell and Larry Sackney

Conflict is any disagreement between two or more parties in which one party believes his or her or their rights are deprived. Conflict occurs when two or more parties discover that what each wants is incompatible with what the other wants.

Many people say they were taught as children to believe that conflict is a bad thing to be feared and avoided at all costs. It turns out that conflict occurs as a regular part of life and could lead to growth. While you don't want to cause conflict just to have some experience, educators should proactively seek out the conflicts that are real and put the issues on the table, rather than allow them to fester. Giving staff a chance to talk about conflicts and their natural response to them will build trust and teamwork.

Lencioni suggests that a team can know if it is having enough conflict by thinking about how an outsider would feel sitting in on a team meeting. Pictured in figure 4.4 is the Conflict Continuum from his book *Overcoming the Five Dysfunctions of a Team* (2002). Lencioni tells us that it's rare to get as far as personal attacks in most teams. You may think you are too far over on the conflict side, but Lencioni says that "a great team will look at least a little strange to an outsider who isn't accustomed to the direct and unfiltered dialogue taking place" (p. 38). Teams may sometimes slip over the midpoint, but then they self-correct and reflect on what happened after everyone has calmed down.

> "When a team recovers from an incident of destructive conflict, it builds confidence that it can survive such an event, which in turn builds trust."
>
> —Patrick Lencioni

Figure 4.4: Lencioni's Conflict Continuum

From *The Five Dysfunctions of a Team: A Leadership Fable*, by Patrick M. Lencioni. Copyright © 2002. Reproduced with permission of John Wiley & Sons, Inc.

According to Lencioni, most teams actually perform at the harmony end and are often terminally nice. They avoid conflict, "fearing that any movement toward the middle is one step closer to murder" (p. 39).

Start Discussions

Activity

Here are some great conversation starters for this topic that can reveal new information about yourself and your team.

- "What percentage of conflicts would you say are not discussed in our school?"

- "What emotions does conflict bring out in you? Do you keep grudges or recover quickly? Do you get it all out or hold it all in?"

- "What were your parents' responses to conflict? Did they openly disagree or disagree in private?"

- "In some workplaces, problems and conflicts are swept under the rug and kept there. Why don't we discuss these issues publicly at meetings where we have a chance? What can we do to put these meaningful issues on the table for resolution?"

- "Where do we fit on the conflict continuum most of the time? Are we okay with this? What bothers us about conflict?"

In addition:

- Discuss the conflict-resolution method shown in the next section, and ask for reactions to it.

- Revisit the norms you established for group meetings, and discuss whether anything needs to be added or revisited to help with handling conflict.

Activity *Try Conflict Resolution*

Robert Bolton's time-honored, three-step method to deal with conflict is shown here. Share this with staff, to use when disagreements arise.

1. Treat the other person with respect. Remember the Golden Rule—do unto others as you would have them do unto you.

2. Listen until you "experience the other side."

3. State your views, needs, and feelings (speak for yourself). (Bolton, 1979, pp. 218–22)

To go deeper with this strategy, turn to the widely used Myers-Briggs Type Indicator (MBTI), which includes a specific analysis about how each of the sixteen personality types deals with conflict. Share everyone's results with the entire team in order to gain insights about the similarities and differences, and then talk about what it means for the trust levels of the participants.

Final Words of Advice on Conflict

Lencioni (2005) writes:

Good conflict among members requires trust, which is all about engaging in unfiltered, passionate debate around issues.

Even among the best teams, conflict will at times be uncomfortable.

Conflict norms, though they vary from team to team, must be discussed and made clear among the team.

The fear of occasional personal conflict should not deter a team from having regular, productive debate and dialogue. (p. 50)

What About the Resistors?

The sleeping dragon metaphor illustrates the duality and complexity of managing resistance. Change agents often tiptoe around this dragon, hoping it will not awaken. If awakened, they fear resistance will wreak havoc. A proactive approach to managing resistance, however, can help staff developers tame the dragon and, thus, turn resistance into a powerful force.

—Monica Janas

I am often asked, What will we do about the resistors? This always strikes me as backward. Resistance is as natural as conflict. If enough trust has been established and plans are developed collaboratively, there will be the normal resistance to anything new, but there won't be the outright hostility and trench warfare that some fear.

Get to know the "resistors" who are whining, blocking, and sabotaging efforts to move ahead. And watch out if there is *no* resistance: silence is rarely golden. Remember times when you have been a resistor. It can have a constructive, legitimate purpose. Take all resistance seriously, and deal with it. Change is hard work. Some people don't find collaboration and teamwork natural and resist leaving the privacy of their world of work.

Three Levels of Resistance

As you read about these three levels from Rick Maurer (1996), think about which level is prevalent in your school.

1. Resistance to the change itself. People like the status quo. The timing may be wrong. This is low-grade resistance.

2. Deeper than the particular change at hand. It is caused by prior broken promises and low trust. Motives are questioned. At this level, people are afraid of losing respect, status, or control. They think that there are too many changes and may feel worn out. (Most resistance is here.)

3. Most deeply embedded and overwhelming. At this level, people are experiencing severe distrust and conflict between values and visions.

Strategies for Understanding Resistance

It may help to understand resistance if we remember times in our lives when we consciously resisted a philosophy or a command with which we didn't agree. Why is it so hard to understand resistance when it comes from others? We often want to ignore hardcore resistors. Instead, we need to move toward expecting and understanding the resistance. Trusting cultures should provide safe places for people to vent and share all points of view.

Don't ignore resistors without trying to find out their reasons. Except for outright saboteurs, you must reach out and include those who resist change. Deal with saboteurs directly, and make it clear what's okay and what's not. Discuss these proactive techniques:

- Start your efforts quietly, and build in small steps. Nothing worthwhile happens overnight.

- Expect varying degrees of commitment. *Predict and prevent* is always better than *react and respond.*

- Work with the informal group leaders.

- Help people believe they have had a part in the plan. Involve and empower people in the decision making in a sincere manner.

- Inspire people with a shared vision of success and goals to get there. Communicate openly.

- Help stakeholders identify potential roadblocks. These may be legitimate, such as lack of funding or failure of the same initiative in the past.

- Work on building and maintaining trust. Be sensitive. Deal with the emotions of the issue even if they are difficult.

- Build support for change. Spend time with one person at a time. Do not hold a group meeting until you have done this.

> Trusting cultures should provide safe places for people to vent and share all points of view.

McKenna and Maister (2002) offer these steps:

1. Describe the situation and how it affects the individual and group: "I need to talk to you about an issue and get your ideas before our next meeting."

2. Discuss the stake you both have in addressing the situation: "I'm thinking of raising the question next week. Any suggestions for how you think we should do this?"

3. Offer options you see, and ask for comments: "Here's my idea. . . . Does that make sense?"

4. Ask for their assistance and support.

5. Express your appreciation.

Critical Questions About Conflict

In most workplaces, great value is placed on the need for collaboration, cooperation, and trust. With so much emphasis on the positive, there is a tendency to discount or ignore the negative—the voice of dissent and resistance. How can we honor resistant behavior? Discuss the three levels of resistance, and decide which you are dealing with at the current time.

Every new undertaking seems to get worse in the middle before it gets better. The middles are the hard work. Team members will appreciate knowing about this and discussing their views about change and conflict. Conversations about the challenges of change and the complexities of conflict and resistance will make a stronger team or school staff. Success belongs to those who persevere.

More Serious Situations

In spite of the fact that you are building trust, you must deal with rare but extreme situations with the seriousness they demand. When issues of incompetence, unprofessional behavior, harassment, sabotage, or insubordination get ugly, they must be dealt with through the formal routes of the organization—that is, through the principal, supervisor, superintendent, or union processes. If you are the victim of an unwarranted amount of conflict, do not hide from these relationships or think you are to blame for them. Stand up for yourself and get help. We have mediation processes and problem-solving methods that we use in student discipline. The same respect must be applied to all adult disputes.

What Now?

Being comfortable with conflict is never easy. It is, however, a necessary mindset to put the real issues on the table without hurting people or being offensive. Dealing with the conflict in itself will build trust. Sharing alternatives and finding solutions will make it more likely that people will be more honest about their resistance to a new idea in the future. They will develop more sophisticated ways of handling inevitable and necessary conflict as part of any growth process.

These experiences will also make it more possible for them to enjoy each other's company and maybe even have some fun together.

Lighten Up and Play More

This strategy is a variation on the personal strategy How Much Fun Am I to Be With? (page 111). Here the question is, "How much fun is it to work here?"

In a culture of distrust or low trust, this strategy would be received with cynicism. However, in a culture of trust it is seen as an appropriate way to relieve tension and stress and get to know each other better.

With trust and respect, the benefits of play—curiosity, enthusiasm, creativity, and learning—can be truly experienced. People trust those they can laugh with. They feel safer to take risks and make mistakes.

The organization of fun at work is a joint responsibility of the leaders and the staff. Staff members can take a major role in designing the fun environment they want for themselves. Success depends heavily on the social committee (the "Cabinet of Fun"), who use their expertise and fun-loving personalities to plan activities for the adults, with special attention to food, decorations, music, and social interaction. They can use their powers of persuasion to make sure all staff members feel invited and welcome—including the quieter ones.

Who's Who?

Activity

1. Ask staff members to find pictures of themselves as children and give them to one person, who will coordinate the activity.

2. Post photos in the staff room without identifying who anyone is.

3. Put a sticky note beside each photo, and invite staff to try to identify who's who and write their guesses on the sticky notes.

4. Give them about a week, and then reveal the identities.

5. Return the photos to their owners.

An extension of this activity is to ask each staff member to write a response to this question and post it beside the photos: "If that picture could talk, what would it say?"

Activity

Our Cup Runneth Over!

Todd Whitaker, speaker and author, focuses on the positive with this activity:

1. Divide the staff into groups of three to five. Provide each group with a piece of chart paper with a large cup or glass drawn on it and a package of sticky notes.

2. Instruct the groups that they are to "fill" their cup with examples of great things happening at their school.

3. Allow 10–15 minutes for them to write brief thoughts and descriptions on the sticky notes and place them inside the cup. Continue working until each cup is filled with positive, productive things.

4. Allow time for them to choose their top five ideas and share them with the entire group.

5. Post these charts for all to read and discuss. (2003, p. 16)

Activity

Celebrate Staff Achievements

Celebrations weave our hearts and souls into a shared destiny. People come together to celebrate beginnings and endings, triumphs and tragedies.

—Lee Bolman and Terrence Deal

Take stock of the traditions and rituals you have developed to celebrate the achievements of the staff. Even short thank you's and mentions of trust-building behaviors will go a long way. You can even celebrate data with the progress of staff as well as students. Make up awards with a sense of humor. For example, ask the staff to nominate their Happiness Heroes, or people who live this philosophy and bring it with them to school every day. Download the *Gratitude Dance* from www.YouTube.com so that everyone can do this dance for his or her Happiness Heroes.

Here are some celebrations from "Applause! Applause! Recognize Behaviors You Want to See More Often" (Richardson, 1998):

*   Super Pats—started by Rick DuFour when he was the principal of Adlai Stevenson High School in Illinois (a play on the phrase "pat on the back")

*   Gummy Worms—for the person who comes first to early morning meetings

*   Golden Plunger Award—a toilet plunger spray-painted gold, for taking a risk and plunging into an assignment

*   Juan Valdez Award—for making coffee for the staff each day

*   Bungee Cord Award—for helping colleagues learn from each other (p. 1)

Activity

Welcome New Staff Members

Many schools have traditions of honoring the contributions of staff members who are leaving the school or retiring. Think about what can be done to welcome new staff members and ease their first few days in a new environment. One suggestions is to make a book called *Your First Day on the Job* and give it to a new teacher with memories from other staff members.

Use Funny Videos

Activity

Whether it's one of those particularly busy times of year like report cards or just a blah week in February, a funny video or video clip can make people laugh and ease the stress. Use these at the beginning of meetings, or put a TV in the staff room with a DVD player and run them at lunchtime. Here are some good ones:

- *Who's on First?*
- *Good Morning, Vietnam*
- *The Joy of Stress* (a Loretta LaRoche video)
- *Patch Adams*

What other movies or videos can you think of that would achieve the same goals? How can you use laughter and humor to strengthen trust in your school?

What Now?

Armed with more knowledge about each other and the skills to have some fun together knowing that along the way they will disagree, staff members are now ready to move ahead to the serious work of deciding what they want to do together to make their school a better place for themselves and their students.

These next three strategies and the activities associated with them fall under the category of building the cognitive side of trusting relationships.

Cognitive Interpersonal Trust: Speaking to the Mind

Thinking about the intellectual complexities of our careers involves research, reflection, and dialogue about professional issues. In an atmosphere of trust, staff members will be more forthcoming about the deeper questions they struggle with and the new mental models they have contemplated forming for themselves at work. This type of trust leads groups to make better decisions for their students and their schools.

Create the Future Together Through Action Planning

The process of action planning can be applied at many levels, with small or large groups, and even with individuals. Here we refer to action planning as it would be used with an entire school staff.

The action planning process requires a quick response. While there is a planning phase, planning should be done quickly so the overall process doesn't become paralyzed. You must push to get to the action phase and the subsequent formulation of a work team so that there is visible proof of the commitment by the principal and the staff to make fundamental changes in the school to improve trust.

The honesty and vulnerability necessary in this process demand a higher level of established trust among the majority of the staff. When staff members trust each other, there is more candor in conversations and less need for anonymity. The facilitation teams need to decide with the principal if the staff is ready for these discussions. If they are not, they will give only lip service and the results will be superficial, with little or no commitment to follow through.

While we have labeled it cognitive, this process is really a blend of visioning and formulating beliefs (emotional and affective) and data analysis and goal setting (rational and cognitive).

The planning process described here was inspired by Suzanne Bailey.

Whole System Change

Many schools are accustomed to a traditional, linear strategic planning process driven by the school board's vision and mission statement and led by a representative group or task force drawn from the staff. Action planning is nontraditional:

- It is whole system—it involves everyone on staff.
- It includes diverse points of view.
- It becomes the staff's plan "wholeheartedly."
- It is achievable and sustainable over time.
- It requires the staff to take action to make it work in the end.

Make every effort to include parents and community leaders as well as students in the process. To see the whole picture, you need the whole group—their voices and dreams are part of the future, too.

With the facilitation team, and possibly assisted by additional facilitators, develop a plan that brings everyone together in one location for a two- or three-day concentrated process. If you can't arrange for one large chunk of time, plan to do it in two or more sessions. The facilitation team should meet at the end of each day or session to go over the feedback and make necessary adjustments to the plan.

The Action Planning Roadmap

Many times you will hear educators talk about their "mission, vision, values, and goals" as if they were one single concept. There is much confusion about the nature of and difference between each of these important parts. You need to become aware of each concept and how it fits into the overall process. None of them can be omitted. The reproducible Action Planning

Roadmap (page 216) shows the component parts of the process within the big picture.

If the group is large and you have extra facilitators, introduce them and their role at the start. The staff will benefit from seeing the big picture, so photocopy the roadmap and agenda for them. Walk them through the agenda, review established norms of behavior, and check the expectations of the group. Share this sequence of seven steps outlined in the following section, and with the group identify any steps that have already been accomplished in whole or in part.

1. Review of the Past

Review the School History Map (page 135). Refer to the stories that were told, and speak honestly about the history of the school. Explain that this is a time to move on and plan the next phase of the school's history. Use the following talking point: "In order to articulate a vision, imagine trying to look into the future as if you were standing on stilts looking out over a maze that you must travel through. The heightened perspective allows you to see where you are now and how far you need to go to see your dreams come true."

2. Shared-Vision Scenario

I have heard people use the terms *vision* and *mission* to mean the same thing, when in fact they are quite different. Vision is located in the future, and mission is found in the present, in what we value and believe right now. On the Action Planning Roadmap, vision is depicted as a puffy cloud in the sky, off in the distance. We can't touch it from the ground, but we can see it and imagine it. This is the critical place to start each and every time you make a plan.

Our vision scenario takes our thinking into the future two, three, even five years. It describes an ideal image and tells the story of a preferred future for our school. It communicates how it will be different from today—how it will feel, what it will look like, and how it will sound. Vision scenarios are:

- Passionate, optimistic, and inspirational
- Hopes and dreams
- Lighthouses or guiding stars showing us the way
- Magnets to pull us toward the future
- Stories or pictures

When we put our dreams into action, the results are powerful. Without a strong vision, we have no confidence that our actions will take us where we need to go. Without a vision we would be like Alice meeting the Cheshire Cat in Lewis Carroll's *Alice in Wonderland*.

Futuring Activity. Part of the visioning step involves "future scanning"—being on the lookout for trends by watching the changes going on around us in the world. To be good at futuring, you need to be open-minded,

Visit **go.solution-tree .com/leadership** to download and print the Action Planning Roadmap.

Activity

Activity

"The pioneers in any endeavor have no maps to study, no guidebooks to read, no pictures to view. They can only imagine the possibilities."

—James Kouzes and Barry Posner

Activity

"Would you tell me, please, which way I ought to go from here?" "That depends a good deal on where you want to get to," said the Cat. "I don't much care where," said Alice. "Then it doesn't matter which way you go," said the Cat.

From Alice in Wonderland, by Lewis Carroll (1865). Drawing from original edition, by Sir John Tenniel, available at Project Gutenberg, www.gutenberg.org.

creative, and willing to explore the possibilities for the future. Then you must decide which are the most probable directions.

Gather five or six short items to read about the trends of the next ten to fifteen years. (You could also use short video clips.) These could include predictions about technology, genetic engineering, global warming, the economy, alternative sources of fuel, and so on. Three websites you could refer to for these items are:

- www.cotf.edu (NASA's Classroom of the Future)
- www.wfs.org (World Future Society)
- www.kiplinger.com (The Kiplinger Newsletter)

After you have the clippings, ask the participants to do the following:

1. Copy sets of these clippings and put them in individual envelopes, one for each group of four to five staff members.

2. Ask each person to jot down some thoughts on notepaper about their own personal hopes and dreams three years from now and how they plan to get there.

3. Ask each group to open their futuring envelopes and share the insights inside with each other for fifteen minutes.

4. Talk about the effect that reading these clippings had on everyone's thinking about the future and the world students will live in when they are adults.

5. Discuss what kinds of communities, schools, teachers, and classrooms would best prepare students for this future. What skills, knowledge, and attitudes will students need to be successful as adults in the future we described? What implications do these changes have for our success?

6. Now ask each group to create and share a story of a day in the life of a student ten years from now.

Visioning Activities. Visioning also uses a global approach to thinking with which some people will be more comfortable than others. Encourage people to be emotional, speak from the heart, and unleash their imaginations.

Share these quotations from *Improving Schools From Within* (Barth, 1990):

Visions of schools are deeply submerged, sometimes fragmentary and seldom articulated. . . . Dreams can come to us in the day as well as the night. The night dreams are often a journey back into the repressed unconscious. Daydreams, on the other hand, are the occasion of a journey forward to what might be, what can be, what we want to be. (p. 148)

Teachers and principals who convey their craft knowledge and their visions to other adults derive enormous personal satisfaction and recognition. Vision unlocked is energy unlocked. (p. 151)

A vision for me is like a star or a compass. It offers a clear, sometimes shining sense of direction, a destination. It is important, therefore, not to ask, "Have we reached the star yet?" or "Are we at north yet?" The more realistic and helpful

"All education springs from some image of the future. If the image of the future is grossly inaccurate, its educational system will betray its youth."

—Alvin Toffler

Activity

question is "How much closer to the star or to the compass course are we today than we were last week?" (p. 157)

There are many ways to get people thinking about the future. Use your imagination for gathering this information with staff members. Some groups may want to go through magazines, clipping pictures for a collage depicting future images. Others may want to role play a scene from a school on the Starship Enterprise.

Another choice is to write discussion starters on posters in different parts of the room and ask people to go to whichever one they want to discuss. Give the people at each poster fifteen minutes of discussion time, and ask them to write or draw a summary chart. Then ask them to report back to the whole group.

- "What is impossible to do right now, which—if it could be done—would make a fundamental difference?"
- "How would things be different if the future was controlling the present rather than the past controlling the present?"
- "When parents walk into our school today, do they feel like they are walking into the past or the future?"
- "If we were to open a new school today, would we recreate what we are already doing? What would we do differently?"
- "What is the kind of school I would like my grandchildren to attend?"
- "What haven't we done yet that might work here?"

Activity

Find Common Ground in the Vision Scenario. Now that everyone has spent time thinking about the future, it's time to craft a vision scenario for the school. Use this sentence as a starter: "In the future, we want this school to be a place where . . ."

Be ambitious—write a vision of greatness. Don't be too practical. A vision has to be idealistic. Focus on the children.

If it's a small staff, you could work together to craft the final scenario. In larger staffs, delegate the job of preparing a draft. When the whole group accepts it, record it in permanent form.

Activity

3. Mission, Values, and Beliefs

While our vision is future-oriented, our mission is what we stand for and believe right now, planted in the ground of the present. The image for the mission, values, and beliefs on the Action Planning Roadmap (page 216) is a flag and flagpole.

In the past, more emphasis was placed on the mission statement than the vision scenario. A school spent often countless months working on its mission statement. Here, however, we mean the general mission, purpose, or credo that we need to be clear on at this point. It isn't important that it be said in twenty-five words or less in a precise, formal way.

The true value lies in articulating the core of the mission—its beliefs and deeper values—so that everyone, including the parents, students, and larger community, understands them. Respected voices say that if behavior can be changed, new values will follow. I dispute that. I believe discussions to clarify and articulate values and beliefs must come first. If behaviors are artificially imposed without the prerequisite values in place, the behaviors will be short lived. Values are:

- Bedrock convictions that we will not compromise

- Principles that guide how we treat other people on a daily basis

- A source of meaning in our work

What do we stand for in public education? What makes this school unique? What difference are we trying to make in the lives of the children and families of our community? Do we think it's important to help all students learn or to just give them a chance to learn? What percentage of kids who aren't successful is acceptable to us? Richard DuFour expressed it this way to me one day: "Would teachers want to send their children to a school where, on the opening day, ten or twenty students were pulled from a group of one hundred and told they were the ones the school didn't care whether or not they learned."

Our Belief Wall. Refer back to the I've Been Framed activity (page 38) and revisit the belief statements developed there. I believe that values are deeply held beliefs, so you may want to call this your Values Wall if it reflects deep discussions.

Activity

Another way to display these beliefs visually is to make a Belief Wall that pictures the shared beliefs of the staff.

1. Cut paper into brick-shaped pieces, and spread them out on the tables.

2. Structure a conversation to discover which beliefs you hold in common.

3. Once you have an agreement, write the beliefs one at a time on the paper bricks, and put them together in a visual display, as a bricklayer would lay rows of bricks.

Parents and students could be invited to join in the process and add their own bricks.

The value of shared beliefs is that they become a filter through which you can judge and prioritize new initiatives and suggested actions. The question will change from How are we going to do this? to Does this fit with our beliefs, and will it get us toward our vision scenario? If the answer to the second question is "no," then it will not become a priority for the school. The test of trust comes when the principal and staff can decide what fits in their school plan. For example, if fun is a core value, there will be permission built in to encourage its behaviors.

As Peters and Waterman (2004) state, time spent discussing and reaching consensus on shared beliefs will be time well spent.

I firmly believe that any organization, in order to survive and achieve success, must have a sound set of beliefs on which it premises all its policies and actions. Next, I believe that the most important single factor in success is faithful adherence to those beliefs. And finally, I believe if an organization is to meet the challenge of a changing world, it must be prepared to change everything about itself except those beliefs as it moves through its life. (p. 280)

4. Current Situation

At this point you have a history map and stories, vision scenario, beliefs, and perhaps a summarizing mission statement. Now it's time to take stock of your current situation. You may have surveys, common assessment scores, and other sources of feedback and information to analyze what's working well and what isn't. Two activities are included here: a SWOT analysis and appreciative inquiry.

Activity

SWOT. SWOT is an acronym for Strengths, Weaknesses, Opportunities, and Threats. It is a quick way to identify boosters and barriers to your action plan. The SWOT Diagram is generally credited to Albert Humphrey, who led a research project at Stanford University in the 1960s and 1970s using data from Fortune 500 companies. The threats and weaknesses will need to be addressed specifically one at a time.

1. Explain the meaning of SWOT to the group and ask them to work in groups with a worksheet and write sticky notes for what they feel fits in each of these categories:

   - **Strengths**—What is the school competent at and known for doing well?

   - **Weaknesses**—Where is the school falling short of its capabilities?

   - **Opportunities**—What is possible that the school isn't seeing or doing?

   - **Threats**—What is causing danger to the success of the school, internally or externally?

2. Post a chart like the one in figure 4.5 with four quadrants, and ask for the sticky notes to be posted in the appropriate quadrant.

3. Stand back and look at what happened. Summarize and share the results with staff members.

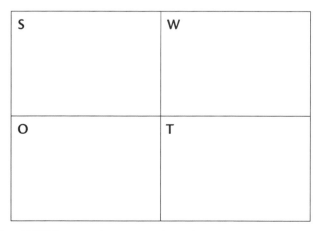

Figure 4.5: Using SWOT to analyze an action plan

Appreciative Inquiry (AI). Appreciative Inquiry extends the strengths and opportunities parts of the SWOT method. It also connects well to the visioning steps already described. But AI is also used as a stand-alone planning process. It involves a collaborative search to find and understand a school's strengths, potential, and greatest opportunities, including its hopes for the future. AI was developed by David Cooperrider, a professor of organizational behavior. It complements earlier themes in this book about the value of conversations and storytelling.

The approach of AI is to focus on what makes the organization work instead of what people don't like and what isn't working. It is a deceptively simple process and philosophy that restores trust and generates hope by having everyone at the table focus on:

- Seeking the best of what is currently in place
- Respecting employees for who they are
- Interviewing and storytelling about what they appreciate most about their workplace
- Inviting the imagination of what could be by involving hearts, minds, and souls
- Taking a positive approach as an antidote to cynicism, anger, and fear

In a typical AI activity, participants develop questions about possibilities from the optimistic perspective that "the glass is half full." Questions might include:

- What is working well at this school that, if we did more of it, would have a significant impact on the future?
- What possibilities exist that we haven't yet considered?
- What's the smallest change that could make the biggest impact?
- What do we do that keeps us interested and energized at work?

Once the conversations are finished, step back and look for the themes and patterns in the stories that were told. Look for stories that are driven by curiosity and a spirit of discovery. Record these themes on paper and use them as a basis for the next step—agreeing on actions that will create this type of workplace.

In 2005, the Toronto District School Board (the fourth largest school system in North America, with over 600 schools in Ontario, Canada) used AI to focus on a vision of what student success would mean from a student perspective. Specially trained students, using specific prepared questions, interviewed over 2,000 students, parents, school staff, and community members. They identified themes and created images of the future in this school board. They then presented to the board recommendations about how the district could help students be more successful in school. It was a very personal approach in what some would see as a large, impersonal school board.

Activity

"We can't ignore problems. We just need to approach them from the other side."

—Thomas White

5. Gap Analysis

Go back to the vision and beliefs, and compare them to your current situation. What actions need to be taken to close the gap and make the vision possible?

Decide on small but significant steps or actions that take your dreams seriously and put them into action.

What to Do and What Not to Do. Although difficult, it is important to create boundaries and sharpen your focus by analyzing the impact that new plans may have on current ones. You will have to decide what to say "no" to and what to not even start. Others may need to be slowed down or postponed indefinitely. Peter Drucker coined the term *organized abandonment* for this collective and conscious process of letting go.

Mark all endings with a ritual or ceremony—even an announcement—heard and understood by all.

6. Action Plans

This is the critical part of the process. To close the knowing-doing gap, you must get going and emphasize actually *doing* things now rather than just knowing what to do and stopping there, as is often the case. The best plan is not worth the paper it is written on if it is not implemented.

- Prioritize your actions into short- and long-term categories.

- Apply the vision test. Ask, Will this get us closer to our vision?

- Focus on three to four goals that will make the most difference. Push for goals that are a stretch—difficult but attainable.

- Form action plans that you all agree on, and then be more specific about each one by writing them as SMART goals. Anne Conzemius and Jan O'Neill introduced this acronym in their book *The Handbook for SMART School Teams* (2002):
  - Strategic and Specific—linked to your priorities and vision
  - Measurable—the impact can be assessed
  - Attainable—within your control, resources and timelines
  - Results-oriented—specific outcomes that can be measured
  - Time-bound—an end-point is clear and urgent (pp. 4–5)

Some actions could be assigned to one person for implementation, but in most cases, a small work team will be the most productive approach to each SMART goal.

7. Evaluate the Process

At this stage, when the planning seems to be finished, you need to pause and reflect on the overall process while it is still fresh in your mind. Capture in writing any recommendations from the feedback and evaluation for future use in the next cycle of planning.

Activity

"It's easier to say 'no' when there is a burning 'yes' inside."

—Stephen R. Covey

Activity

What Now?

When I dream alone, it is just a dream.
When we dream together, it is the beginning of reality.
When we work together, following our dream,
it is the creation of heaven on earth.

—Brazilian poverb

If this process is successful, it will have a positive impact on the staff members. They will have planned their future goals together. But don't rest or stop here. Put your goals into action and measure the progress. Over the years, you may want to revisit this process. New staff members will have to learn it, but the rest of the staff members will be familiar with it. Work teams can also use it on smaller parts of the overall vision.

Once the action planning process is complete, the last two strategies will be needed: collaborating and working in teams and making decisions together. These final strategies provide the tools to make your goals come alive.

Collaborate Through Teams

Never doubt that a small group of thoughtful, committed citizens can change the world. Indeed, it is the only thing that ever has.

—Margaret Mead

It is time to establish new work teams to implement your goals. The facilitation team should retain an overall coordination role, but many more staff need to be involved to move the school forward and continue to develop trust. All (including teaching and support staff) must feel invited and included in at least one team—maybe even several—and must participate in this growing culture of trust.

Team learning is the antithesis of the traditional professional development day with everyone gathered in the same room. Teams are not as visible; they meet at various times during the day to talk and plan without any fanfare. The facilitation team monitors each team's overall progress, but the work team itself will have its own mandate or charter and its own team leader. Open communication lines between and among the work teams, the principal, and the facilitation team will make a more effective structure.

This strategy, which is both interpersonal and organizational, focuses on the benefits of collaboration and teamwork. Take time to consider the type of teams that would suit your overall plan. Some teams will require more coaching, while others will be strong from the start. Make your teams match your goals. While the principal and assistant principal(s) could be seen as automatic members of all teams, decisions need to be made about which teams require an administrator as a full-time member.

> All must feel invited and included in at least one team.

Activities are included for building the capacity of the work teams. Some can be done with the whole staff, and others can be shared with team leaders for use directly with their specific teams. Each team will develop a unique personality and needs time to establish its own level of trust and identity.

Collaborate for Staff and Student Learning

The assumption in this strategy is that collaboration is beneficial. Consider these advantages:

- Working together usually reduces isolation, loneliness, and stress.
- A synergy of ideas leads to higher quality solutions to complex problems.
- New teachers feel supported when they are part of a team.
- Staff members working together leads to better results for students.
- Working in teams doesn't mean giving up individuality or working independently. Each of these work styles has an appropriate time.

Here are three higher-risk examples of what teamwork looks like in a school that has passed the early or developing stage of trust:

- The expertise on staff should be tapped. If one teacher is a cooperative learning specialist, ask him or her to share that skill with others by running lunch 'n' learn sessions and then inviting interested staff into the classroom to actually observe how it's done. Some teachers go as far as recording themselves so others can see inside the world of their classroom.

- Use senior teachers who are approaching retirement as coaches or mentors. While you can always find expert curriculum and instructional coaches or consultants who can come into the school from outside and collaborate with staff, why not honor the expertise within the school first and build trusting relationships among colleagues at the same time?

- Honor the expertise within the school. Schedule a significant number of hours for specific staff members to support teachers as coaches or facilitators. These in-school instructional coaches are often used for literacy or numeracy. Based on your SMART goals, you may also have other goals in mind for this type of coach.

Instead of sending one person to workshops or institutes outside the school, send a team so that they can confer at the session about how the content would apply in your school and classrooms. Research done in the late 1980s by Bruce Joyce, Beverly Showers, and Barrie Bennett (1987) revealed a startling fact: The impact of attending a training session had only about a 5 percent chance of implementation back at the school if the person went alone. If several colleagues went together and coached each other when they returned, the chance of implementation jumped to a whopping 90 percent.

The Pat Carrigan Story

A concrete example of this level of collaboration and trust existed in the automobile industry during the 1970s under Pat Carrigan, who led a General Motors (GM) parts assembly plant in Bay City, Michigan. Her approach, based on trust, teamwork, and strong union partnerships, spread throughout the relationships in this plant and was the subject of a television documentary (Peters, 2008).

Carrigan started out as an elementary school teacher, then became a college professor with a doctorate in clinical psychology. At GM she started in human resources, and then became the first female plant manager in GM history. There were years of cynicism and distrust for her to overcome. GM was losing money and wanted to close down this older plant.

As a plant manager, she achieved extraordinary change, improving trust and quality through the following policies and innovations (Peters, 2008):

- She was the first plant manager to be visible and spend time on the factory floor saying hello, shaking everyone's hands, and listening to her employees.
- She had an open-door policy, unlike any previous manager there.
- She turned the executive dining room into a work area and converted the separate dining room for white-collar workers into an aerobics classroom.
- She was said to know the name of everybody who worked in the plant.
- She had a style that was supporting, enabling, and empowering.

The results were revolutionary:

- Productivity increased by 40 percent.
- The number of rejected parts was reduced 44 percent.
- The budget was reduced by millions of dollars.
- Employee grievances and discipline incidents were reduced dramatically.

The partnership in joint decision-making she developed with the United Auto Workers Union was ground-breaking and reversed a long-standing atmosphere of tense relationships (Peters, 2008). She told the union to challenge and test rules and talk to her about them, leading to streamlined and more humane procedures. (In chapter 5, we look more closely at union-management partnerships and return to the example of General Motors.)

One man in a middle management role said, "In a traditional financial role . . . you are taught 'Don't trust people.' Let's look at the documents. Pat Carrigan's philosophy was to let people have the information, let them have the control and it will work out. And it did" (Peters, 2008 [television broadcast]).

Her leadership style focused on people as the most important component of the job. She also led a major structural change, forming voluntary, self-managing work teams based on strong interpersonal relationships. They kept their own statistics and did their own quality control.

Through her caring style and shared leadership, Pat was able to unite four previously isolated groups—unions reps, employees, front-line supervisors, and middle managers—into one group with a common mission to ensure the future of the company. As Tom Peters (2008) says, "Pat Carrigan's thing was people!"

Form Inclusive Teams

Collaboration "by invitation" just doesn't work in Rick and Becky DuFour's and Bob Eaker's view of learning communities. Simply asking people to work together will not get them to move out of the comfortable, isolated working styles teachers have been accustomed to. Organizational structures and systems must be created that require teachers to work in collaborative teams. Everyone needs to be involved. Otherwise, people tend to distance themselves and criticize the work of others.

The exciting types of collaborative work teams that are possible include the following:

- The facilitation team that facilitates this entire process

- Work teams that take on the responsibility of a specific part of the action plan

- Grade teams (such as third grade teachers), division teams (for example, teachers from grades 6–8), or departmental teams (such as physical education teachers)

- Integrated teams consisting of teachers from different grades or subjects working together to teach a curriculum that brings the common content, themes, or skills of each together in a new form (for example, a teacher of science and a teacher of technology working together on an integrated unit that they will share over several months)

- Study groups that meet with a specific action research mandate to explore together (for example, teachers and staff members from across the school who want to improve student behavior in the yard and in the hallways)

- Peer partnerships, such as peer coaching, mentoring, and team teaching

There must be a deliberate and concentrated focus on staff and student learning for each work team. Members of new teams will naturally feel vulnerable as they get to know each other and clarify their task. The first team meeting will be especially important in setting the tone. All of the team-building strategies they have done will put them in a better position to accelerate through the necessary relationship building. Trust must be built and maintained—just as in any lasting relationship. Each person hopes the other team members will be trustworthy. Each team has to sort out performing issues with regard to their task, or "what we do" (competence), and relationship issues with regard to their interactions, or "what we say" (character). They need to know how they can help each other, be dependable, and do the job as a team—as well as care about each other as individuals.

Peter Drucker, one of the foremost American experts on business management of the twentieth century, urged managers to give employees an environment where they could do their best work and experience a sense of community. Writing in the *Harvard Business Review*, he made this observation about different models of teams:

> There's a lot of nonsense in team talk, as if teams were something new. We have always worked in teams, and while sports gives us hundreds of team styles, there are only a few basic models to choose from. The critical decision is to select the right kind for the job. You can't mix soccer and doubles tennis. It's predictable that in a few years, the most traditional team will come back in fashion, the one that does research first, then passes the idea to engineering to develop, and then on to manufacturing to make. It's like a baseball team. . . . the greatest strength of baseball teams is that you can concentrate. You take Joe, who is the batter, and you work on batting. There is almost no interaction, nothing at all like the soccer team or the jazz combo, the implicit model of many teams today. This soccer team moves in unison but everyone holds the same relative position. The jazz combo has incredible flexibility because everyone knows each other so well that they all sense when the trumpet is about to solo. The combo model takes great discipline and may eventually fall out of favor. (Drucker, 1993, p. 121)

Which team model best suits the purpose of each of your teams? Let them decide and experiment with different types of team interaction.

The biggest challenge for many teams is learning to work with colleagues for a common purpose; such efforts stimulate continual professional development as well. Here is how one teacher talks about his experience in teams:

> When I first began team teaching on a four-person team . . . I was motivated to leave my social studies hallway and venture into other areas of the building. It always amused me when colleagues in other departments either kindly or jokingly asked, "Are you lost? Can I help you?"

> Despite evidence that teaming can have a positive impact on teacher and student attitudes, performance, and growth, high schools and teachers resist teaming. They may fear scheduling conflicts, personality conflicts and losing control. I've participated on largely dysfunctional and even somewhat stressful teams, but they were still better than being isolated as a teacher because our students formed a community and I knew exactly who their other teachers were. (Spies, 2003, p. 61)

Once SMART goals are established and decisions have been made as to which teams should continue, the staff needs to decide which new teams need to be formed. Then invite staff members to join one or more of these teams. Teams of three to five are best, but teams as large as seven to nine can work well too. In a large school, there may be a temptation to include more people on each team, but if a team gets too large, it can't function. To involve more people, set up the core teams but have additional people on standby for their opinions and feedback.

Specific tasks for these teams include:

- Speed progress by agreeing on the scope of the task and explicit SMART goals through the action planning process. Having team members agree on an inspiring vision of success and engage in meaningful conversations using their own expertise will be critical. Some teams go as far as making learning contracts or charters with each other.

- Take time to get to know each other better and open up.

- Develop and commit to a few essential norms specific to their team, especially for sharing the workload, solving conflict, and reaching decisions—while having some fun, too.

- Agree on meeting times and places and develop a schedule of dates.

- Decide on roles and assign responsibilities such as who will be the team leader or facilitator.

- Decide who will take on the additional roles of recorder, spokesperson/reporter, time-keeper, and process observer (listens, observes, and provides feedback to the group).

- Request resources as needed.

- Decide on a system to report back through the team leader to the facilitation team and principal.

- Focus on action rather than overdrawn planning.

- Review progress, effectiveness, and results at regular intervals, and celebrate success.

- Address any violation of team norms quickly and with sensitivity.

These actions will build the trust necessary to accomplish fundamental change.

Team Structure Map

As a first step, the facilitation team should take on the task of developing a visual map of the current team structure in the school. This would include any group, committee, or team—even teams that cut across the school, like the social committee. Ask each team to briefly communicate its mandate, how often they meet, and who its current members are.

Once this visual map of current teams is drawn, share it with all staff so they can see the connections and overall structure. Sharing this information may have an impact on several teams.

Violations of Team Norms

As teams move from early to higher levels of trust, it is critically important to address team norms that aren't being honored. Being reliable and living up to agreements is a key norm in team behavior. This issue was discussed in a book by Kerry Patterson, Joseph Grenny, Ron McMillan, and Al Switzler:

The worst teams walk away from problems. . . . In good teams, the boss eventually deals with problem behavior. In the best teams, every team member is part of the system of accountability. If team members see others violate a team agreement, they speak up immediately and directly. It's dangerous to wait for or expect the boss to do what good teammates should do themselves. . . . Success does not depend on perfect compliance with new expectations, but on teammates who hold crucial conversations with one another when others appear to be reverting to old patterns. (2002, p. 197)

Build the Capacity of Teams

Forming the teams and setting them off with a charter isn't enough. They need support and training to build higher-performing trust. Team building is a process of helping groups to improve the way they accomplish tasks while enhancing each individual's ability to function effectively as a member.

Among the hundreds of possibilities, several team-building activities are included here to help teams develop trust. The best way to build a team is for people to do real work together and enjoy the results! Always make sure that team-building activities you choose are related to the task and personally safe for members.

Basics First

Activity

If team members still don't know each other well, use the What's in My Name? (page 134) or the Shoebox (page 65) activities to start building relationships. Nametags may be necessary for a few meetings to learn names. Attend to basic needs like this first.

Develop Team Norms

Activity

Even though the school staff has developed norms for its behavior, each team needs to do the same thing. Ask each person to take a moment and complete this statement: "Team members trust each other when . . ."

Share the responses around the table, and record the key thoughts on a chart for all to see. Use this list to develop norms of behavior for your team. Review the process found in chapter 2 if necessary.

Form an Identity

Activity

Spend some time brainstorming a team identity or name for the group that members can relate to and that suits their task. Have a sense of humor in forming team names. Group photos that capture the spirit of the team can help people learn names, and they're fun too.

Listen for Understanding

Activity

Form pairs around the table. Sit face to face with your partner. One of you is the speaker, the other the listener. The speaker makes a statement he or she believes to be true. The listener responds with, "Do you mean . . . ?" to indicate

"Seek first to understand, . . . then to be understood."

—Stephen R. Covey

Activity

whether or not she or he has understood. The aim is for the listener to get three "yeses." Switch roles and repeat the exercise.

Reflect on Progress

After several meetings and a few months into your work, take a break and do the following:

1. Distribute a feedback form, and have team members discuss their progress. Here are some sample discussion points:

   · I know the team norms we established.

   · Members of my team are living up to the team norms.

   · I am following the team norms.

   · We talk about it when norms are violated.

   · We are making progress on our SMART goals.

   · We feel supported by our team leader.

   · We feel supported by our principal.

   · Our team uses humor and a supportive approach.

   · We have the resources needed to complete our task.

   · There is a high level of trust on our team.

2. Tabulate the results, and talk about what's working well and what needs improving.

Facilitate Teams

Facilitators are part of the team, but they take on the special task of making it easier for the team to get its job done and to involve everybody. Specifically, a facilitator or team leader:

- Assists in the formulation of agendas and follow-up

- Ensures that there are food and drinks

- Ensures that the seating arrangements maximize discussion

- Places the chairs so that they face away from the door to lessen distractions

- Organizes resources such as chart stands, flipchart paper, pens, and masking tape

- Is a guide for the group

- Is a good listener and intervenes appropriately

- Summarizes when needed

- Provides written feedback or brief minutes within a few days

Maintain Visual Group Memory

An additional responsibility the facilitator can assume, or delegate to another team member, is maintaining the visual group memory. Visual group memory refers to agendas, activity charts, banners, and other paperwork that is generated and used by the team. These are organized ahead of and used during the meetings and need to be stored carefully afterward for future reference.

When people have visual information in front of them, it leads to greater focus on the task and creates more ownership in the long run. Putting up the results of the last meeting brings everyone back to the reason they are there and increases the continuity of the process. These tasks can be delegated to team members.

Other advantages of group visual memory are that it:

- Frees individuals from having to take notes

- Depersonalizes ideas as people focus on the walls

- Prevents repetition and wheel-spinning

- Enables each person to check and make sure his or her ideas are being recorded accurately

- Makes it easy for latecomers to catch up

- Makes everyone accountable with regard to who is doing what and when (Doyle & Strauss, 1986)

Switch Hats   *Activity*

Sometimes facilitators want to participate as team members and devise visual signals to communicate which role they are in. For example, they could put on a ball cap when they step into the facilitator role. Other team members should take the roles of timekeeper, process observer, and record keeper to help the facilitator.

Write a Team Charter   *Activity*

The final step is to put in writing a plan or charter so the team can organize itself and begin to manage its work. Copy the reproducible Team Charter (page 217), or visit **go.solution-tree.com/leadership** to download and print one.

The plan is only the beginning, not the end. Don't get stuck planning. Do something.

The true measure of a great team is the relationships it forms and the results from it.

What Now?

Team leaders may want to share experiences within the school with other facilitators. They could also take advantage of specific facilitation skills training outside the school to expand their repertoire.

Make Decisions Together

Decisions are part of the everyday life of a school. Sometimes they must be made quickly, and sometimes there is time to consult and deliberate. Staff members often think that *all* decisions should be made together in order to become more collaborative and build trust. In fact, the degree of collaboration before a decision is reached depends on its nature and importance, and the choice of decision-making techniques is also significant.

This strategy is designed to expand the repertoire of methods and skills of teams (large and small) and their facilitators around decision making. It starts with the initial processes of gathering information and the subsequent processes of narrowing the options to make a decision. It builds on the strategies already covered that include the Abilene Paradox (page 71), developing norms (page 58), being ready for resistance and conflict (page 138), and working in teams (page 156). When higher levels of trust and consultation exist, more honest discussion of the issues and their effects will take place, and better decisions will be made for students and the school.

Getting Started

How are decisions typically made at your school? Is there one method, such as voting by a show of hands, or are a variety of methods used depending on the situation? What would you like to change about decision making at your school?

One way to begin a discussion on group decision making is to have the staff watch how another group makes decisions. You could use the 1995 film *Apollo 13,* dramatizing the ill-fated lunar mission of 1970.

Show team members a segment from the film in which the teams of engineers have to decide how to deal with an oxygen shortage in the three-man spaceship. Ask them to observe the skills and attitudes used. How was the problem solved? (In this case, urgency led to creative teamwork that demanded a high degree of trust between the ground crew and the astronauts.)

The following are some of the characteristics of an effective decision:

- The resources and skills of team members are fully utilized.
- All viewpoints are "on the table" before calling for a decision.
- Time is well spent.
- The decision is of high quality.
- The decision is implemented.
- The problem-solving ability of the team is enhanced.

The Decision-Making Scale

In choosing the degree of collaboration for a decision, it helps to envision a continuum: on one end, one person takes or is given the authority to decide, while at the other end is unanimous consent. The Decision-Making Scale (page 219) shows the range of possibilities.

Pin the Tail on the Decision

Make a chart or slide of the scale so everyone has a copy. Explain that the intention in a collaborative, trusting culture is to aim for the upper ranges whenever the decision merits it. Discuss when it would be acceptable for a decision to be made:

- By one person without any discussion
- By a subgroup or committee
- With a 70 percent vote
- Only if there is unanimous consent

Each point on the scale has its pros and cons. Which decision method will lead to the best decisions for the school and the team? Who decides which method is used? Is it negotiable?

For example, a school may decide that it needs at least 80 percent of the parents to support a new school uniform policy *before* its adoption. If they don't have this degree of support to start with, then the odds of the policy being successfully implemented are not good. Getting the support up front may be time consuming, but it saves time in the end.

As you move up the scale, trust, ownership, and commitment increase along with the likelihood of implementation.

What Is Consensus Decision Making?

Steven Saint and James Lawson define *consensus* in their practical book *Rules for Reaching Consensus* as "a state of mutual agreement among members where all legitimate concerns of individuals have been addressed to the satisfaction of the group" (1994, p. xii). In *Building Team Power,* Thomas Kayser (1994) says that consensus is a cooperative effort to find a solution that's acceptable to everyone instead of one that no one will be happy with.

Consensus does not have to mean a long, arduous process. It isn't a unanimous or a majority vote. It doesn't mean everyone is satisfied. It does, however, mean finding a proposal acceptable enough so that all members will say they support it and not criticize or oppose it outside the meeting.

It is not in the best interests of a team to try and make every decision by consensus. It *is* required when ownership and commitment are needed for major decisions, as in the action-planning process. Consensus could also be effectively used to turn the decision making over to a small group. Many methods exist that, when used at the right time, will help people move toward a feeling of consensus.

Chapter 5 highlights two successful workplaces with high-performing trust. One of them is General Motor's Saturn division (page 182). Work teams at Saturn make decisions by consensus—defined in a unique way:

Activity

Visit **go.solution-tree .com/leadership** to download and print the Decision-Making Scale.

Consensus doesn't mean everyone is satisfied. It does mean finding a proposal acceptable enough so that all members will support it.

The Saturn model for consensus decision making doesn't require that every person in the group agree with the decision 100 percent. We tell people they need to get 70 percent comfortable with the decision, but when they leave the room they must support the decision 100 percent. Even if a person can't muster a 70 percent comfort level, she can't block a popular decision unless she can come up with an alternative or point the team in another direction. This caveat breaks the gridlock that can sometimes plague consensus decision making. (Geber, 1992, p. 31)

This method therefore uses the highest level of agreement without dividing the participants into factions.

As shown in the reproducible Four-Phase Decision-Making Model (page 220), decision making can also be broken down into four phases.

Expanding the Information Base

In the strategy Invite Feedback on Staff Trust (page 47), you were introduced to the SWOT method, which can be used here. Other sources of data will also be useful in helping staff members to make a decision. The following are five additional methods for expanding the information base:

1. Stick 'Em Up!

2. Carousel Brainstorming

3. The Force Field

4. Focus Groups

5. Help Line

Visit **go.solution-tree .com/leadership** to download and print the Four-Phase Decision-Making Model.

Activity

Stick 'Em Up!

This is a quick method to get a lot of information in a short time. It is also relatively anonymous. Decide on the key questions you have and write each one separately at the top of a piece of chart paper.

Give each person enough sticky notes for the number of questions there are. After each person numbers his or her sticky notes to match the numbered questions, ask people to stick their responses on corresponding posters. Next, ask them to break up into groups corresponding to the number of posters and read the responses for each poster. Then ask each group to report out to the whole. In large groups, the questions can be duplicated on two or three sets of chart paper and the whole group split into sets. Using the example of the school uniform decision, here are four sample questions:

1. "What do you think the benefits of students wearing uniforms will be for the tone of the school?"

2. "What will the concerns be from the students?"

3. "How do you think we should inform the parents of this idea and get their opinions?"

4. "What will be the drawbacks?"

Carousel Brainstorming

Activity

This method is similar to the previous one, except that participants move around from poster to poster, in small groups of five or six.

Once again, write the questions you have developed on a topic or issue at the top of pieces of chart paper. Divide the whole group up into smaller groups to match the number of questions. Ask each group to stand in front of one of the questions, one group to each question. Give each group a different color of marker pen. Give them five minutes for each question, depending on its complexity. A recorder writes their responses as quickly as possible on the charts. Then, give a signal for the groups to move clockwise to the next question.

Once they have moved to the next poster, ask them to read the comments that previous groups have written. They should add only new comments or indicate their agreement with previous ones. Repeat this process until each group has answered each question.

Once they are back at the question they started with, ask each group to review the comments written by all the other groups. At this point, groups could report out to the whole, or the charts could be analyzed by a smaller group that would prepare a summary.

Participants tend to like this method because it gets them standing up and moving around and encourages creative thinking. This activity can generate a lot of information in a short time, collaboratively.

The Force Field

Activity

The Force-Field, or Barriers and Aids Diagram, developed by Kurt Lewin (1943) provides a method for identifying the factors opposing the change and those pushing for the change.

The leader of this activity identifies and describes the desired, in contrast to the current, situation as well as what will happen if no action takes place. Suppose that the situation being discussed is the establishment of a school uniform policy. The recorder draws a vertical line down the middle of a piece of chart paper, as shown in figure 4.6, and the group then follows the steps shown.

1. The group members brainstorm all of the forces that they perceive as working against or restraining the change in the status quo on the left side of the chart. For example:

    Force A—Many parents will not have the money.
    Force B—Some students will object.
    Force C—The uniform policy will have to be enforced.
    Force D—A uniform manufacturer will have to be found.
    Force E—The student handbook will have to be revised.

2. The group members then brainstorm all the forces driving the change toward the desired situation. These forces are listed on the right side of the chart.

Force 1—Uniforms eliminate competition between students.

Force 2—They help poorer students "fit in."

Force 3—The policy eliminates extreme clothing styles.

Force 4—Many parents have lobbied for uniforms.

Force 5—Competing schools have uniforms. The policy may help with enrollment.

Force 6 –There will be fewer discipline problems, as students can be differentiated from intruders.

Equilibrium

Forces Against Change		Forces For Change
Force A ⟶ 25		25 ⟵ Force 1
Force B ⟶ 35		5 ⟵ Force 2
Force C ⟶ 25		10 ⟵ Force 3
Force D ⟶ 10		25 ⟵ Force 4
Force E ⟶ 5		30 ⟵ Force 5
		5 ⟵ Force 6

Figure 4.6: Analyzing the component forces of a decision

"Defining the Field at a Given Time" (1943) *Psychological Review. 50*: 292–310. Republished in *Resolving Social Conflicts & Field Theory in Social Science,* Washington, D.C.: American Psychological Association. Copyright © 1997 by the American Psychological Association. Reproduced with permission. The use of APA information does not imply endorsement by the APA.

3. The group members then step back and discuss all the forces. Which ones are the strongest? Can any of them be changed? How can the restraining forces be diminished? How might the resistance express itself? What resources are available to counteract the resistance? For example, the discussion of the forces against the change may produce the idea of specifying only the colors and basic style of uniforms as a way to make them easier and more affordable for students than ordering specific items from a manufacturer would be. Families could purchase or make their own, as long as they were the right colors. This would also allow some creativity for the students.

4. At this point, a score between one and fifty is allocated to each force using the following scale, with one being extremely weak and fifty being extremely strong.

5. Decide whether the change is viable based on the weighted totals of the forces for and against. In the example shown, it is clear that the forces are greater in favor of the uniform decision than against it.

6. If you go ahead with a decision, keep in mind that as implementation occurs, new forces may emerge that need to be discussed.

Experience has shown that this is a high-payoff strategy—one that gets the greatest results with the least expenditure of resources. The group may want to consider what it can do to increase the intensity of the forces working in favor of the change. Experience indicates, however, that without deliberate efforts to diminish resistance, the more one pushes the forces for change, the more likely one is to stimulate natural increases in resistance.

Focus Groups

Activity

Like carousel brainstorming, focus groups can yield a great amount of feedback to specific issues in a short period of time. Staff members are divided into small groups and organized to meet with the facilitators for about one hour each during the day. Ideally, the groups would be made up of staff members who wouldn't normally meet and talk together.

Two facilitators are ideal: one to guide the group and one to record the responses on chart paper. The advantage of focus groups is that people feel more comfortable talking about critical issues in small groups. They also tend to participate more when they can hear the opinions of others in a small group. In some cases, you may want to encourage written submissions in addition or instead of the face-to-face focus groups.

The facilitators generate a summary report and then share it with the whole group.

One approach to focus groups involves the participation of the whole staff over a period of one or two days. Another approach is to select a cross-section of the staff and have a focus group with them only.

To use the school uniform example again, focus groups might be used to delve more deeply into such new issues as:

- Consequences they would support for students who refuse to wear a uniform
- How to help families that cannot afford a uniform for their children
- Whether or not there should be days when students can wear their street clothes

Help Line

Activity

This method is designed to help staff members talk to a number of other staff members one at a time instead of in groups. There needs to be a central topic of discussion, with the freedom to allow each person to get advice on a question she or he has about it. For example, the Help Line might have a central topic like consistency of teacher supervision of students before and after school. Each teacher would approach the topic from a different point of view. Creativity often emerges in this method as people bounce ideas off each other.

1. Set up two rows of chairs, row A and row B, facing each other about one foot apart.
2. Ask everyone to take a chair.

3. Ask the people in row A to stay in their seats throughout the activity, and ask the people in row B to move, at a signal, one chair to their right.

4. The facing partners will have a discussion of about three minutes, at which point row B moves and everyone has a new partner.

5. Repeat this process so that each person has four or five conversations. Initially, those in row A make suggestions, while those in row B listen and ask for clarification. After four or five rotations, switch the roles and ask row B to make suggestions and row A to listen and respond.

It will become very noisy during this activity, so make sure you give the instructions clearly before everyone starts. Interrupt them only to signal when it's time for row B to move over. Allow thirty to forty minutes for this in total.

Take time at the end of the activity to talk about ideas that were generated, share what has been learned, and reflect on the overall value of this activity, which depends on willingness to collaborate. This can also be done with participants arranged in an inner and an outer circle.

Useful Phrases for Facilitators

The language we use with teams affects their decisions. Here are some open-ended questions that will help groups (Hirsch & Murphy, 1991):

- "Let's begin by getting a reaction from everyone in the group."

- "Let me summarize what I hear you saying."

- "Are we all comfortable with this recommendation?"

- "Is this the way a team with high trust would behave?"

- "Is anyone uncomfortable with this recommendation? Please tell us why."

- "Does everyone feel that he or she has had the opportunity to express an opinion?"

- "Let me see if I can pull together a recommendation."

- "Let's take five minutes to reevaluate our positions and prepare a response."

- "Let's think about this decision overnight and discuss it when we are fresh tomorrow."

Narrowing the Options

Once all of the information has been shared and discussed and people feel ready to move on, then it is time to start honing in on solutions, narrowing down the options, and finally making a decision—all of which is done collaboratively. Each of the methods has as its goal reaching consensus and then putting the words into action.

Now that there is more trust, anonymity and secret ballots may no longer be such an issue, and people are more comfortable with openly saying or showing their preferences in front of others. Methods such as the following would never have been feasible or appropriate in low-trust cultures:

- Voting without paper
- Compression planning and forced choice
- Nominal group process with reverse weighting

Secret paper ballots have their place but they aren't needed as much in groups with higher trust. Here are several unique methods for arriving at decisions quickly:

Voting With Your Feet

Activity

This enables people to visually see the differences of opinion in a group. Post signs on both sides of the room indicating yes and no responses.

Ask everyone to stand in the middle of the room. Ask one question at a time and tell participants to make a yes or no decision and then move to the appropriate side. Ask them to also discuss their rationale with people near them. Then each side appoints a spokesperson who speaks for that side and shares the reasons they have for being there. The patterns formed when they move tell a group a lot about the decision before it is discussed.

Thumbs Up, Even, or Down

Activity

Ask people to visually signal one of three choices with their thumb in the air so all can see. Then count the responses for each choice.

> Thumbs up = Yes
> Thumbs even = Not sure or don't care
> Thumbs down = No

Fist to Five

Activity

Post a response chart outlining the following five choices, and ask for a show of fingers:

- One finger—I cannot accept this solution/decision or be part of it. I will take actions that will prevent this from happening. I will not support it in public.

- Two fingers—I strongly disagree and believe it will have negative implications, but I will not stand in the way of the group. I will support it in public.

- Three fingers—The solution/decision does not make much difference to me.

- Four fingers—I think that this solution/decision should be given a high priority, and you can count on me.

- Five fingers—This solution/decision is a high priority for me, and you can count on my strong support. High five!

(Fletcher, 2002)

We've seen two choices, three choices, and five choices. Now refer to the ten-point scale, shown again in table 4.2.

Table 4.2: Commitment Continuum

Levels of Yes and No		Level of Contribution and Support
Strong Agreement *I think this is the best option.*	10 9 8	Maximum Support *I will lead/support the implementation.*
Agreement *I think it's workable.*	7 6	Proactive Support *I'll help to plan and implement.*
Disagreement *I have some concerns.*	5 4 3	Moderate Support *I will look for things I can do to support this.*
Strong Disagreement *I think this is a mistake.*	2 1 0	Minimal Support *I'll do what is necessary to support this.*

Visit **go.solution-tree.com/ leadership** to download and print this chart.

Once everyone understands the scale, you can proceed in several ways to end up with a vivid display of opinions.

1. Make a chart of the ten-point scale.

2. Pose the questions.

3. Give participants a colored sticky dot, and ask them to come up to the chart and place it beside the number that fits their decision. This can also be done with two different colored dots in two steps: first for the level of yes or no; second for the level of contribution and support.

4. Tally the dots and see if you find any agreement. Are there enough dots in the maximum and proactive levels to ensure implementation? Ask for clarification from those who disagreed. Repeat the process if new points are raised.

5. Once the top two levels have sufficient dots, the decision is declared and implementation can begin.

Activity

Compression Planning and Forced Choice

Compression planning is used to sort and cluster information into categories. These categories or clusters could become alternative choices.

1. Give the group a problem or challenge that needs a solution.

2. Distribute sticky notes and ask each person to write possible solutions on them—five sticky notes per person and one idea per sticky note. Allow five to ten minutes.

3. Post all the solutions on a chart, read each one, and then sort them into categories or clusters.

4. Give each cluster of sticky notes a label.

5. Ask the group to discuss the choices in pairs or trios.

6. Use the sticky dots again to force a choice. This time you could give each pair or trio five dots that they can "spend," either by voting with them all for one choice or by weighting their vote by spreading the dots among several choices.

7. Tally the results.

Reverse Weighting

Activity

This process (easier than it sounds) involves gathering and ranking many solutions to make a decision.

1. Ask for participants to make suggestions for solutions and share ideas about the merits of their suggestions. Continue the process until every member has contributed.

2. After the alternative solutions are generated in a list on a chart, assign each one a number.

3. Ideas can be clarified as they are presented or after all the ideas are on the chart. The intention here is not to change or eliminate ideas but to make sure everyone understands the options.

4. Ask participants to select the three options they feel will work best, and assign three points for their first choice, two points for their second choice, and one point for their third choice. (Some choices will receive no points.) This is called a reverse-weight chart.

5. Go around to the individuals or groups and ask for their choices, writing down the number of points beside each option.

6. Tally the totals and revise the list to show the top three options (the ones with the highest numbers of points).

7. Repeat the process again with three choices only.

The end product should be one clear decision.

Three Final Questions

At the end of any decision-making process, the group needs to be asked three final questions:

1. Can everyone say they have been listened to by all members?

2. Can we live with the decision?

3. Will we support it publicly?

Resolving an Impasse

If there is a lack of consensus, the group should consider these questions:

1. Can anyone suggest a compromise we could all support?

2. Under what conditions would you support this solution?

3. What part of the solution do you oppose, and what parts would you modify?

4. What would be required for you to live with the solution for a limited time?

5. Would you be willing to live with the solution until we revisit it in the future?

6. What would be a reasonable time before we reassess the decision?

Closing the Decision

Now attention needs to turn to implementing the plans and getting on with it. If there has been strong conflict and disagreement, feelings need time to heal in order to move ahead. Give these tough decisions a few months in action, and then revisit them again with fresh eyes.

Teams with high trust will be more generous with each other and set aside their point of view more easily for the will of the group. There will always be another time to face another challenge together.

What Now?

Many groups are used to voting either by a show of hands or a private ballot. Like voting, all of the methods described in this strategy require everyone's participation, but they are more rooted in trust, sharing, and listening. Consider that consensus has been reached when you have met these criteria:

1. I believe that you understand my point of view.

2. I believe that I understand your point of view.

3. Whether or not I prefer this idea or concept, I will support it because it was reached openly and fairly.

4. I can live with this decision. (Ouchi, 1997, p. 3)

Key Messages

1. Medium-risk strategies build on a foundation of early trust.

2. Attention to personal strategies continues to be as important as interpersonal strategies, as you refine your Trust Touchstones.

3. Leaders new to a school or opening new schools have unique challenges.

4. Relearning the art of conversation is critical to early trust.

5. Knowledge of the change process and conflict resolution is required to build trust.

6. An Action Planning Roadmap that encompasses future visioning, clarification of mission, values, and beliefs, and analysis of the current situation will make goal setting more strategic and effective.

7. Work teams need to be structured to bring life to each action plan. These teams need attention and guidance as they work through their own growth stages.

8. Groups need a variety of decision-making strategies as they gather information and narrow their choices to reach consensus where everyone can support the decision in public.

9. Schools can reach higher levels of trust if they commit the time and effort to continue learning and talking together.

Questions

1. What surprises are you discovering as you continue to build self-trust?

2. Describe the transition as the group moves from distrust and early trust.

3. In the issues that have surfaced, is competence or character a root cause or is it a combination of both?

4. Are there indications that conflict is now being seen as a positive and inevitable in the trust-building process?

5. Is it more common to hear genuine laughter in hallways, offices, and meetings—maybe even in classrooms?

6. How does the Action Planning Roadmap compare to the planning processes you used to follow? What pieces were missing or undervalued?

7. Which new teams are forming? Are people willingly volunteering to join them?

8. What are the results of alternative decision-making processes you are using as compared to traditional majority voting?

9. Do you feel and think there is a desire to continue working towards higher levels of trust?

Further Resources

Adams, P. (1993). *Gesundheit! Bringing Good Health to You, the Medical System, and Society Through Physician Service, Complementary Therapies, Humor and Joy.* Rochester, VT: Healing Arts Press.

Alban, B., & Benedict Bunker, B. (2006). *Large Group Interventions: Engaging the Whole System for Rapid Change.* San Francisco, CA: Jossey-Bass.

Briggs-Meyers, I., with Myers, P. (1995). *Gifts Differing: Understanding Personality Type.* Mountain View, CA: Davies-Black Publishing.

Brown Easton, L. (2004). *Powerful Designs for Professional Learning.* Oxford, OH: National Staff Development Council.

Cooperrider, D., Whitney, D., & Stavros, J. M. (2008). *Appreciative Inquiry Handbook: For Leaders of Change.* LaVergne, TN: Ingram Publishing Services.

Holden, R. (1998). *Happiness Now! Timeless Wisdom for Feeling Good Fast.* Carlsbad, CA: Hay House Books.

Johnson, S. (1998). *Who Moved My Cheese? An Amazing Way to Deal With Change in Your Work and in Your Life.* New York: Putnam and Sons.

Killion, J. (2008). *Assessing Impact: Evaluating Staff Development.* Thousand Oaks, CA: Corwin Press.

Magruder, J., & Mohr, B. (2001). *Appreciative Inquiry: Change at the Speed of Imagination.* San Francisco: Jossey-Bass/Pfeiffer.

Martin, R. (2007) *The Psychology of Humor: An Integrative Approach.* St. Louis, MO: Elsevier Academic Press.

Stephenson, S. (2001). When Your Heart Is in Your Dreams. *Register, 3*(3) , 28–31.

Stephenson, S. (2003). Saying "NO" to the Unimportant. *Register, 5*(2), 21–24.

Wooten, P. (2002) *Compassionate Laughter: Jest for Your Health.* Santa Cruz, CA: Jest Press.

Videos

Cap Gemini is an excellent video for an overview of Appreciative Inquiry. Several businesses are featured with interviews from employees and leaders.

Time to Lead is a DVD and resource booklet, Ontario Principals' Council.

Websites

www.worldlaughtertour.com—Steve Wilson website

www.aath.org—Association for Applied and Therapeutic Humor (AATH) website

www.reflectivehappiness.com—Martin Seligman website

www.stressed.com—Loretta LaRoche website

Websites for Self-Assessments

- Stephen M. R. Covey (www.speedoftrust.com)
- Emotional Intelligence EQi Assessment (www.danielgoleman.info)
- Insights® (www.insights.com)
- Myers-Briggs Type Indicator (www.myersbriggs.org)
- The Passion Test (www.mypassiontest.com)
- My Personality Dimensions® (www.personalitydimensions.com)
- Reina Trust Building® Measurement Surveys (www.reinatrustbuilding.com)
- Theory of Multiple Intelligences (www.education-world.com)

- True Colors® (www.true-colors.com)
- 4MAT Learning Styles (www.aboutlearning.com)

VIPs

Take time and reflect on the Very Important Points you feel were made in this chapter. What resonated with you the most?

The Courage to Create High-Trust Cultures

Most innovation in the future will demand that historically adversarial relations: (1) between many functions in the firm, (2) between labor and management, (3) between suppliers and the firm, (4) between the firm and its distributors/customers—be replaced by co-operative relations. Establishing new relationships requires listening, creating a climate of respect and trust and coming to understand the mutual benefits that will ensue if partnership relationships are firmly established.

—Tom Peters

In this chapter, we talk about places where people love to work, appreciate how they are treated, and feel they are making a difference. People in high-trust environments have challenged the status quo to achieve something better. These people go the extra mile for the customer—which in our case is our students!

As explained earlier, a symphony orchestra is a good metaphor for this high level of identification-based trust. While it is true that very few relationships make it to this final stage, in those that do, people experience a high degree of empathy and begin to think, feel, and respond like their fellow members.

High levels of trust produce synergy and creativity in unexpected ways.

They understand each other so well that they can act on one another's behalf. High levels of trust produce synergy and creativity in unexpected ways.

Schools that get this far in the trust-building process have reached a transforming phase of achievement. They have faced the barriers to trust and found solutions. While the barriers are never gone entirely, people can talk openly about their fears and how to tame them.

The Great Place to Work Institute holds a yearly competition to determine the best workplaces, both in the United States and Canada. Their Trust Index survey instrument, used by organizations around the world, cites three primary trust-building dimensions found in the best workplaces—credibility, respect, and fairness—plus two additional factors, pride and camaraderie.

The level of high trust experienced by companies rated as Best Workplaces is rare in the educational world. The following two corporate success stories serve as best-case examples—Southwest Airlines and Saturn automobiles. Although the automobile industry as a whole has undergone sweeping changes as it tries to respond to changing demand and newer technologies, the Saturn story remains relevant. As we look at these two examples of excellent corporations, we should ask ourselves how their strategies could be applied to education. What would high-performing, mature trust look like in schools, and which of these practices would work there?

The Southwest Airlines Story

Jody Hoffer Gittell captured the essence of Southwest Airlines' passionate focus on relationships in her book *The Southwest Airlines Way* (2003), one of many books written about this company. This is an airline that doesn't need frills—just good service, lower fares, and dependability. Gittell writes that "it is the only airline to have won the airline industry's 'Triple Crown'—the fewest delays, the fewest complaints and the fewest mishandled bags . . . for entire years from 1992 through 1996" (2003, p. 7). To achieve the shortest turnarounds in the airline industry, they use only one aircraft type (Boeing 737), fly into less congested airports, offer no in-flight meals or baggage transfer to other airlines, and provide a unique approach to reserving seating online by groups. It is also known for its safety record. Southwest Airlines seems to give customers what they value most. It achieves this level of excellence with the following philosophy and actions:

- Unions and management accept each other as partners working on something together, rather than as adversaries. Their work agreement includes flexible job descriptions, which ask workers to do whatever is needed to enhance the overall operation. This incredible concession on the part of the unions is an outcome of negotiations that occurred repeatedly over time and is indicative of the huge amount of trust built up between management and labor.

- Shared goals, shared knowledge, and mutual respect are key to their relationships.

- The credibility of the leaders depends on their honesty in daily conversations with employees. Leaders achieved "high levels of credibility through repeated, consistent episodes of 'telling it straight' whether the news was good or bad" (Gittell, 2003, p. 251). This level of credibility, where people trust that you are telling them the truth, takes years to develop. And along with credibility through trust, employees come to believe the leaders truly care about their well-being.

- Teamwork is identified as the most necessary trait of employees. When a group is first formed at Southwest, team-building activities are used to establish group identity and the scope of their responsibilities. Gittell writes that "as the group gains a sense of its identity and begins to develop its own ways of dealing with task and organizational issues, the manager . . . can gradually withdraw from prominence in the group activities" (2003, p. 82). The critical skills they learn go beyond the technical aspects of their job to include soft skills such as customer orientation and teamwork ability. Employees learn more about each other's jobs through job exchanges. Southwest invested heavily in the position of "boundary spanners," who manage the flow of information and build relationships across twelve distinct functional boundaries, from pilots to ticket agents to caterers to ground crew (much like the facilitation team concept).

- Southwest takes considerable time finding the right people to hire and then spends time training them. Hiring for relational competence (trust and the ability to relate effectively with others) is considered an important means for determining who will go above and beyond. As Gittell (2003) writes, "Southwest watches newcomers carefully at the outset, to identify and correct potential hiring mistakes" (p. 87). Each newly hired employee receives both classroom and on-the-job training guided by a training coordinator.

- Conflicts are seen as a fact of life, with interdependent teams coming from different "thought-worlds." Supervisors coach new employees while modeling problem-solving skills. These local managers are trained to help employees resolve differences on the floor. Gittell describes how top managers began to push resolution of employee-to-employee problems to the extent that these resolutions actually occurred in information gathering meetings. She contrasts this atmosphere with the usual one: "Whereas it's warfare at other airlines, here the goal is to maintain the esteem of everybody" (2003, p. 103).

- Southwest employees are given the freedom to be themselves at work and are expected to be friendly and open. The many Cultural Committees at Southwest Airlines were started to plan social events for themselves and charitable events for the community. They have been known to plan carnivals, cruises, and casino nights for employees and their families. Celebrations are used to reward people and teams for good performances. Employees at Southwest also care about each other as if they were members of a family. An example of this is their Catastrophic Fund, which provides for members in dire financial straits. They also try to help each other achieve a work-life balance so they have time for their friends and families as well as work.

The Saturn Story

Saul Rubinstein and Thomas Kochan's book *Learning From Saturn* (2001) documents the story of the Saturn Corporation—the first new nameplate for General Motors since 1917. Saturn was set up with dual objectives—"to make small cars profitably . . . and to create (or retain) good jobs for American workers and UAW members" (2001, p. 9). When the first car was unveiled, the Saturn concept and design revolutionized the industry. Its sales approach was the opposite of the prevailing one: no pressure, no haggling, clear pricing, a commitment to exceed customer expectations, and a thirty-day, money-back guarantee. Customer service was based on a Golden-Rule philosophy. Saturn cars became sought after. Seventy percent of first-time visitors returned to the showroom, and a whopping 90 percent of owners recommended the car to their friends. Saturn reshaped the way automakers build and sell cars with its philosophy and actions:

- Their mission, philosophy, and values were all directed to achieving world-class levels of quality and customer enthusiasm.

- In 1983, Saturn launched a bold experiment in corporate governance and employee relationships, promising "to serve as a learning laboratory for a new partnership model from which labor, management and government policy makers might learn" (Rubinstein & Kochan, 2001, p. 6). Both the company and the union leaders shared the basic view that more participative approaches to labor relations were needed, from the shop floor to the decision-making meeting rooms (Rubinstein & Kochan, 2001).

- Saturn began a "different kind of company and a different kind of car" with a remarkable twenty-eight-page Memorandum of Agreement (instead of the usual four hundred pages), that states the principles that both parties, labor and management, commit to follow and hold each other accountable for.

> But what is more striking about this labor agreement than its specific terms and conditions are the tone and the language used to convey the principles of mutual trust and respect that the parties hoped to build into their relationship through principles of joint consensus-based decision making . . . and a shared vision of what a world-class company and employment relationship of the 1980's should be. (Rubinstein & Kochan, 2001, p. 25)

- It was the UAW's vision to share with workers the problem solving, management, and governance of the enterprise. Workers' skills and capability were seen by management as essential to securing their own long-term careers in the new economy and adding value both to their enterprises and the national economy: "In order for the partnership and consensus process to mean anything, each party puts . . . themselves at risk, on the line, for performance" (Rubinstein & Kochan, 2001, p. 33).

- They flattened the hierarchies by using networks with many horizontal links to communicate and to solve problems. They did this through the placement of hundreds of union representatives in the operations and staff management structure (Rubinstein & Kochan, 2001). The format for organizational governance they adopted would enable management and the local union to jointly manage the business with high quality and productivity. The union viewed the UAW members elected to serve in these co-management roles as supplementing the local union's elected leadership. Both partners approved payroll, overtime, and purchase orders. However, they did not discharge, hire, or discipline workers.

- The leaders at Saturn knew that they needed to begin by hiring or selecting employees and supervisors who displayed the relational trust they felt was absolutely necessary for teamwork, decision making, and problem solving to flourish. At Saturn, skills and abilities, not seniority, were the key ingredients in hiring.

- Saturn's frontline teams and, more specifically, their team members turned out to be the key asset and source of competitive advantage to the company, and were trained in work team organization, problem solving, decision making, and conflict resolution. Furthermore, they developed skills in areas traditionally reserved for management, including budgeting, record keeping, and data analysis. Saturn had a passion for training, with employees receiving 5 percent of their work time for learning—ninety-two hours each year!

- Saturn used Decision Rings (joint labor-management committees) as the communication medium to get the word out to the floor about what was going on, what changes were coming, and what procedural changes were being made. Although decisions took longer, they were usually better, because there was buy-in from everyone. A union executive board member described communications this way:

> At my old job, you were never a part of identifying problems. You were always out there bitching and moaning about problems, but when it came time to get into a huddle in the room and resolve it, you were never part of that. You were never part of the conversation. Management would go off into one room and do their thing, and we would go off in our room and do our thing. We would get back together, and they would lay their plan in front of you and want you to buy into it. Well, it's a lot harder to buy into a plan you haven't been part of. . . . You are always suspicious. (Rubinstein & Kochan, 2001, p. 50)

Saturn's management practices paid off in the popularity of their cars and the number of repeat buyers—as well as in the contentment of their workforce. Whatever the fate of the beleaguered automobile industry, the success of Saturn's workplace innovations is undisputed. The original champions were motivated because they believed in Saturn's mission and philosophy and felt ownership of it. Subsequent generations will need to find their own motivation.

Creating High-Trust Cultures in Learning Communities

People can learn from one another, build shared knowledge, and develop and transfer skill and wisdom only in a "sharing culture" . . . a climate in which people talk and interact comfortably, in part, because they are not competing against each other.

— Richard DuFour, Robert Eaker, and Rebecca DuFour

Like many other sectors of the economy, public education has reached a crossroads. At a time when we know more than ever what students need to learn effectively, our accountability to them and to a larger public is challenged by the decrease in overall student population and the increase in choice in school settings. Those involved in public education have a responsibility to provide the best school governance models possible. We want the publicly funded education system to thrive.

With these examples of high-trust workplaces, Southwest and Saturn, to learn from, the question becomes: How do schools create their own stories and sustain them over time as staff members and leaders change and cope with the forces swirling around outside of the school itself in the local area, state or province, and country? At Saturn, a division of a larger company created its own culture, and at Southwest, relationships were placed at the heart of the serious business of air travel. How can an individual school do the same thing as part of a larger school system? What can we take from this?

Specific factors work together collectively to create high-performing trust in schools. One or even a couple of them may bring about small change, but the cumulative effect of all of them working together creates true sustainable change in what Stoll and Fink (1996) call a "moving" school (see figure 3.2, page 86).

These are the core characteristics of a school with high-performing trust:

- People and relationships first and foremost ("me" becomes "we")

- A strong sense of moral purpose and passion for student learning (Dreams are taken seriously, and it is believed they make a difference in the lives of students.)

- Openness and information (candor, free speech, honesty)

- True inclusion of and buy-in from all staff members in their shared vision

- Flattened and flexible structure for empowerment (sharing power, control and decision making) to find new solutions through new knowledge bases

- Courage to innovate and be creative (taking risks and being vulnerable)

- Regarding mistakes and successes as part of learning and capacity building

- Seeing conflict as inevitable and dealt with at the source wherever possible

We are not talking about tinkering with the existing structure. In high-trust cultures, major, substantive change and drastically different ways of doing business are necessary. As DuFour, Eaker, and DuFour (2005) write:

> Significant transformations will require more than changes in structure—the policies, programs, and procedures of a school. Substantive and lasting change will ultimately require a transformation of culture—the beliefs, assumptions, expectations and habits that constitute the norm for the people throughout the organization. Principals and teachers can be placed in new structures and go through the motions of new practices but unless they eventually develop new competencies and new commitments that lead to true school reculturing, they will continue to be under the inexorable pull of their traditional practices and the assumptions that drive them. If schools are to be successful in developing their capacity as PLCs, new assumptions must ultimately prevail over long-standing traditional beliefs. (p. 12)

School decision making must work for both adults and students alike. The key task for school leadership involves getting the right balance. This entails a constant moderation between demonstrating a personal regard for faculty while steadfastly advancing the primary mission of the school. When conflicts arise, organizational integrity must be preserved. Ultimately, adult behavior must be understood as directed toward the betterment of children (Bryk & Schneider, 2002).

Finally, let's examine the following conditions that need to be in place for a school to consider reaching for high-performing trust. As you read them, think about which of these conditions are currently well in place at your school and which ones could become your future goals.

Union-Management Partnerships Are the Foundation

If you want people to be committed to a decision, engage them in the decision-making process.

—Stephen R. Covey

Just as in the two case studies we looked at, schools with high-performing trust need a foundation of strong partnership between union and management. This includes all unions—support staff unions, teacher unions, substitute teacher unions and principal unions or associations. Some teacher unions are proactively trying to bargain for more minutes of learning time each day and to influence the productive use of staff meetings and their agendas. Every person must be invited to participate equally in the process. This will lead to stronger relational trust between staff members and the union representatives or stewards among them.

Because of the greater degree of vulnerability, low trust is typically protected by lengthy contracts with litigious language and penalties built in for both parties in case things go badly. For example, if a clause in the contract is broken, there is an investigation and the possibility of a grievance or subsequent discipline for one of the parties. These factors contribute to a "win-lose" mentality, with only one winner and one loser.

With high trust in a school, union and management have to decide together which clauses of the contract should have more flexibility and which clauses stay in effect. Don't try to get around the collective agreement. You must work within it. Principals cannot make special deals with individual teachers or staff members. It's against the law.

Partnerships will work depending on the issue—they will work when advice or support is needed, but won't work in a supervision or disciplinary issue. A memorandum of agreement or respectful relations policy can be as useful in schools as it is at Saturn for enabling both sides to experience a win-win solution. Progress won't be smooth, but in a high-trust school, people will support each other even if they mess up.

Weekly meetings with union representatives and the principal, with a "no surprise policy," can help in the beginning. One Canadian union leader who has used this process for years told me she always told principals and superintendents, "If you ever lie to me or spring something on me, my trusting relationship with you is over." She said it has always worked for her at the school and district levels, even when there was no time to build through stages of trust. These meetings give a chance for a "heads-up" on issues, time for advice and planning. Issues don't simmer and boil over.

Hiring and Firing Issues

The capacity to remove or "counsel out" incompetent principals, teachers, and other staff members remains a complicated issue that everyone will have to confront. Distinctions need to be made between staff members who can become competent with coaching and instruction and those who cannot improve or will not take advantage of any assistance. Some school systems give the principal the authority to hire and fire, while many do not. Although there will be bumps along the way, there must be avenues for staff members who cannot or will not commit themselves to the skills, knowledge, and attitudes of a high-trust school to leave with dignity:

> Teachers [and all staff members] who are unwilling to take on the hard work of change and align with colleagues around a common reform must leave. Only when participants demonstrate their commitment to engage in such work and see others doing the same can a genuine professional community grounded

---

Partnerships between union and management will work when advice or support is needed, but won't work in a supervision or disciplinary issue.

There must be avenues for staff members who cannot commit themselves to the skills, knowledge, and attitudes of a high-trust school to leave with dignity.

in relational trust emerge. . . . Interestingly, such authority may rarely need to be invoked thereafter once these new norms are firmly established. (Bryk & Schneider, 2002, p. 138)

Unions have considerable print and media resources available for professional learning and can offer their expertise and consultants as resources to assist the school—perhaps even sources of funding.

It Starts With the Interview and Hiring Process

The hiring process is an intentional process of gathering trust-relevant information on both sides of the hiring decision.

—Megan Tschannen-Moran

Interview and hiring practices should include emphasis on the presence and importance of relational trust. New staff members will need to be carefully selected to work in collaborative teams. Interviewers need to develop character-based as well as competence-based questions to ask. Both the interview and reference-check process should explore past experiences with trust and respect. Any potential new staff members need to know the high-trust culture of the school they are applying to and the level of commitment and teamwork that will be demanded. A probationary period should be established which allows for exit counseling with support from both labor and management. People new to their roles must be supported and mentored (teachers and administrators).

New Organizational Structures Support Team Learning

Typical school structures do not provide sufficient flexibility or autonomy for school people to approach the mysteries and perplexities and problems of teaching and learning. Organizational capacity entails creating a flexible system that is open to all sorts of ideas, that welcomes the eccentric and unusual as well as the tried and true.

—Coral Mitchell and Larry Sackney

Capacity building needs to be focused and sustained in all three areas: personal, interpersonal, and organizational. Previous strategies have been organized around developing personal and interpersonal capacity for trust. Without attending to additional organizational capacity and the supportive structure for it in a school, any progress made by individuals or teams will be short-lived, and there will be little time for personal growth.

Every school is unique and will have to make its own decisions about the structure that would best suit its students, staff, and community. Decisions that alter the structure of a school should not be made by one person or a small elite group. This authoritarian type of change would rewind the trust-tape to zero if, after all this, unilateral changes were made without a collaborative process among a trusting staff. There must be a tight, "puzzle-

Decisions that alter the structure of a school should not be made by one person or any small, elite group.

piece" fit between the vision, mission, beliefs, action plans, and work teams and the organization or architecture of the school.

While some organizational changes are relatively easy, others involve major restructuring and upheaval. Take time to analyze the current structure, and resist quick-fixes and add-ons in favor of planning a comprehensive structure. To make significant changes without the support and will of the group would be disastrous.

Three features of the organizational structures common to all high-trust cultures are:

- An administration team
- A central facilitation team
- Work teams for each defined action plan

Members of an administration team must be carefully matched so that they work well together. These teams should be left in place long enough to make a difference and to build relationships without the fear that they will end prematurely.

At Southwest they called them boundary spanners. In schools, this connecting role can be played by the facilitation team members. In a high-trust culture, the dynamics of the facilitation team will be more automatic and accepted by the staff and won't need to be written in contractual language. People know what to do already and decide how to do it for themselves. Identify one or more staff members who might be the leader of the facilitation team. School staffs need to be asked to formally commit to working in work team structures. Entry and exit strategies also need to be explored, as school staffing does fluctuate both during and at the end of each school year. Newcomers—even new administrators—need to be welcomed to the staff and paired with mentors.

This type of deep change will bring a totally different approach to team-work in which people:

- Voice valuable, opposing ideas in a safe environment.
- Feel a sense of control and involvement not usually found in teams.
- Take risks and generate new ideas in an atmosphere of creativity and play.

When classroom and office doors are open and staff break free from their past isolation, the possibilities of what they can achieve are endless. Here are some examples of new organizational structures that might take shape in a high-trust culture involving new approaches to the school calendar and the school day:

- Multi-age and multi-grade level groupings
- Biweekly, grade-team meetings at which the administration (or another staff member such as the librarian) takes the students together to free up the teachers so they can meet
- Integrated disciplines in high schools that cut across former subjects, such as global issues; creativity; and equity-based learning

        focusing on integrated curriculum, bringing teachers together from several subject disciplines, and perhaps team teaching

- Year-round schools with built-in periods of remediation and review and shorter but more frequent breaks

Obviously, the teaching timetable has to include noninstructional time when staff members can collaborate during the day. The timetable structure has to enable this type of trust and not be a direct impediment to it. The challenge is to evaluate your existing organizational structures and design new organizational structures for the workplace where needed to provide the time for work teams and other forms of collaboration.

In spite of the complexities and perplexities surrounding the notion of restructuring, there appears to be a clear link between professional learning and structural arrangements. As Firestone (1996) points out:

> It is fairly clear that attending to the knowledge base of teachers without considering organizational arrangements is likely to lead to a situation where new ideas are adopted by a minority of practitioners and are weakly institutionalized. However, changing organizational arrangements without a clear sense of what teaching and learning should be like can lead to goal displacement, where these arrangements become ends in themselves and do not contribute to the educational outcomes they are expected to produce. (as quoted in Mitchell & Sackney, 2001, p. 83)

Once there is an organizational structure in place based on high trust, everyone will be free to open their doors even wider, take some risks and invent new realities for themselves and for students.

New Roles and Responsibilities Are Defined

People need to know what others expect of them. Roles and responsibilities may need redefining for each of the following people or groups:

- Principal and assistant principal
- Facilitation team and its leader
- Staff members
- Work teams
- Outside facilitators and central office staff

There will be always be decisions that only the principal can make, but many decisions can be made collaboratively when it's appropriate and if there is sufficient time. Power and control need to be shared by the principal and accepted by the facilitation team and staff members. Information about such core issues as the overall budget, sources of revenue, and purchasing power of the school need to be made transparent so requests can be realistic. The principal will play a pivotal role in the success of the school organization and its structures.

"Principals who are successful in creating a sense of shared responsibility for improvement create school cultures built on a strong sense of purpose and profound commitment to children and learning. These cultures support innovation, teamwork, shared leadership and on-going professional development."

—Anne Conzemius

Staff must feel comfortable enough to raise questions and challenge any rule or procedure that doesn't reflect high levels of trust.

It is important to remember that many principals were teachers at one time and have their own vision of success for themselves and the school. Mitchell and Sackney (2001) describe four ways a principal can be approached or co-opted into trying a new school structure:

1. Outside-in—the principal is approached from an outside source such as a central board consultant or university researcher.

2. Inside-out—the principal believes change is needed and initiates it on his or her own.

3. Bottom-up—the idea begins with an individual teacher or group of teachers who persist and receive the support of the principal (more likely in a high-trust culture with a principal who is an active learner).

4. Top-down—a more typical, hierarchical approach begins with a superintendent or central official.

Principals (and teachers) tend to resist top-down approaches:

Unless the top-down approach is handled with extreme sensitivity, it is not as likely as the other strategies to lead to commitment on the part of principals and to profound improvement in the school. . . . Unless a top-down approach facilitates the creation of a community of leaders, it is not likely to stand the test of time. (Mitchell & Sackney, 2001, p. 115)

Staff members have to get involved in the leadership of the school and feel more comfortable in leadership roles outside of their classrooms or offices. Their primary job is to teach their students, but to do this better, they have to speak up, become involved, and trust others. Staff must feel comfortable enough to raise questions and challenge any rule or procedure that doesn't reflect high levels of trust. Principals must guard against creating rules or procedures that are applied to everyone but only needed by a few.

The principal must also build a strong relationship with the facilitation team and work closely with them at every step. As Wayne Hulley and Linda Dier write (2005):

The importance of the principal to the functioning of the Coordinating Council [facilitation team] cannot be overstated. When principals consistently deliver the message that they want everyone to feel part of the process, they can work with reluctant staff to ensure that opting out is not an alternative. A large part of the principal's role is to anticipate the barriers to success and plan for ways to overcome them. (p. 75)

Other work teams in the school will have much the same structure as the facilitation team, except their purpose will be to implement one aspect of the action plan.

Finally, consider the support you can count on from central office consultants and outside facilitators for advice, coaching and sometimes facilitating and presenting certain parts of the strategies or working directly with work teams. In low-trust cultures, staff members are wary of an outsider offering expert advice or coming into their classrooms. With greater trust, central office staff become a welcome part of the team.

All Meetings Are Productive

If you want to get some quick feedback on how well your meetings are going, use this technique from Jonathan Fox and Playback Theatre. Ask the participants to improvise three 3-minute skits about:

- How meetings used to look.

- How meetings are done now.

- How they would like meetings to be done real soon.

As the three scenes are acted out, listen and watch. The skits will tell you what the staff think of their meetings.

Meetings will take on new structures and purposes in a high-trust school. Full staff meetings will be carefully planned by the facilitation team to fully utilize this special time with the staff together in one room. Activities the staff think are worthwhile will be their focus. Many other means can also be used to share basic information such as online bulletin boards, weekly bulletins, or a simple, open binder of information in a central location that staff can refer to regularly. Access to information is important, but meeting time is too valuable to use for these items.

Grade level, department meetings and work team meetings will take place more often. More meeting spaces will have to be carved out of school floor plans and equipped with chart stands, LCD projectors and round tables for team discussions. The staff room will be an important learning space in the school and may need new furniture and equipment too.

Productive meetings are a good use of people's time when they set the agenda.

High-Quality Professional Learning Is the Norm

Every educator engages in effective professional learning every day so every student achieves.

—National Staff Development Council, 2008

Inappropriate staff development was cited in chapter 1 as one of the five main barriers to establishing trust in a school. Increasing workload and stress are huge factors in this issue. When many teachers think about professional development, they think mainly of PD days or pro-d days (professional development days), which are few and far between and considered to be more of a one-shot event rather than part of a well-designed plan. For this reason the term professional learning more accurately describes the wide range of formal and informal types of learning of teachers. Formal learning includes conferences, keynote speakers, courses, workshops, and meetings with mandatory attendance. Informal learning comes from professional

"The support that teachers provided to each other resulted in a positive energy that gathered momentum. Bi-weekly professional development meetings were established at which staff teams made presentations to each other about new insights and their work with children. Teachers came to understand and appreciate each other's strengths and gifts as teachers."

—Wayne Hulley
and Linda Dier

reading, networking on the Internet or in person, and discussions with trusted colleagues.

Whatever role our school leaders have, they need to be strong communicators, great at power sharing and creating shared values and a common purpose, willing to deal with conflicts, and in possession of superb negotiation and conflict resolution skills. Planned professional learning opportunities need to be in place in every school district for these skills to be developed and refined over time.

We now have the best-qualified teachers and principals compared to any previous era in teacher training. The majority of educators do engage in ongoing learning. However, many educators report a loss of autonomy and an increase in workload, which makes finding time for their own learning very difficult. Educators know the kind of professional learning they like, and "one size doesn't fit all." Pre-service teacher education courses and principal qualification courses both need to emphasize learning communities and the need to develop high levels of trust both with colleagues and students.

Part time on-site mentors for new administrators, like the new-teacher induction program, would help, especially for those administrators with very few years of teaching experience to start with. The best quality professional learning must be routine. Staff members need to speak up if what they need in order to learn isn't provided. Training for principals is needed in conflict resolution and de-escalation of strong feelings.

Here are some goals and characteristics of high-quality professional learning in a school:

- Focused on improving learning and success for every student
- Offering a wide range of opportunities to meet diverse learning styles, career stages and ages
- Based on results for staff and students
- Inclusive of all staff—principals, teachers and support staff
- Based on people's wants and needs
- Based on adult learning models and principles—relevance, choice and follow-up
- Reflective of knowledge of the change process
- Based on research and best practices
- Offering modeling, demonstration, coaching and feedback over time
- Offering choices that account for differences in years of experience and career stage
- Embedded in work and taking place most often during the school day
- Founded on a sense of collegiality and trust—learning from and with each other
- Allowing physical space in the school for adult learning, with a staff room and smaller meeting rooms

This poignant comment clearly communicates the frustration felt by teachers and principals about the lack of time to accomplish all this:

> It came down to a timing issue. There's not enough time going around for anybody—It was essentially, here's the dates [for implementation], here's how to do it . . . We tried to do it through . . . a concerted effort in some ways to free up the students on various themes and that would then free up the staff so we might have forty minutes here or there, and it worked for a while but then it just sort of disintegrated because it just became overwhelming. It became . . . a logistics nightmare . . . I don't think we really got a handle on it. And I would guess that we're probably just an average kind of example of what's going on out there. (Clark et al., 2007, p. 51)

This feeling of anxiety and frustration is all too common among teachers and principals who are seriously trying to learn and improve without the time to do it professionally.

Many of the issues raised here are directly controlled by policies at the state or provincial education level. Others are locally negotiated in collective agreements between school boards and teacher unions. While it is beyond the scope of this book to discuss these further, the following recommendations are made concerning major structural changes at these levels:

- Less instructional time and more learning time each day for collaboration and planning. Some reports recommend a minimum of 25 percent learning time daily during the regular workday.

- More autonomy and respect for teachers' professionalism and ability to make choices for themselves to suit their needs

- Significantly more funding for professional learning

- Partnerships between unions and school boards for planning formal learning activities and encouraging more informal learning among groups

- Reduction of the number of formal PD days and re-allocating the time and money to individual schools to suit their action plans

Principals, teachers, and support staff are finding innovative ways to achieve high-quality learning. Schools that work closely not only with school board personnel but also with union personnel increase their sources of funding and chances for sustainability over time and broaden their wealth of experiences. When staff members feel respected for their professionalism and are given (or find) additional time for learning, novel ways to learn are more likely to emerge. Here are five examples of the new wave of higher-trust professional learning models:

- Teacher collaboration through vibrant online communities to get and give advice for both beginning and experienced teachers

- Summer institutes with teams comprised of principals and teachers attending together instead of separately

- Formal team planning time built into the timetable

- Partnerships between schools, colleges, and universities around the world via the web.

- Job-embedded learning for new teachers that focuses on their needs, including a school-based mentor (where both mentor and protégé learn)

Three examples of organizations committed to professional learning are:

- The Association for Supervision and Curriculum Development (ASCD). This organization develops programs, products, and services essential to the way educators learn, teach, and lead. To learn more, go to www.ascd.org.

- The National Staff Development Council (NSDC). This association is committed to ensuring success for all students through staff development and school improvement. To explore the benefits of this organization and their *Twelve Standards for Staff Development* and how they can be useful in evaluating your school's professional learning plans, go to www.nsdc.org.

- The Ontario Teacher's Federation (OTF). This is the professional organization for teachers in Ontario, Canada. A recent OTF publication, *Beyond PD Days: Teachers' Work and Learning in Canada* (Clark et al., 2007), summarizes the results of ten years of federally funded research into the workload issues and learning habits of Canadian teachers. A seventeen-minute DVD called *No Two Alike: PD That Works* accompanies the book. It shares a wealth of research and and includes the learning of two teaching groups that are often over-looked: substitute teachers and internationally educated teachers. To learn more, go to www.otffeo.on.ca.

What other organizations are available in your state or province? Are there local affiliates of national organizations that you could join? What does your local union and school board offer that would help you and your school?

The ultimate result in a high-trust culture is staff members who are excited about their own learning, who have time to do more of it during the day, and who generate their own ideas for improving themselves and the school.

Roland Barth captures the essence of effective professional learning in the following:

> Over the years, staff development has come to take on quite a different meaning for me. I now see it as listening in a hundred different ways for a question to emanate from teachers. It usually takes the form of, "Here's what I want to try." And staff development means being ready to supply assistance or encouragement in a hundred different ways. (1990, p. 57)

Communication Lines Are Open

Regular meetings should be scheduled for problem solving and decision making. A multitude of venues should be used to convey information among staff (that is, memos, newsletters, teleconferencing, meetings, emails, voice-mail). Good teaching is determined by individual social understandings of schooling. These individual understandings must be shared and transmitted through group norms and social cues expressed in everyday interactions among individuals. Administrators need to be in their schools on a regular basis and when they are there, get out into the school each day to listen to staff members and pick up concerns and questions.

Fun and Camaraderie Are Encouraged

Many ideas have been shared in previous pages as to how to lighten up and play more at work. At this point the staff should be responsible for their own plans for having fun at work, developing friendships and supporting each other. Take your work seriously but yourself lightly. The contrast in the overall experience of staff members in schools that have built high levels of trust and continue to innovate and those that are stuck in old patterns of distrust can perhaps be summed up in figures 5.1 and 5.2.

Figure 5.1: The distrusting school

Reproduced with permission of the artist, Kristin Morrison

Figure 5.2: The high-trusting school

Reproduced with permission of the artist, Kristin Morrison

The higher level of trust described in this chapter is far from where most schools are now, but though these high-trust schools may be rare, the educational community needs to share its own stories of schools that have reached this level. These schools are self-organizing learning labs, where individuality as well as team learning is respected. What were the factors that made a difference? Did these schools have support from their school boards or communities? What can others learn from the experiences of the trailblazers?

It will always be a work in progress, and the going will be tough. There must be no complacency that the end has been reached. Especially after people have committed a great deal of energy to a major innovation, they may not want to hear bad news and will take out their frustrations on the few staff members who speak up about what is not going as expected. But while people must sometimes work on what they are doing for a while and not try anything additional that is new, it is important to constantly step back and measure progress, in spite of the fact that there are complex, multiple innovations being implemented.

I believe that all people want to be involved in decisions that affect them, care about their job and each other, take pride in themselves and in their contributions, and want to share in the success of their efforts.

This level has no roadmaps—only clues and the odd story. Each school will have to work it out itself. Share your stories of high-trust schools and teams. Let's work together to provide more best-case scenarios.

These are some of the positive changes experienced in high-trust schools:

- Friendships are formed.
- Individual personalities and strengths are recognized and utilized.
- Different attitudes and opinions are accepted.
- Masks are removed—people can be themselves.
- Barriers come down—more candor and honesty.
- Communication is clear and transparent.
- Conflict and confrontation are risked—and valued.
- Data flows more freely.
- Students and staff are learning at higher levels.
- The high level of trust is sustained over time and continues to improve over future generations.

"Employees may come to characterize themselves in relationship to their teammates or firm as 'we' and may derive psychic benefits from being part of a successful enterprise. Identity-based trust is relational trust at its broadest."

—Denise Rousseau, Sim Sitkin, Ronald Burt, & Colin Camerer

The Chinese Bamboo Tree Story

Zig Ziglar tells the incredible, but true, story of the Chinese bamboo tree. He credits his friend Joel Weldon, an outstanding speaker from Phoenix, Arizona, as the source of the story:

> The Chinese plant the seed; they water and fertilize it, but the first year nothing happens. The second year they water and fertilize it, and still nothing happens. The third and fourth years they water and fertilize it, and nothing happens. The fifth year they water and fertilize it, and sometime during the course of the fifth year, in a period of approximately six weeks, the Chinese bamboo tree grows roughly ninety feet.

> The question is, did it grow ninety feet in six weeks or did it grow ninety feet in five years? The obvious answer is that it grew ninety feet in five years, because if they had not applied the water and fertilizer each year there would have been no Chinese bamboo tree. (Ziglar, 1985, p. 225)

Trust is much like the growing process of the Chinese bamboo tree. It is often discouraging. We seemingly do the right thing and nothing happens. But for those who do the right thing and are persistent, good things will happen. At some point, we begin to receive the rewards. Perhaps we have never had the patience to stay long enough with the plans for trust to grow.

Key Messages

1. People in high-trust cultures have successfully challenged the status quo to achieve something better through synergy and creativity.

2. Very few relationships make it to this high level of trust. Nevertheless, it should be a goal for all schools.

3. Studying the organizational structure of high-trust workplaces such as Southwest and Saturn can guide us to be more like them.

4. Camaraderie is a key factor in all high-trust workplaces. Employees can be themselves and have fun at work.

5. Relationships between unions and management do not have to be adversarial. True partnerships between these groups are critical for high trust.

6. Educators need to learn teamwork skills to work effectively in administrative teams, facilitation teams and work teams. Students need the same skills.

7. People and relationships have to come first. Things and procedures will follow.

Questions

1. Do you know of other companies, agencies, or teams that exhibit high-level trust?

2. Describe the closest you have come in your career to being part of a high-performing team. How did this experience reflect the five dimensions of trust from a Great Place to Work: credibility, respect, fairness, pride, and camaraderie?

3. How would you defend the need for union-management partnerships with a person who disagreed with you?

4. How would you take these messages and apply them to "parent and teacher trust" and "student and teacher trust"? In what ways would your ideas change if administrators were in the equation instead of teachers?

5. Could you have high-level trust for a person you didn't necessarily like?

6. In what ways are you personally:
   - Learning to deal constructively with conflict?
   - Risking innovation and vulnerability?
   - Focusing on deeper relationships?

7. Is it your experience that happy people are also trusting people? What is the relationship of happiness and trust?

Further Resources

Crother, C. (2004). *Catch! A Fishmonger's Guide to Greatness.* San Francisco: Berrett-Koehler.

Sisodia, R. S., Wolfe, D., & Sheth, J. (2007). *Firms of Endearment: How World-Class Companies Profit From Passion and Purpose.* Philadelphia: Wharton School Publishing.

Yokoyama, J., & Mitchell, J. (2004). *When Fish Fly: Lessons for Creating A Vital And Energized Workplace.* New York: Hyperion.

Websites

www.greatplacetowork.com

www.greatplacetowork.ca

VIPs

Take time to reflect on the Very Important Points you feel were made in this chapter. What resonated with you the most?

6

Higher-Risk Strategies for High-Trust Cultures

A culture of high-trust encourages people to take risks, to step out in a new direction, to fail gloriously as well as succeed beautifully.

—Coral Mitchell

A number of strategies with many activities have been suggested throughout this book. In this high-performing stage of trust, groups often are able to develop their own focusing on what the natural next step should be. Three final strategies are added here for your consideration.

Letting Go of the Past

While the new changes will be highly anticipated and carry their own sense of excitement, people need some help with "letting go" of what is ending as part of the healing process. Review the activity in chapter 4 called "Walk Your Talk" (page 120) with a focus on interpersonal behavior. Pay special attention to the section called "The Difficulty of Transitions."

Ending Phase

It's natural to want to stay with the familiar, even if it isn't working. Feelings of loss of identity and uneasiness are often experienced when phases of our lives come to an end. Sometimes a ritual like burning or burying something symbolic of the old way of doing things will assist in letting go. The metaphor of home renovations is quite appropriate here, with all its stages. Stress what will continue from the past and let people talk about how they feel emotionally. Celebrate with staff what they are ending to formally recognize the value it had in its time and the effort people put into making it work for students. Each person will have varying degrees of ties to the old way of doing things. Ending rituals can be spread out over several weeks or months.

Neutral Zone

Help each individual with his or her own personal transition through the "neutral zone" of disorientation and confusion. This is a necessary time for reflection and discussion. Give people time to experience this so they are ready to move on.

New Beginnings

Going into this stage as a member of a team will give everyone strength. Having visual reminders of the vision and the action plans they agreed on will act like a lifeline to hold on to. Celebrate this stage too.

Fuller's Trim Tab Theory

The late engineer and architect Buckminster Fuller is often cited for his use of trim tabs as a metaphor for leadership and personal empowerment. Fuller said (1972):

> Something hit me very hard once, thinking about what one little man could do. Think of the *Queen Mary*—the whole ship goes by and then comes the rudder. And there's a tiny thing at the edge of the rudder called a trim tab.
>
> It's a miniature rudder. Just moving the little trim tab builds a low pressure that pulls the rudder around. Takes almost no effort at all. So I said that the little individual can be a trim tab. Society thinks it's going right by you, that it's left you altogether. But if you're doing dynamic things mentally, the fact is that you can just put your foot out like that and the whole big ship of state is going to go. (p. 1)

In the same way, the steps a school makes to create high-trust are like a trim tab in the sense it can be one small thing that moves the whole school. It goes against our natural instincts to push from the "nose" of the ship. By pushing at the back on the trim tab, and with less effort, the whole ship can be made to move. It takes a while for the change to be felt, but it does happen after a while. All we need to do is to find the point at which minimum change will have maximum impact on the learning of staff and students.

The final two strategies are meant to help you find your school's "trim tab."

Open Space Technology (OST)

This method combines all four phases of the decision making process—with the least structure of all them. Harrison Owen, a management consultant, developed this method—in which participants are asked to co-create the meeting agenda and then move into small group break-out sessions—when he listened to people rave about the great conversations they had at meetings *outside* of the formal sessions. He observed: "The only times when people held adult conversations seemed to be the coffee breaks. . . . So I created a meeting format that was like one long coffee break" (as quoted in Deutsch, 1984, p. 23). His method has two basic premises:

1. The best people to discuss a subject are the ones who want to, not the ones who are forced to; employees who have a chance to discuss things are the ones most likely to improve them.

2. The participants must focus on a real issue that is of passionate concern to those who work together. Without passion, nobody will be interested.

Here's how it works:

1. Find a space large enough for the staff with only a circle of chairs around the edge and a bulletin board or several chart stands.

2. A facilitator introduces the theme of the meeting, the expectations, and the process in its simplicity. Staff members with an issue they are passionate about related to the central theme go to the center of the circle, write their name and the issue they will host on a sheet of paper, and tape it on the chart or bulletin board. Keep doing this until people are finished generating new topics.

3. People decide which discussion groups to join and sign up on the charts provided.

4. Impromptu groups move to separate rooms or locations and work intensely on their particular issue. Recommendations from each group are recorded and shared in hard copy or electronically.

This works extremely well with large groups and can span two or three days, with the smaller groups reconvening as a large group at the beginning and end of the day to share their news and reflect on their progress working toward specific action plans. It can be repeated in the future if the staff thinks it would work for a purpose they have at the time.

It won't work if the leaders are determined to implement a certain outcome before the discussion, if there is manipulation of the topics, or if people don't want to hear the truth.

Central themes for schools using OST could come out of the action planning process in order to generate the specific actions. Other broad themes could be:

- How to structure the professional development of staff

- Revision of the staff and student handbooks to reflect responsibility and trust in both groups
- New approaches to the use of time during the school day and year to increase collaboration of teachers and student learning
- A plan to welcome new staff to the school

The norms for Open Space Technology are:

- Whoever comes, they are the right people.
- Whatever happens, it is the only thing that could happen.
- Whenever it ends, it's over.
- The Law of Two Feet—if you are not learning or contributing, use your two feet and go to another group.

When open-space meetings work, they can yield creative and unexpected results that have a greater potential for implementation because the plans come from the passion, energy—and trust—of the group.

A simplified version of OST is to select four topics and have people choose from them by moving to one of the four corners of the room to discuss that topic and record their suggestions.

Organizational Sculpting

Organizational sculpting involves recreating a system in motion in order to "see" the system and "hear" from the parts as a way of informing future decisions. This high-risk intervention, which Suzanne Bailey taught me, must be used with great care and sensitivity. It is a powerful way to see the true structures in your school.

The staff members stand in an open room and one key staff member acts as the "sculptor" for this strategy. The sculptor can stand on a chair or ladder to see the whole group from above. One group at a time, the sculptor arranges people to stand together to represent the present organization of the school. The groups are named and arranged according to the sculptor's view of how things happen and how groups interact. Instructions can be given for specific people or groups in the organizational sculpture to stand or move or make noises in certain ways.

Once the sculptor is satisfied with the structure, he or she stops, and the members of the group look at what has happened in the room. What are the groups that were formed? Is there a hierarchy? Is anyone standing alone? What are the movements and sounds like?

Then everyone breaks free from the sculpture and relaxes for a while. The sculptor then starts again only this time the sculpture represents the desired organizational structure or a possible one.

This is a powerful strategy and can help people see where their trim tab could be. When people kinesthetically act this out at the directions of the sculptor, they feel what it must feel like to walk in other people's shoes and do their jobs. Interviews and feedback from the participants can reveal how it feels to be in a particular role and in a particular place in the organization. Various sculptors could take turns trying out different formations to see if they show improvements and create the school system they need.

As more schools develop high-trust cultures, more strategies will be discovered to take them to transformational stages we can only imagine now. Are there other strategies you would add that work well with high-trust cultures?

One School Scenario

Go to **go.solution-tree.com/leadership** to download and print Composite Middle and High School: A Fictional Scenario (page 221). This scenario demonstrates the principles and practices outlined in *Leading With Trust*.

Future Directions

Strong professional learning communities do not occur by accident. It is critical that union contracts, district calendars, and teacher's schedules be designed to support results-driven, team-focused professional learning and collaboration that are part of teachers' work-days. It is also critical that principals and teacher leaders be equipped with knowledge and skills that enable them to build and sustain performance-oriented cultures that have at their heart high-quality interpersonal relationships founded on trust and respect.

—Dennis Sparks

I had two purposes in writing this book: first, to communicate what is currently known about the importance of trust in school relationships—the research; and second, to suggest what we can do to improve trust in schools—the strategies. I recognize that the road ahead won't be easy. It never is when people are asked to live at the edge or even outside of their comfort zone, but you *can* do it. You will need courage. Following these precepts will keep you going during your toughest moments and allow you to sustain your vision:

- Start with yourself and confront your own fears.
- Speak up and seek the truth.
- Confront your negative emotions and darker side.
- Start conversations and talk together as friends would, actively listening to different viewpoints.
- Deal with the uncomfortable feelings that come with change.
- Act, rather than just talk about change.
- Remain hopeful.
- Be willing to change the system from the top down and the bottom up.
- Use creative and novel solutions.
- Be a follower as well as a leader.

- Resist the urge to jump on new bandwagons. Finish what you start.
- Persevere if you fail the first time.

When you find the courage to take risks, you'll find freedom from your fears. My mother gave me a book called *The Aquarian Conspiracy* many years ago. Its message concerning risks remains vivid to me to this day:

> Risk brings its own rewards; the exhilaration of breaking through, of getting to the other side, the relief of a conflict healed, the clarity when a paradox dissolves. Whoever teaches us this is the agent of our liberation. Eventually we know deeply that the other side of every fear is freedom. Finally, we must take charge of the journey, urging ourselves past our own reluctance and misgivings and confusion, to new freedom. (Ferguson, 1980, p. 294)

Allow for failures. Expect setbacks and learn from the lessons that each setback brings. Let the lessons guide you, not destroy you. Instead of dwelling on what's wrong, focus on the possibilities. Remember that many other people around you have the same dreams of more trusting relationships in schools.

I experienced this lesson when I had the privilege of opening a new school. Some of the staff members had volunteered to leave their schools, and the rest of the staff were hired from interviews I conducted with the leaders I had assembled. While we implemented many innovative technologies and team learning structures, we did have our challenges. One day, while having a quick break with my assistant principal Liz, I was kicking myself for a bad staffing decision we had made. She stopped me and said, "That wasn't your decision, that was *our* decision. We all share in the blame for that one."

That one conversation was an example of the mature level of trust and teamwork that we developed over our few years together. Our school motto was "If it is to be, it is up to me." In reality, it should have been "It is up to *we*." It was in this school that I worked with Brenda Martin—the woman in the dedication of this book—as a member of the leadership team. We all trusted that we each had the best interests of our students in mind as we worked with the families in a very challenging neighborhood known for its poverty and violence. While I have worked with several other high-trust teams in my career, this one was the best for everyone. I truly felt like people had each others' backs.

Even though barriers to trust diminish as you build it, they never disappear. Be ready for them. The barriers of fear and betrayal will remain the most challenging. Educators need to identify and face the fears they have about each other. Reduce the fear people have of each other by encouraging them to tell stories and have meaningful conversations. Small issues may not strike you as important when they occur, but they could mushroom into huge interpersonal issues and barriers if ignored. Admittedly, this takes a bit of courage, as the cowardly lion in *The Wizard of Oz* reminds us:

> **Cowardly Lion**: Courage! What makes a king out of a slave? Courage! What makes the flag on the mast to wave? Courage! What makes the elephant charge

his tusk in the misty mist, or the dusky dusk? What makes the muskrat guard his musk? Courage! What makes the sphinx the seventh wonder? Courage! What makes the dawn come up like thunder? Courage! What makes the Hottentot so hot? What puts the "ape" in apricot? What have they got that I ain't got?

Dorothy, Scarecrow, Tin Woodsman: Courage!

Cowardly Lion: You can say that again! Huh? (Freed & Vidor, 1937)

You will need to be proactive with the other three identified barriers as well. Inappropriate staff development, mandated changes, and lack of ownership can prevent schools from having the time to focus on their unique needs. A balance must be found between "Prison PD" and self-directed professional learning. The carousel of leadership is starting to slow down; more and more school districts understand the need to leave administrators in a school long enough to build trusting relationships. Concerted dialogue among all parties needs to focus on union-management relationships that are less adversarial and more productive. It can be done.

You may be met with skepticism about all of these changes. Be open to new ideas and curious about the possibilities and results. Remain focused on the purpose of your efforts: improved learning for all students. As your vision begins to yield positive results, the skeptics will be persuaded.

Where to Go From Here

Leading With Trust is the continuation of an important discussion of trust in schools, but it is not definitive. Research needs to extend to trust in school staffs and work teams. Schools that have spent years developing learning communities would be ideal sources of research and success stories.

Quantitative and qualitative analyses with more sophisticated data collection are called for in these areas:

- Union-management partnerships in education
- Larger samples with a wider cross-section of schools, including those in areas of high poverty
- The use of dispute resolution and peer mediation for trust repair in adult relationships in schools
- The role of students, parents, school trustees, and the community
- Implications for larger schools—both elementary and secondary
- Secondary schools with strong departments that are more like small towns than communities
- Opening up the relationships among teachers and assistant principals and principals. We need administrators to lead and also be led by teacher leaders as team members. Facilitation skills need to be honed as well.

- Cultural differences as they pertain to trust and trust building with persistently resistant and incompetent staff members and administrators

An untrusting culture will always prevent gains in student learning and achievement. Conversely, a trusting environment will open the doors to creative, new ways of meeting students' needs. As educators, we must remember that our world is changing rapidly and those changes will happen whether we want them to or not. For the sake of our children, we must not let the past control our professional lives. Use the resources of this book to challenge and extend your thinking and your practices in any way that works for you and your staff. Be proactive rather than reactive, so that your school looks to the future and builds toward it. I extend an invitation to all readers to learn together and share their stories of trusting cultures that grew out of distrusting workplaces.

Key Messages

1. Strategies that have been effective in rising out of distrust and building early trust will continue to be as effective in reaching for high-trust.

2. There are strategies that will only be effective when high-trust exists in a team.

3. High-trust cultures believe in the merit of each person's ideas and contributions and invite these openly.

Questions

1. What other strategies could you add to this chapter from your experience?

2. Do high-trust cultures even need strategies, or are they so finely tuned that they function as self-directed teams and seek help when they need it?

3. How hopeful are you that your school could reach this rare level of high-trust?

VIPs

Take time and reflect on the Very Important Points you feel were made in this chapter. What resonated with you the most?

Reproducible Resources

The following section contains a selection of the tools and activities presented in this book in reproducible form. Please feel free to photocopy these resources and use them as you and your school explore the trust-building process.

Visit **go.solution-tree.com/leadership** to download reproducibles and read other materials associated with this book.

Leader Self-Assessment

Indicate the extent to which you agree or disagree with each of the statements about your school by circling a number in the columns on the right.

0 = Completely Disagree   1 = Strongly Disagree   2 = Disagree   3 = Uncertain   4 = Agree   5 = Strongly Agree

	Leader Self-Assessment	CD	SD	D	U	A	SA
1	Teachers in this school are candid with me.	0	1	2	3	4	5
2	I have confidence in the expertise of my teachers.	0	1	2	3	4	5
3	I have confidence in the commitment of my staff.	0	1	2	3	4	5
4	I am willing to accept ideas proposed by others.	0	1	2	3	4	5
5	Staff work collaboratively to benefit the school and students.	0	1	2	3	4	5
6	I openly share my thoughts and feelings with staff.	0	1	2	3	4	5
7	Students and staff really care about this school.	0	1	2	3	4	5
8	Honesty is a "norm" with both staff and students.	0	1	2	3	4	5
9	Making suggestions for improvement is valued at this school.	0	1	2	3	4	5
10	I feel proud of this school.	0	1	2	3	4	5
	Column Totals:						
	Reflection Score:						

Once you have completed your reflection, add up your score. This will range between 0 and 50. The higher the score, the more positive your situation is.

Using table 2.2, reflect on your score, using the middle and right columns to see how it correlates to the trust scale. Share your analysis with a trusted friend for additional insights.

Table 2.2: Trust Level Indicators

Score	Level	Indicator
0—09	-1	Distrust
10—19	0	No Trust
20—29	+1	Early Trust
30—39	+2	Developing Trust
40—50	+3	Mature Trust

Consider whether the score reflects your opinion of the overall trust level you feel you have in yourself.

Staff Feedback About Leader

The purpose of this survey is the professional growth of the leader. Your constructive honesty is important. All staff members have been invited, but participation is voluntary. Your responses should be anonymous and will be kept confidential. The results will be summarized and shared with the group.

0 = Completely Disagree   1 = Strongly Disagree   2 = Disagree   3 = Uncertain   4 = Agree   5 = Strongly Agree

	Staff Feedback About Leader	CD	SD	D	U	A	SA
1	I can be candid with the leader(s) of this school.	0	1	2	3	4	5
2	I feel that the leader(s) has confidence in my expertise.	0	1	2	3	4	5
3	The leader(s) is committed to the job and will follow through on expectations.	0	1	2	3	4	5
4	The leader(s) willingly listens to all ideas proposed by staff.	0	1	2	3	4	5
5	Staff work collaboratively with the leader(s) to benefit the school and students.	0	1	2	3	4	5
6	Thoughts and feelings are openly shared with the leader(s).	0	1	2	3	4	5
7	The leader(s) demonstrates sincere care about this school.	0	1	2	3	4	5
8	Honesty is a "norm" between staff and the leader(s).	0	1	2	3	4	5
9	Making suggestions for improvement is valued at this school.	0	1	2	3	4	5
10	I feel valued by the leader(s) of this school.	0	1	2	3	4	5
	Column Totals:						
	Reflection Score:						

On a second page, you are invited to type your responses to these two questions:

1. What are three strengths, three concerns, and three possible actions with regard to how the leader builds trust?

2. What five words describe the current culture of the school?

Staff Trust Survey

The purpose of this survey is to investigate the element of trust and credibility among school staff in order to assist in future planning. The results will be compiled and taken seriously. Indicate the extent to which you agree or disagree with each of the statements by circling a number in one of the columns at the right.

0 = Completely Disagree   1 = Strongly Disagree   2 = Disagree   3 = Uncertain   4 = Agree   5 = Strongly Agree

	Staff Trust Survey Questions	CD	SD	D	U	A	SA
1	Staff openly share their thoughts and feelings with each other.	0	1	2	3	4	5
2	Staff work as equals within the school environment.	0	1	2	3	4	5
3	The staff are accepting of individual differences and opinion.	0	1	2	3	4	5
4	Teachers in this school treat each other with respect.	0	1	2	3	4	5
5	Input for decisions is valued from all staff members.	0	1	2	3	4	5
6	I feel that my work and my contributions are valued by others.	0	1	2	3	4	5
7	Staff work together effectively to achieve school goals.	0	1	2	3	4	5
8	I enjoy coming to work.	0	1	2	3	4	5
9	I would not leave this school for an equivalent job anywhere else.	0	1	2	3	4	5
10	I would recommend this school to others.	0	1	2	3	4	5
	Column Totals:						
	Reflection Score:						

Commitment Continuum

There are many shades between yes and no when making decisions. This continuum gives us a clear and easy method to see both your level of agreement or disagreement and also your level of intended contribution to the issue being discussed. For each issue, we will use either a private ballot or a show of hands.

Levels of Yes and No		Level of Contribution and Support
Strong agreement *I think this is the best option.*	10 9 8	Maximum Support *I will lead/support the implementation.*
Agreement *I think it's workable.*	7 6	Proactive Support *I'll help to plan and implement.*
Disagreement *I have some concerns.*	5 4 3	Moderate Support *I will look for things I can do to support this.*
Strong Disagreement *I think this is a mistake.*	2 1 0	Minimal Support *I'll do what is necessary to support this.*

Stages of Trust and Team Development and School Culture

This graphic represents a synthesis of Lewicki's Stages of Trust Repair, Tuckman's Stages of Team Development, and Stoll and Fink's Five Types of School Culture. Use this chart to start discussions about where your school or group seems to be. Is there a danger of moving backward? What would help the school move upward on the graph?

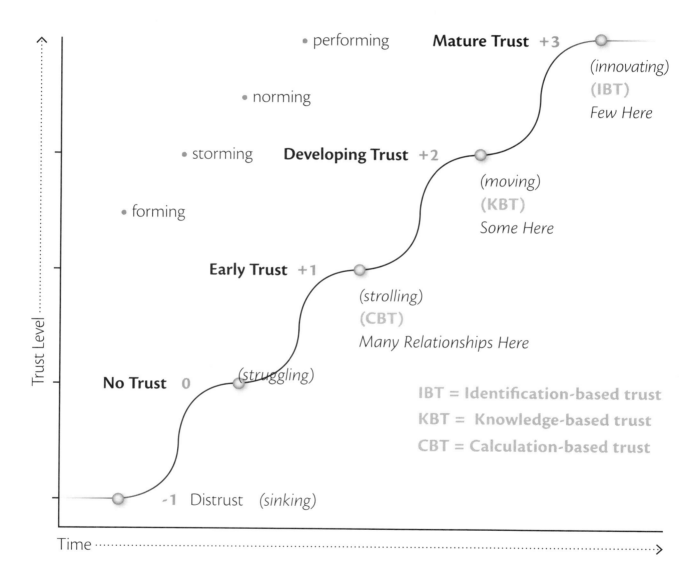

- performing   **Mature Trust** +3

(innovating)
(IBT)
Few Here

- norming

- storming   **Developing Trust** +2

(moving)
(KBT)
Some Here

- forming

Early Trust +1

(strolling)
(CBT)
Many Relationships Here

No Trust 0   *(struggling)*

IBT = Identification-based trust

KBT = Knowledge-based trust

CBT = Calculation-based trust

-1 Distrust *(sinking)*

Trust Level

Time

Berens Personality Analogy

Although people have one core set of values and needs, they can adapt to the behaviors of others. But this requires both observation and sensitivity.

Looking at the image of the tree trunk, reflect on your own core needs and values. How deep inside you are they? Are your behaviors aligned with your core needs and values? Do you talents get a chance to shine in true authentic happiness?

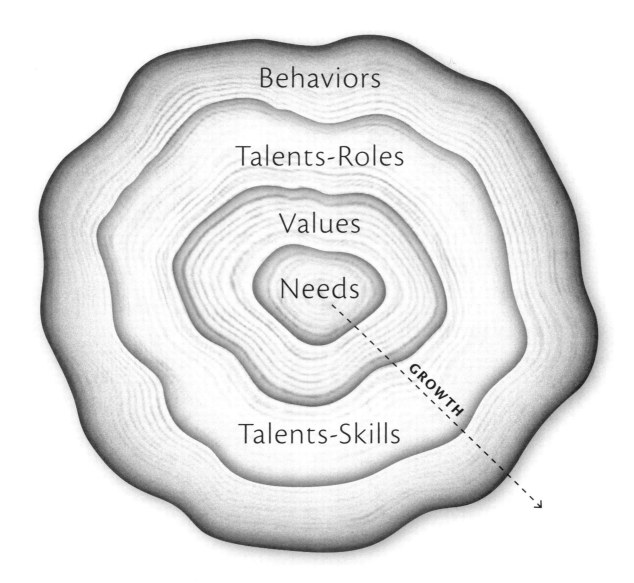

From *Understanding Yourself and Others: An Introduction to Temperament,* by Linda Berens. Telos Publications. © 2000 United Media Group: Used with permission.

Your Johari Window

Reflect on the four regions of your own Johari Window to better understand yourself.

Consider how comfortable you feel disclosing information about yourself to others. People vary greatly in this regard. What behaviors do you freely show to others?

Would you be interested to know what other people know about you that you aren't aware of? Do you have hidden talents you'd like to know more about? This is a vital area for feedback from others.

What do you keep secret or private about yourself? Are there things about you that you should tell other people in order to work better with them? While you may have sensitivities and fears that you don't want to reveal about yourself, there may be not-so-personal information that could be disclosed. These reveal your core needs and values. As trust builds, fear and vulnerability decrease and region three shrinks in size and importance.

As you reflect more and invite feedback from others, there will be less in this unknown region.

From Luft, Joseph, *Group Processes: An Introduction to Group Dynamics*, 3rd Edition. © 1984. Reprinted with permission of The McGraw-Hill Companies.

Draw your own Johari Window below with the four regions scaled in size to reflect how you see yourself. Then answer the following questions:

1. If you continue to build self-trust and trust with others, how do you imagine the relative sizes of the four regions you have drawn will change over the next year?

2. Schedule some time to discuss your conclusions with a friend, another administrator, or trusted colleague. Does your self-assessment match their knowledge about you?

3. How does this activity relate to Your Personal Trust Scale? What have you learned about yourself from doing these two activities?

Consider using this activity with facilitation team members individually and then sharing the results as a team.

My Trust Touchstones

Think of a touchstone as a rule, a basis for comparison, or a reference point against which other things can be evaluated. This culminating activity will identify the trust touchstones you need to use as a guide for the future. They can always be refined over the years.

To start, refer back to your Pain-to-Power Chart. Is there anything you want to add to it now?

Review all of the feedback you've received not only from your own reflections but also from others. Now, step back from all the information you have compiled and synthesize what you have learned.

Use two headings to organize your thoughts: Personal and Interpersonal. You could have any number of trust touchstones in each category—it's up to you to decide. Feel free to add other categories that will help you build your capacity to grow.

The conclusions that rise to the top as you work on this activity are your Trust Touchstones—reminders to yourself about trust. What do you want to remember the most from this reflection and dialogue you have had about yourself? Use positive language about what you *will* do. Hope and optimism should shine through.

Visit **go.solution-tree.com/leadership** to download and print the Personal Trust Touchstones Planner.

Personal Touchstones

Interpersonal Touchstones

Action Planning Roadmap

Use this graphic organizer to work backward from your shared vision in order to close the gap between the present and future. It is important to agree on what actions to take, what actions to stop taking, and what actions you will take more slowly. Measure your success at several intervals along the way.

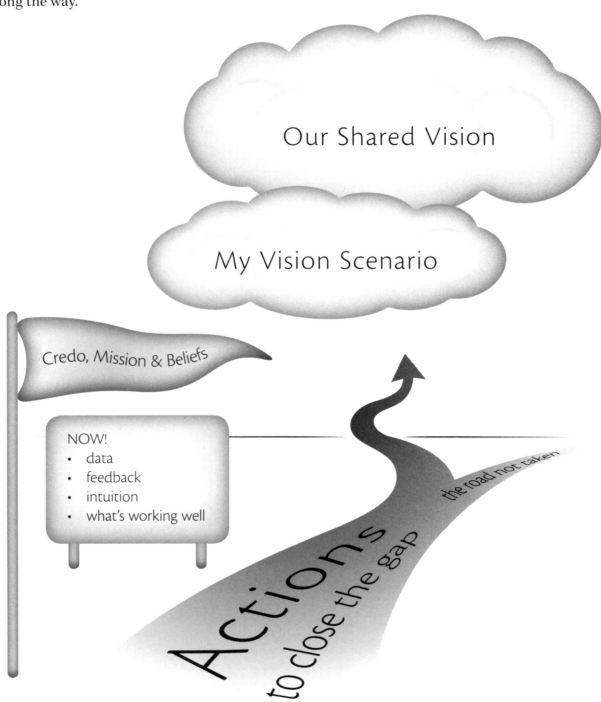

Team Charter

Work Team Focus: Clarify exactly what your team is expected to do and the timeline.

Team Members: List members and specific roles. For example facilitator, timekeeper, recorder, group member & process observer. Ask for signatures.

Name   Signature

Vision Check: Explain how this action will be part of achieving the vision.

Resources Needed: Identify what is needed and the costs if any.

Measuring Progress: Establish indicators of success. Decide when to measure.

Celebrating Success: Acknowledge progress at each meeting.

continued >

Team Charter (cont'd)

Steps and Methods: Describe what, how, when, and by whom.

Specific Action	Who	Timeline

The Decision-Making Scale

Use this scale to determine the appropriate level of commitment for decisions you face as a team or school. Although there may be occasions when mandates are imposed, teams in high-trusting cultures aim for the top half of the scale, where there is more buy-in and a greater chance of implementation.

Unanimous Consent – Everyone agrees enthusiastically.

Common Ground – What points do we all agree on?

Consensus – Everyone accepts the decision.

Collaboration – Synergy produces a new option.

Super Majority – The decision is made with a large majority.

Most Popular Alternative Chosen – The decision is made after the alternatives have been weighed.

Simple Majority – Approval requires that the ayes have at least one more vote than the nays.

Average or Compromise – A decision is made without voting.

Flip a Coin, Roll the Dice – The group uses this method for unimportant decisions.

Minority or Subgroup – The authority to decide or recommend is delegated.

Leader (Authority or an Expert) – The leader decides after discussion and input.

Tweaking – A plan that already exists is tweaked.

Leader (Authority or an Expert) – A leader makes the decision on his or her own.

Mandate – The decision comes from outside the group or someone other than the leader.

The Four-Phase Decision-Making Model

Decision making can be broken down into four phases, each with its own unique dynamic. Place this graphic alongside the Decision-Making Scale as you work through the four phases.

Allow sufficient time for each phase, and agree on when it's time to move to the next phase. Traditionally, groups move too quickly through phases two and four to come to a premature closing. Is this your experience? Each phase is important to the implementation of the decision. Remember "The Abilene Paradox," in which phase four was assumed to have happened and a decision was made that no one wanted.

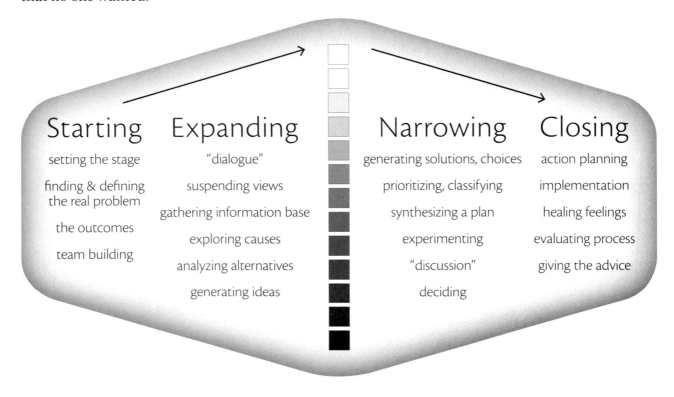

Starting

setting the stage

finding & defining the real problem

the outcomes

team building

Expanding

"dialogue"

suspending views

gathering information base

exploring causes

analyzing alternatives

generating ideas

Narrowing

generating solutions, choices

prioritizing, classifying

synthesizing a plan

experimenting

"discussion"

deciding

Closing

action planning

implementation

healing feelings

evaluating process

giving the advice

Composite Middle and High School: A Fictional Scenario

Principal Harold Hope has written three progress reports over three years, first assessing the current situation at his school and then outlining next steps, as we often do in education. Sometimes, as you will see, the results of the actions he takes are intended and positive; sometimes they are unintended and positive; and sometimes they are unintended and negative. Read through his reports to see if any of the people, relationships, patterns of behavior, and conflicts apply to your situation. Follow this school on its journey to trust.

The Administrators

Harold Hopes

Harold is the principal of the new school. He has been at the school for two years—the first year as an assistant principal and the second as a principal replacing Sarah Solo, who retired. This is his second assignment as an administrator but his first in a school with middle school students.

Norma Newby

Norma, the assistant principal, is new to the position and to the school district. She was appointed when Harold became principal. One of her strengths, due to her many years as an instruction and assessment consultant, is staff development.

The Students

The school has a population of 1000, with a 30:70 ratio of middle to high school students. Most come from upper-middle-class farm families. These are well-established, wealthy farm businesses. However, a new housing development has brought low-income, immigrant families to the area, who typically are employed on the farms as laborers. The majority of children in this housing development are elementary and middle school students, resulting in expected growth in this section of the school.

The Staff

The middle and secondary school teachers have separate staff rooms. Neither group knows much about the other, but there is an active rumor mill and destructive gossip about how easy it is to teach "on the other side." Each side feels betrayed, but no one is talking about it openly. Morale is also low not just because of the integration but also because of the remnants of the autocratic style of the previous principal and the challenges of the new student population. The two union representatives don't speak to each other. The calendar contains no social activities.

continued >

Composite Middle and High School: A Fictional Scenario (cont'd)

Five Key Staff Members

Ashira Accountable has been promoted to a newly created position of elementary literacy facilitator for the school (E.L.F.) and has high expectations of raising the literacy levels in the middle grades.

Coretta Character is a senior grade-7 teacher who has been a champion for a character-education program to improve behavior. She had been resistant to the amalgamation of the two schools because of the poor behavior of the high school students.

Connie Collaborative is a new high school union steward, voted in by a strong majority and with a mandate to change from the combative relationship between the previous principal and the last union steward to a more collaborative one.

Pablo Proud is the high school languages department head. His efforts at building a strong team have started to pay off this year. He also applied to be the literacy facilitator, the position that Ashira got.

Victor Vigilant is a long-standing union steward representing the elementary staff. He has been making sure that the move from the middle school doesn't create added workload for the teachers.

Progress Report: End of Year One

During the summer, as a key part of my entry plan and because of my lack of experience with middle school students, I met several times with Jake Kinder, the principal from the JK–5 school nearby who became my mentor.

From my observations and experiences as assistant principal here under Sarah Solo, I knew that morale was low.

I believe there were four causes of this at the time of my entry plan as principal for both schools:

1. Consequences for student misbehavior were not seen to be appropriate and consistent.

2. The lengthy memos issued by Sarah Solo reprimanded everyone for the mistakes of a few. This created lingering resentment.

3. Sarah took on too many new initiatives without consultation with the staff, who saw them as political bandwagons created solely for her benefit. They want a say in the direction of the school.

4. The middle school staff is upset at losing their school building and moving in with us.

My Long-Term Goals Over the Coming Years

1. To rebuild staff morale and productive working relationships

2. To bring the two school cultures together into one, based on a compelling vision for the future

3. To improve student achievement in literacy in middle grades (as per the board-mandated program)

continued >

Composite Middle and High School: A Fictional Scenario (cont'd)

My Specific Short-Term Goals for This Year

These were set last June in my entry plan as principal:

1. To build productive relationships between staff and administration during the year

    Action (September onward): Be visible in the hallways and make rounds to visit each teacher's classroom at least once a week. Tell them why this will become a routine of mine.

    > **Positive Consequence**: I am beginning to make connections with both middle school and secondary staff. This has given us new insights about each other. I didn't realize the amount of time middle school teachers spend on their room design.

    Action (monthly): To meet with my mentor Jake (JK–grade 5 Principal) at least once a month to be more knowledgeable of the middle school grades and therefore a more respected leader.

    > **Positive Consequence**: I have learned so much in the areas of identifying special needs children, the importance of involving parents in decisions we make about their children, and the different kinds of time demands facing grades 6–8 teachers with limited planning time and hours of work to prepare manipulative materials and activities. When Jake walks through the halls and classrooms with me, the staff can see how serious I am about learning about their world.

2. To form an effective administration team with Norma Newby during the year

    Norma has many skills that complement mine. I was surprised by her commitment to work through the personal strategies. She told me it gave her valuable insights into her own levels of self-trust. She also had the courage to take the initiative and ask for feedback from the staff. I had seen it as just more "self-help" jargon and ignored it. I was wrong. She was right.

    Action (middle of November): Administer the trust survey with Norma first, and assess the results.

    > **Unintended Positive Consequence:** I was afraid of asking the whole staff, so I started with Norma. This led to a valuable discussion during which she told me that I had embarrassed her by correcting her in front of staff and students and by often taking over situations that she could handle. I apologized to her for this. We have agreed to meet more regularly and to share the workload.

3. To identify the core issues around our low staff morale in the fall term and act on the results over the winter and spring terms by establishing a facilitation team to work with me.

    I was starting to find out how deep the resentment of the secondary staff toward the last principal went. I have learned that Ms. Solo didn't involve the staff in decision making about new initiatives and took credit for the work others did. She was not into teamwork and kept all the control herself. Many staff felt undervalued and bitter. I needed to visibly implement a more collaborative leadership style.

    Action (since last June): I made it my practice to stop taking on new initiatives without staff approval, stop the lengthy memos "from on high," and deal directly with individuals who weren't following procedures instead of reprimanding the whole group.

    > **Positive Consequence:** Changes were all well received by staff and gave me some time to achieve other goals rather than take on new initiatives.

    Action (February): Established a facilitation team that is representative of the staff.

continued >

Composite Middle and High School: A Fictional Scenario (cont'd)

Positive Consequences:

a. I presented my rationale for this new group at a special staff meeting and gave them a week to consider it. After a discussion at the next staff meeting, there were three nominations and two volunteers. We agreed to include each of these five people on the facilitation team so no vote was needed (thankfully). The members ended up being: Victor Vigilant, Connie Collaborative, Coretta Character and Norma Newby and Pablo Proud.

b. They quickly elected Pablo Proud as the leader of the facilitation team because of his success with teamwork in his department.

c. (March) After two lengthy meetings getting to know each other and clarifying their mandate with me, the facilitation team decided to lead a discussion at the April staff meeting of an article called *Improving Relationships in the Schoolhouse*.

d. (April) The discussion of the article was effective, because both staff groups met together for this first time. They were organized into small, mixed groups (middle and high school) to get to know each other better.

e. Connie Collaborative suggested at the end of the meeting that we should hold joint staff meetings whenever possible with both the middle and high school staff together. A show of hands indicated almost everyone agreed.

f. (May and June) The facilitation team added the Rumor Mill activity at the end of joint staff meetings in May and June to correct misinformation.

This brought out a surprising assumption, namely that both the middle school and secondary teacher groups each thought the other group had an easier job than theirs! This was informative for everyone. We also learned more about the effects of the previous principal's style and why there is such a fear of speaking up. This will be a regular agenda item for future staff meetings.

4. To assist the merging of two schools into one

   Action (May and June): The final two staff meetings were held jointly.

   Positive consequence: Having everyone in the same room at meetings is building stronger relationships. They are learning each other's names to begin with.

   Actions That Didn't Work:

   a. I asked for curriculum plans from each grade and department.

      Negative Consequences: Only a few plans were submitted. Ashira told me in the parking lot one night that the middle school staff currently plans their curriculum as individuals and, therefore my request was impossible—and they didn't know how to tell me this. She said that if they started to plan more as grade teams in the future, I could try this again next year.

   b. I decided to share my personal vision with the staff at the May meeting.

      Negative Consequences: When I shared my vision for the school, it was received with blank stares and silence instead of the positive reaction I expected. It may have been premature and I should have coordinated this message with the facilitation team's plans. It was a noble gesture but everyone wondered why I did it.

continued >

Composite Middle and High School: A Fictional Scenario (cont'd)

My Goals for Next Year

1. (September) Get to know the staff members better—all of them.

    How: Tell the staff before they leave for the summer that I am going to schedule individual meetings beginning next September.

2. (Ongoing) Reach out and include more people to help me, and use the expertise on staff.

    How: The facilitation team will be a good start, but I need to involve other strong people who do so much around the school, like Noel Network and Paul Peacemaker

3. (September) Conduct a trust survey about myself with the staff.

    How: Seek advice from Norma on how she did it, and get going.

4. (Ongoing) Build my professional relationship with Norma.

    How: Hold weekly meetings with her to clear the air, debrief what happened recently, and plan together for the coming week.

5. Learn more about leading a middle school staff.

    How: Continue meetings with Jake Kinder, and talk more with other middle school principals at our meetings.

6. Work on the literacy mandate.

    How: Include Norma Newby and Ashira Accountable in getting the data we need for literacy baselines as a start. Involve them in planning.

7. Work with the new facilitation team under the leadership of Pablo Proud to do the following:

    - Establish school norms for meetings (involve both staffs)
    - Conduct a staff trust survey
    - Reestablish the social committee in order to plan fall and winter activities and have fun together, especially at the first staff meeting.
    - Continue to bring the two groups together as one staff.

Progress Report: End of Year Two
My Long-Term Goals Over the Coming Years

1. To continue to build the two schools so that we become one school with one compelling vision
2. To continue to improve student achievement in literacy in grades 6 to 8

My Short-Term Goals for This Year

1. To get to know the staff better through scheduled one-on-one meetings

    Action (September): Although I intended to conduct all the meetings myself, this quickly became too time consuming, so Norma and I decided divide the staff between us. We completed this task by the end of October.

continued >

Composite Middle and High School: A Fictional Scenario (cont'd)

Positive Consequences: Norma's staff development background was useful in helping me develop a set of questions for the staff to find out about their hopes and dreams, their achievements, and their expertise. We gave these questions out ahead of time and used many of the principles of appreciative inquiry she had read about. We also included all support staff—secretaries, caretakers, educational assistants—and outside staff from the district level who are liaisons with our school. Being candid with the staff prevented a lot of "fear-mongering."

2. To do a trust survey about myself

   Action (Beginning of Oct.): I summoned up the courage to do my trust survey with the staff.

   Positive Consequences: It was a stroke of brilliance to ask Jake Kinder to administer, score, and share the results with my staff.

   Key results about me from the Trust Survey:

   - I need to have more confidence in the expertise and commitment of my staff.
   - I scored well on "honesty" and "openness to listen to candid comments" questions.
   - There were several anecdotal comments about my being a welcome change from the last principal and the team spirit I have encouraged. (Someone suggested doing a trust survey with the facilitation team as a focus. Good idea!)

   Negative Consequence: Several people scored me very low on almost all of the questions. (Were they middle school teachers, or the ones who remain loyal to Sarah, or maybe they read the scoring scale backward?)

3. (Ongoing) To strengthen my professional relationship with Norma

   Action: Set regular meetings with Norma Newby.

   Positive Consequence: We have started having quick "huddles" during the day to share information. She appreciates having me as a sounding board and coach. We debrief sensitive events and decisions and respect each other's viewpoints even though we sometimes disagree. Doing this privately works better than the way I used to do it.

   She told me recently that she and Jake are thinking of requesting permission to swap jobs next year for a term to grow professionally and build relationships with the JK-5 school. This was initially exciting news, but later I worried about such a huge change.

4. (October) To learn more about instruction and assessment in grades 6–8.

   Action: Study the curriculum documents for these grades. Then, to get a better understanding, ask Victor and Ashira to teach me about the differences I should expect to see from my high school perspective.

   Positive Consequences: We had three in-depth conversations. I developed a greater respect for the complexity in these grades. We continued our lessons over the month. I started to do more "walk-throughs" in these classrooms to observe more.

5. (October) To develop a literacy plan based on the data from Norma and Ashira.

   Action: Ashira and the middle school teachers met with me, and she led us through the research and graphs from Bryk and Schneider on math and literacy (and staff trust in the principal) from their research in Chicago schools.

continued >

Composite Middle and High School: A Fictional Scenario (cont'd)

Positive Consequences: Ashira was able to provide data for the past three years about each of our students and talked about using a Data Wall next year to track their literacy levels. She gave us several articles to read about Data Walls. Pablo heard about this at a facilitation team meeting and wants his Languages Department to be invited to future meetings.

The teachers are starting to understand the use of data and seem less fearful of talking about it.

Norma has suggested we explore the growing need for ESL classes next year due to the new school population.

They decided to start a remedial literacy room in the spring term and asked if the smaller staff room could be converted for this purpose by then. This accidentally solved the problem of our two separate staff rooms and everyone started using one staff room in March.

Negative Consequence: Victor reported to me that several teachers had approached him with concerns that the Data Walls were going to make confidential information publicly accessible. I redirected him to share his message with Norma and Connie.

6. (Oct—Dec.) Support the facilitation team as they help us establish staff meeting norms, conduct their own staff trust survey and re-establish the social committee to bring the two schools together.

Action: To assist the facilitation team to develop a team identity and staff meeting norms.

Positive Consequences: We held two evening meetings in October to accomplish this and asked Norma to be the facilitator. These became monthly meetings and have become the highlight of my job. The facilitation team members are so talented and they do this on top of their teaching duties, often wearing multiple hats and responsibilities. Norma and I want to think of an appropriate recognition for them.

Action: To mediate the conflict between Connie and Victor

Positive Consequences: Norma and I had a special dinner meeting with Connie and Victor. Victor later wrote me a note of appreciation that I will keep forever in my archive folder.

Action: The facilitation team will administer the staff trust survey.

Positive Consequences: Pablo and the facilitation team set the stage well and administered the Staff Trust Survey at the end of October. Victor took a lead role in the process because of his experience doing staff surveys for the union.

Negative Consequences: We were surprised to see in the results the extent of the distrust the staff have for each other. Overall, the scores were very low on these three items:

- At least four staff members indicated that they wouldn't recommend this school to others (question 10) and might leave the school.

The middle and secondary groups differed in some of the results:

- Middle-school results were very low for question 2 (about working as equals). They feel the secondary staff "has more" than they do. They want more planning time, larger budgets, and time to prepare their anecdotal report cards.

- Secondary staff scored level 3 or 4 (high) on question one: "Staff openly share their thoughts and feelings with each other." (Not as good as it could be, but higher than their elementary colleagues.)

continued >

Composite Middle and High School: A Fictional Scenario (cont'd)

- There were hurt feelings in the middle school staff about losing their school and concern about my lack of experience in leading a middle school.

- Anecdotal comments revealed that staff members don't trust administrators to deal with student misbehavior fairly and consistently and also that staff members are not consistent in applying school rules themselves. We are definitely not a "sinking" school anymore, but we are still "struggling" as we develop more trust.

- Because of the survey, we decided to take the following action.

Action: The facilitation team adapted the Abilene Paradox to suit our community and acted it out for the staff to encourage them to speak up and make suggestions.

> **Positive Consequences:** These suggestions and actions arose from the activity.

- The staff decided to form middle school grade teams to plan instruction and assessment together. We need to find a way to provide time for this during the day.

- Teachers volunteered to teach in different grades. For example, a grade 6 teacher is going to teach grade 9 and 10 mathematics next year and a secondary phys ed teacher is going to take a grade 6 homeroom and do middle school health and phys ed classes too. Victor and Connie are going to oversee the process. Maybe I can encourage more of that kind of voluntary integration.

- The facilitation team members divided up the staff into mixed groups (middle school and secondary) and became facilitation team contacts to open up communication lines. Victor voiced his concern about additional workload because of this. We agreed to look at ways to provide release time for the facilitation team.

- The facilitation team decided on a goal for the whole staff to collaboratively develop a school vision and action plans based on their beliefs and values by the end of May.

- The staff worked in two separate groups on the I've Been Framed activity. We all were pleasantly surprised to see the similarity of the beliefs about teaching and learning in both middle school and secondary staff groups. When they saw this they decided to make a common Belief Wall in the staff room representative of the whole staff. It was the first concrete step to unite the two groups into one.

- This led to a joint session for building norms for our staff meetings, based on the premise that we are one school and not two schools in one building. It grew into a discussion about norms for the organization of the school. The heated debate was made manageable by the logical process we followed.

- When the norms were complete, Connie suggested that the two staffs line up facing each other. Then she reshaped the group into a circle. It was very symbolic of the change they were experiencing—even more so as she is a union rep. We were finally one school!

7. (Ongoing) To reach out and include more people to help me and use the expertise on staff more effectively.

> **Action:** To form a social committee to involve more people and have more fun.

> **Positive Consequences:** Our social committee (in consultation with the facilitation team and admin) has taken on a new life with Noel's leadership. She formed a small committee

continued >

Composite Middle and High School: A Fictional Scenario (cont'd)

with the intention of having more fun and having people get to know each other better. They led the Personal Histories and Shoebox activities at the December staff meeting. People just kept talking and didn't want to leave.

They planned an honorable ending for the elementary school in January. Both school staffs prepared their own history maps separately and then presented them to each other. That was an eye-opener. There was a public celebration and formal ending ceremony featuring the creation of a hallway with historical photos, memorabilia, and bricks from the other building. All the former staff members were invited. There was a special assembly for all the students, and many parents came as well.

Unexpected Positive Consequences: I was surprised at how quickly a team formed to organize a year-end staff retreat to celebrate our year and honor the work of the former middle school teachers and their school that closed.

Parents are being invited to sit on the planning team. Both union reps want to be on the team. (A great idea to get them to work on something meaningful together.) They want to administer the staff trust survey again and present the results to see if there has been any positive movement in trust levels. We will have presentations from Ashira about literacy levels and Data Walls, and trust-building activities such as:

- A speaker on laughter and humor at work
- Activities like What's in My Name? and Childhood Photos
- Giving awards for staff involvement

Norma and Jake Kinder agreed to swap positions for a second term next year.

Actions that didn't work and unintended results: When we asked staff to give their preferences for which grade and subjects they wanted to teach next year, five staff members opted to transfer to another school. Two were loyal to Sarah Solo; one felt our school was "just fine the way it was before me" and was "cruising" on past achievements; and two others didn't want to be in a school with high school students. The warning signs were there in the survey results when I looked back at them.

Pablo was successful in a promotion he applied for and is leaving the school to become an assistant principal in the district.

The facilitation team had planned to begin the action planning process with staff this spring but wisely postponed it when they ran out of time.

My Goals for Next Year

1. Develop higher levels of trust on the staff so we can learn more collaboratively with the ultimate goal of improving our results with all of our students.

2. Develop an interview process with the staff that focuses on trust, collaboration, and risk taking. This would include a plan for induction and mentoring of new teachers that join the staff.

3. Support the facilitation team as we:
   - Choose a new leader, due to Pablo's promotion
   - Develop action plans for the decisions made at the June retreat

continued >

Composite Middle and High School: A Fictional Scenario (cont'd)

- Follow through on the plans to lead the staff and student conversations about our vision scenario and develop action plans based on it (This never took place this year due to time constraints.)

- Develop a new English as a Second Language Program

- Co-ordinate with the literacy team to plan a professional learning session on the purpose and procedures of data walls to track student progress and improve results

4. Seek funding from the superintendent for the facilitation team and other key people to attend a conference with me during the January exam break about learning communities and assessment

Progress Report: End of Year Three
Our Long Term Goals Over the Coming Years

1. To develop stronger relationships with the JK–grade 5 school in our community

2. To identify the impact of the growth patterns in the community schools in the vicinity

3. To develop higher levels of trust on the staff so we can learn more collaboratively with the ultimate goal of improving our results with all of our students

My Immediate Goals Over the Summer Break

During the summer, I devoted time to four goals that needed action before the next school year began.

Goal 1 (August)

Seek funding from the superintendent for the facilitation team and other key people to attend a conference with me during the January exam break with two results: To learn more about learning communities and assessment and to build trust on the team.

- **Action.** I met with the superintendent to ask for funding.

- **Positive Consequences.** Sonya Superintendent wanted to meet with our facilitation team and listen to their reasons for wanting to attend this conference/institute.

Goal 2 (August)

Meet with the facilitation team during the summer break to get a head start on the school year

Action. I invited the facilitation team to an afternoon meeting followed by a barbeque dinner at my house in August. I also invited Sonya Superintendent, Jake Kinder, and everyone's spouses or partners to join us later for dinner.

Positive Consequences:

1. Norma brought a flip chart and we sat in a semicircle around it in the backyard. When I raised the issue of finding a replacement for Pablo, Victor nominated Connie as the new facilitation team leader and everyone agreed—including Connie. I had worried about how this decision would be made. In the end it was easier than I thought it would be.

continued >

Composite Middle and High School: A Fictional Scenario (cont'd)

2. I shared the results of my meeting with our superintendent about the conference in January and our obligations. They want to include Noel Network and Paul Peacemaker and the ESL teacher we hire, if we could afford it. Connie and Victor pointed out that there is funding available from the unions as well.

3. Then we reflected on the success of the retreat at the end of June and recorded the priorities and ideas that arose from it:

   - Increasing lateral trust levels among staff members, as measured by the staff trust survey

   - A greater understanding of the data wall concept thanks to Ashira and her team

   - Permission to have fun as a staff and to enjoy benefits of laughter and humor, both in our own personal lives and in our classrooms.

Note: The dinner speaker we hired to speak to us on the topic "Happiness at Work" not only gave us permission to have fun as a staff but also opened doors to the benefits of laughter and humor, both in our personal lives and in our classrooms. This speaker exceeded our expectations. Inviting Jake Kinder to join us for the dinner speaker segment enabled staff to get to know him better in the informal conversations that took place.

4. I shared with them the dates of the interview/hiring process during the last week of August. We developed four interview questions that included:

   - Our focus on building trust and teamwork with this unique Grade 6–12 staff

   - Credibility-competence and character examples

   - Concrete examples of risk-taking and teamwork behaviors

   - Willingness to work hard but to also have fun and be creative at work

   They also developed the format of the interview including a tour of the school.

Goal 3 (July)

Learn more about the elementary contract between the district and the union.

Action: I met with Jake Kinder over several breakfast meetings to continue our mentoring relationship.

Positive Consequences: Jake was extremely helpful pointing out key clauses in the elementary contract that could cause me problems, possibly resulting in a grievance if I weren't careful. We have entered into more of a coaching relationship this summer, as he is now asking me questions about high school cultures in preparation for his switch with Norma in February.

Goal 4 (End of August)

Conduct the interviews for vacant positions from a trust-based perspective.

Action: Norma and I redesigned the process for filling six vacant positions.

Positive Consequences: We were able to hire six new staff members and found the expertise we needed. One was an ESL teacher for many years and was prepared to help us start this new program. Two were beginning teachers who said they were drawn to this school because of our

continued >

Composite Middle and High School:
A Fictional Scenario (cont'd)

reputation for teamwork and creativity, and they liked that trust. I believe the specific questions we asked told us more about their character in addition to their competence to teach.

Unintended Negative Consequence: It became apparent early in September, (after the week of interviews for new staff in August), that I was expecting far more than the facilitation team could deliver in terms of time commitment. Norma sensed their frustration early on.

Action: We quickly called a meeting with the facilitation team to examine our operating procedures.

Positive Consequence: They all concurred with Norma's intuition. They didn't know how to tell me it was a little too much responsibility for them. Coretta suggested that the facilitation team had to see itself as a co-coordinating leadership team and we needed to identify other interdependent teams that would have specific responsibilities and share the workload. We identified the teams already in place that would liaise with the facilitation team:

- Social committee with Noel Network as the leader
- Literacy team with Ashira as the leader
- Breakfast and Snack team

This meeting was a turning point in maintaining the willingness of the facilitation team to continue and to manage their role on top of their teaching duties. They said this was workable.

Our Three Short-Term Goals for This Year

Goal 1 (Ongoing)

Support the facilitation team.

Action: Met with the facilitation team and other team leaders as a group to work out our operating procedures and agree on our structure with the overall coordination of the facilitation team.

Action: Noel suggested that the facilitation team start to use the in-school email system to hold online conferences and share ideas quickly before meetings.

Goal 2 (Ongoing)

Support the facilitation team's plans to build high-trust staff relationships, especially with new staff members, by listening, sharing my expertise, and providing resources.

Action: Examine the results of the staff trust survey, looking for specific areas to address.

Positive Consequences: The experienced teachers we hired were paired up with a buddy in their department or division who guided them through the first weeks of school. They were expected to explain our staff meeting norms, our progress over the last two years since the two schools merged, the role of the facilitation team and other interdependent teams, and the shared leadership role of the principal and assistant principal.

New teachers were assigned a formal mentor for their first two years. The mentors had much the same role as the buddies, with additional responsibilities involving guidance with instructional strategies and classroom management.

All new staff were given a copy of Roland Barth's article and discussed it with their buddy or mentor.

continued >

Composite Middle and High School: A Fictional Scenario (cont'd)

The facilitation team members decided to share their own work on personal trust, their self-assessments, and their trust touchstones with each of their contact groups at lunchtime meetings. (This led many staff members to conduct personal trust surveys with their colleagues and develop touchstones themselves.)

Negative Consequences: We learned from the trust survey results that our elementary staff in general reported greater fear of speaking up and raising issues.

Because of these results, a professional learning session on Personality, Conflict Patterns and Problem-Solving was offered in October. Most staff members attended and reported it was very helpful in understanding that conflict is to be expected and how to deal with their own fears about conflict and resistance. There were many requests for follow-up discussions from the feedback forms.

Action: Norma came back in March to help me administer a trust survey with all staff about myself. (I felt I should do this survey again mainly because of new staff.)

Positive Consequence: The middle school teachers gave me higher scores this time round, most notably in my levels of competence and my willingness to learn more, both from them and from Jake. I had impressed them with my actions, and their trust in me had grown.

Because of the results, I decided to make it a priority to share information more transparently by:

- Continuing my morning walkabouts whenever possible to talk with staff one on one
- Starting an open binder in the staff room with announcements, critical papers
- Writing key messages on the blackboard in the staff room (Jake's suggestion)

Goal 3 (November PD Day)

Support the facilitation team as they lead the staff, parent and student conversations about our vision scenario, our beliefs and core values, and subsequent action plans.

Action: They asked me to introduce this important action planning series of activities at the October staff meeting by explaining why I believed students and parents should be involved as well as staff for the full-day session in November.

Positive Consequence: When they realized that many of the activities we had done over the past two years were actually components of the action planning model, Connie suggested that if we broke up into work groups we might be able to develop our goals (in draft form) in one day. We had compiled data related to literacy and we had our History Maps completed. If we hadn't built a base of trust, I think it would have been an impossible task to complete in one day. Their enthusiasm showed me how much progress we had made in just over two years.

Action: The facilitation team met twice to co-ordinate the plans for the PD Day and included the Student Council President and the chair of the Parent Advisory Council. They established these work groups for the day:

a. A personal vision work group. They were asked to develop a suggested process for staff members to use.

b. A 'future-oriented' work group that would craft a first draft of our school Vision Scenario.

continued >

Composite Middle and High School:
A Fictional Scenario (cont'd)

   c. A core values work group that would base its work on our Belief Wall to identify our core vales and, if possible, develop a draft school mission statement or credo.

   d. An appreciative inquiry work group to identify what is already working well.

   e. A data analysis work group that started with the Tree activity to identify what is in the bud, bloom, full flower, and withering flower stage.

Staff members had their choice of which work group they would join. Student Council and Parent Advisory Council members also joined in. Each work group took its turn in the first part of the morning and gathered information and ideas from everyone assembled in the library. For example, the vision scenario group distributed post-it notes and asked for everyone's response to a question.

Then all the work groups dispersed to different locations, analyzed their information, and prepared a progress report for the whole group. We met together for lunch and listened to spokespeople for each work group describe the progress they had made and answer any questions we had for them. By midafternoon, each work group was ready to report, and we met back in the library. By the end of the day, we had created:

   · A guideline for each staff member to use to develop his or her own personal vision

   · A draft vision scenario for the school

   · A draft document with our core values, beliefs, and school credo (They preferred this term to "mission statement.")

   · A draft list, organized into categories, of what the staff thought was working well

   · A large chart replicating the Tree activity with sticky notes in each section. This helped us see what we could let go of or slow down on in order to make time for our new goals.

Unintended negative consequence: We all noticed one staff member who was continually marking test papers during the morning. (This violated one of our agreed upon norms—focus on the task.) When Paul Peacemaker directly asked her at lunch to respect our meeting norms, she quickly put everything away. I followed up the next day with a private chat with her. She explained that she was way behind with her marking and couldn't catch up at home because her kids were sick. We explored some ways she could get reliable assessments of student progress without bringing her work to staff meetings. She agreed with the necessity of following meetings norms and apologized.

Positive Consequences: We were all truly impressed by what we achieved in one day. All of the work was reproduced for distribution later that week so that staff could reflect on it before the next staff meeting. The parents and students had made it all the more real. They had valuable contributions to make, and they learned a lot that day about us too. People commented about how hopeful this had made them for the future of the school. Our higher levels of trust enabled us to face these daunting tasks together with honesty and integrity for the good of the school.

Action: At the staff meeting early in December, we reviewed the results from the PD Day and discussed each aspect. We reached common ground to proceed on four major goals to enable us to reach our future vision scenario.

The facilitation team's task was to establish any necessary new work teams and help them develop their own detailed action plan with timelines, responsibilities and resources to achieve their

continued >

Composite Middle and High School:
A Fictional Scenario (cont'd)

mandate. Systems had to be put in place to measure progress at regular intervals. At the same time, the facilitation team had to coordinate the plans, the timing, and the resources each work team requested. They aimed to have the work teams in place by the February staff meeting. Major decisions had to be made by each work team during the spring in preparation for the following school year.

These are the four goals and highlights of the plans with the work teams.

A. To restructure the school to enable all students to learn to their potential.

Work Team 1: Structure and Timetable

The goal here is to have multi-age, multi-grade groupings instead of set grades, so that students can proceed at their own rate. New students could enter at their own language level and advance at their own rate. Staff will be grouped into interdisciplinary teaching teams ranging from entry level (grade 6 to graduation level (grade 12). The timetable will be structured to provide common planning time for groups of teachers and a weekly meeting block of time for the facilitation team. Jake will work with the new teacher who was hired because of her expertise in this type of timetabling.

Work Team 2: Literacy

Continue the work of the literacy team to include the development of a new ESL program to meet the needs of students with English as their second or third language.

B. To continue to focus on trust as a core school value

Work Team 3: Trust

The facilitation team wanted to teach the staff what it had learned about trust and also to expand the use of trust surveys for ongoing feedback. They planned to include students and parents in this work team. They especially wanted to explore what impact even higher levels of trust would have on staff relationships and student learning and what that could look like. They saw themselves more of a study group and wanted to read more on the topic and seek further speakers and resources.

C. To change the name of the school and therefore establish a new identity for the future

Work Team 4: New Name and Identity

Finally, it became apparent that choosing a new name to reflect our school vision and core values, and also our history, was not going to be as easy as we thought. A small work team of one parent, one student, one senior community member, and one teacher (Hank Historical) was formed to develop an inclusive process to honor the history of the school in the community and come up with three or four possibilities, with a rationale for each, before the end of March.

Unintended Positive Consequence: Sonya Superintendent revealed at a principals' meeting that she had advance knowledge of a new 'Focus on the Arts' system mandate for next year. I took this back to the facilitation team to discuss how we should handle this, since this was *not* going to be our focus. They decided to wait and see what latitude we had when, and if, the board mandated it. They appreciated the heads-up I gave them and were determined to fight for our decision. I am optimistic that there is room to negotiate with Sarah, as she is supportive of our focus on trust.

continued >

Composite Middle and High School: A Fictional Scenario (cont'd)

Goal 4 (End of August)

Reward the efforts of the facilitation team and provide an opportunity for long-range planning

> **Action:** Go to a conference with a team from this school and the JK–grade 5 school to learn about the current thinking, to assess our results so far, to plan for our next steps, and to build trust
>
> After much planning for our substitute teachers and Norma's willingness to supervise both schools while we were away, we attended the conference. It gave us much needed time to get to know each other better. We quickly realized that we were well ahead of many other schools in developing learning communities. Many schools were interested in our background with trust as a core value.
>
> Later in April, Sarah Superintendent asked me to become principal of a new high school, and I declined the offer. While it was a compliment to me, I knew I needed to stay with this staff, which had worked so hard and made so much progress. We had built significant trust in each other and I knew they wouldn't want me to leave.
>
> Jake and Norma decided to make their job switch permanent. We began planning for Victor's retirement. (I know the district union will want to be on the planning team for that.) When Ashira announced she would be going on a maternity leave, the new ESL teacher volunteered to chair the literacy team until she returned.

My Reflections at the End of Three Years

As this third year comes to and end and I have made the commitment to continue as principal, I can feel how much I have grown as a leader. I now understand that trusting others and being trustworthy myself have a wide-ranging impact. My time is spent in more meetings than before, but they are now action-oriented and not simply focused on information dissemination. There are definitely decisions that only I can make, but they are the exception rather than the rule.

Teacher leaders on staff extended their trust in me and now the facilitation team is deeply embedded in our organizational structure. I saw each staff member who took a leadership role grow over the three years, both personally and interpersonally.

Connie Collaborative wants to leave her role as union rep but remain as leader of the facilitation team. The staff has decided that they only need one union rep for the whole staff now.

Ashira Accountable made the successful transition from classroom teacher to in-school ELF and is thinking of applying for a central consultant position that will open up in a year or two. Our literacy program is so much stronger because of her.

Our high school has benefited greatly with the addition of the middle school grades. In fact, I am glad we were thrown together. We are far more prepared to meet the needs of our existing families as well as our new families. We have programs in place for basic needs like food for breakfast and lunch, and high-quality instruction and remediation for all of our students. Creative ideas are flowing. Enthusiasm is showing. Excitement is growing.

I look forward with anticipation to working with this amazing staff and students for years to come. We have a sense of direction and trust each other to take risks, speak up, and be honest about our progress and our challenges. Morale is better than ever, but not as good as it could be. We can finally call ourselves a school that's 'moving.' I believe that we can only do this together!

References

Achinstein, B. (2002). Conflict amid community: The micropolitics of teacher collaboration. *Teachers' College Record, 104*(3), 421–455.

Adams, S. (1996a). *The Dilbert principle: A cubicle's eye view of bosses, meetings, management fads, and other workplace afflictions.* New York: Harper-Collins Books.

Adams, S. (1996b). *Dogbert's management handbook.* New York: Harper-Collins Books.

Ashton, P., & Webb, R. (1986). *Making a difference: Teachers' sense of efficacy and student achievement.* New York: Longman.

Atkinson, S., & Butcher, D. (2003). Trust in managerial relationships. *Journal of Managerial Psychology, 18*(4), 282–304.

Barth, R. (1990). *Improving schools from within.* San Francisco: Jossey-Bass.

Barth, R. (2002). The culture builder. *Educational Leadership, 59*(8), 6–11.

Barth, R. (2006). Improving relationships within the schoolhouse. *Educational Leadership, 63*(6), 8–13.

Bellman, G. (1992). *Getting things done when you are not in charge.* New York: Simon & Schuster.

Berens, L. (2000). *Understanding yourself and others: An introduction to temperament.* Huntington Beach, CA: Telos.

Bolman, L., & Deal, T. (1995). *Leading with soul.* San Francisco: Jossey-Bass.

Bolton, R. (1979). *People skills.* New York: Simon and Schuster.

Bridges, W. (1980). *Transitions: Making sense of life's changes.* Cambridge, MA: Da Capo Press.

British Association for the Advancement of Science. (2002). *LaughLab: The scientific quest for the world's funniest joke.* London: Arrow Books.

Bryk, A., & Schneider, B. (2002). *Trust in schools: A core resource for improvement.* New York: Russell Sage Foundation.

Clark, R., Antonelli, F., Lacavera, D., Livingstone, D., Pollock, K., Smaller, H., Strachan, J., & Tarc, P. (2007). *Beyond PD days: Teachers' work and learning in Canada.* Toronto: Ontario Teachers' Federation.

Conzemius, A. (1999). Ally in the office. *Journal of Staff Development, 20*(4), 31–34.

Conzemius, A., & O'Neill, J. (2002). *The handbook for SMART school teams.* Bloomington, IN: Solution Tree Press.

Covey, R., Merrill, A. R., & Merrill, R. (1994). *First things first.* New York: Simon & Schuster.

Covey, S. M. R. (2006). *The speed of trust: The one thing that changes everything.* New York: Free Press.

Crowson, B. (2005). *The joy is in the journey.* Bloomington, IN: AuthorHouse.

Croyle, J. (1996). *Bringing out the winner in your child.* Nashville, TN: Cumberland House.

Dale, E. (1969). *The cone of learning.* Accessed at www.cals.ncsu.edu/agexed/sae/ppt1/sld012.htm on December 26, 2008.

Deutsch, C. (1984). Round-table meetings with no agendas, no tables. *New York Times,* p. 23.

Doyle, M., & Strauss, D. (1986). *How to make meetings work: The new interaction method.* New York: Berkeley Publishing Group.

Drucker, P., & Hams, G. (1993). The post-capitalist executive: An interview with Peter F. Drucker. *Harvard Business Review, 73*(1), 121.

DuFour, R., DuFour, R., & Eaker, R. (2002). *Getting started: Reculturing schools to become professional learning communities.* Bloomington, IN: Solution Tree Press.

DuFour, R., DuFour R., Eaker, R., & Many, R. (2006). *Learning by doing: A handbook for professional learning communities at work.* Bloomington, IN: Solution Tree Press.

DuFour, R., Eaker, R., & DuFour, R. (Eds.). (2005). *On common ground: The power of professional learning communities.* Bloomington, IN: Solution Tree Press.

Eisley, L. (1979). *The star thrower.* New York: Random House.

Erikson, E. (1963). *Childhood and society.* New York: W.W. Norton & Company.

Ferguson, M. (1980). *The Aquarian conspiracy.* New York: Penguin Putnam.

Fletcher, A. (2002). *FireStarter Youth Power Curriculum: Participant guidebook.* Olympia, WA: Freechild Project.

Freed, A. (Producer), & Vidor, K. (Director). (1937). *The wizard of oz* [Motion picture]. United States: Metro-Goldwyn-Mayer.

Freedman, G., & Werbe, S. (Producers). (1990). *Learning in America: Schools that work* [Television broadcast]. Arlington, VA: MacNeil/Lehrer Productions.

Fullan, M. (2003). *The moral imperative of school leadership.* Thousand Oaks, CA: Corwin Press.

Fullan, M. (2006). *Turnaround leadership.* San Francisco: Jossey-Bass.

Fullan, M. (2008). *What's worth fighting for in the principalship?* New York: Teachers College Press.

Fuller, B. (1972). *Trimtab: BFI's membership newsletter.* Accessed at http://bfi.org/our_programs/publications/trimtab on December 8, 2008.

Geber, B. (1992). Saturn's grand experiment. *Training, 29*(6), 27–35.

Gittell, J. (2003). *The Southwest Airlines way: Using the power of relationships to achieve high performance.* New York: McGraw-Hill.

Gordon, D. (2002). Fuel for reform: The importance of trust in changing schools—Are good social relationships key to school improvement? *Harvard Education Letter, 18*(4), 1–8.

Grabmeier, J. (2002). *Business people win when they apologize, take personal blame for mistakes.* Accessed at http://researchnews.osu.edu/archive/bustrust.htm on January 2, 2007.

Greer, J. (1997). *How could you do this to ME? Learning to trust after betrayal.* New York: Doubleday.

Hargreaves, A. (1994). The new professionalism: The synthesis of professional and institutional development. *Teaching and Teacher Education, 104*(4), 423–438.

Hargreaves, A. (2002). Teaching and betrayal. *Teachers and Teaching: Theory and Practice, 8*(3/4), 393–407.

Hargreaves, A., & Fink, D. (2004). The seven principles of sustainable leadership. *Educational Leadership, 61*(7), 8–13.

Hargreaves, A., & Fink, D. (2006). *Sustainable leadership.* San Francisco: Jossey-Bass.

Harvey, J. (1988). *The Abilene paradox and other meditations on management.* New York: John Wiley.

Hedva, B. (2001). *Betrayal, trust and forgiveness: A guide to emotional healing and self-renewal.* Berkeley, CA: Ten Speed Press.

Hirsh, S., & Murphy, M. (1991). *Useful consensus building phrases: School improvement manual.* Oxford, OH: National Staff Development Council.

Hoffman, C., & Ness, J. (2004, April). Putting sense into consensus. *Tools for Schools,* 1–2.

Hoy, W., & Kupersmith, W. (1984). Principal authenticity and faculty trust: Key elements in organizational behavior. *Planning and Changing, 15*(2), 80–88.

Hulley, W., & Dier, D. (2005). *Harbors of hope: The planning for school and student success process.* Bloomington, IN: Solution Tree Press.

Janas, M. (1998). Shhhh, the dragon is sleeping and its name is Resistance. *Journal of Staff Development, 19*(3), 13–16.

Jeffers, S. (1989). *Feel the fear and do it anyway.* New York: Random House.

Johnson, D., & Johnson, F. (1989). *Leading the cooperative school.* Edina, MN: Interaction Book Company.

Johnson, D., & Johnson, F. (1997). *Joining together: Group theory and group skills.* Boston: Allyn & Bacon.

Jones, J. E., & Bearley, W. (1996). *360 degree feedback: Strategies, tactics and techniques for developing leaders.* Amherst, MA: Human Resources Press.

Joyce, B., Showers, B., & Bennett, B. (1987). Synthesis of research on staff development: A framework for future study and state-of-the-art analysis. *Educational Leadership, 45*(3), 77–87.

Katz, J. (2007). *Trust in the workplace: By the numbers.* Accessed at industryweek.com/PrintArticle.aspx?ArticleID=14351 on November 11, 2007.

Kayser, T. (1994). *Building team power.* New York: McGraw-Hill.

Kelsey D., & Plumb, P. (2004). *Great meetings! Great results: A practical guide for facilitating successful, productive meetings.* Portland, ME: Hanson Park Press.

Kidder, R., & Born, P. (2002). Moral courage in a world of dilemmas. *School Administrator, 59*(2), 14–20.

King, S. (1982). *Different seasons.* London: Penguin Books.

Kochanek, J. (2005). *Building trust for better schools: Research-based practices.* Thousand Oaks, CA: Corwin Press.

Kouzes, J., & Posner, B. (1987). *The leadership challenge.* San Francisco: Jossey-Bass.

Kouzes, J., & Posner, B. (1993). *Credibility: How leaders gain and lose it, why people demand it.* San Francisco: Jossey-Bass.

Kouzes, J., & Posner, B. (2002). *The leadership challenge.* San Francisco: Jossey-Bass.

Kouzes, J., & Posner, B. (2004, July/August). A prescription for leading in cynical times. *Ivy Business Journal* (Reprint #9B04TD02).

Kramer, R., & Tyler, T. (Eds.) (1995). *Trust in organizations: Frontiers in theory and research.* Los Angeles: Sage Publications.

Lambert, L. (1998). How to build leadership capacity. *Educational Leadership, 55*(7), 17–19.

LaRoche, L. (1996). *Happy talk: Fun ways to talk to yourself.* Plymouth, MA: Lighthearted Productions.

Lawton, V. (1998, March 8). Read this if you're a sucker. *Toronto Star,* p. A12.

Leithwood, K. (2006). *Teacher working conditions that matter: Evidence for change.* Toronto: Elementary Teachers' Federation of Ontario.

Lencioni, P. (2002). *The five dysfunctions of a team: A leadership fable.* New York: John Wiley & Sons.

Lencioni, P. (2002). *Overcoming the five dysfunctions of a team: A field guide.* San Francisco: Jossey-Bass.

Levering, R. (2000). *A great place to work.* San Francisco: Great Place to Work Institute.

Lewicki, R. (2006). *The impact of culture on trust repair: What we know and what we don't.* Accessed at business.brookes.ac.uk/ research/esrc/ TrustRepairCulture4.pdf on November 30, 2008.

Lewicki, R., & Bunker, B. (1996). Developing and maintaining trust in work relationships. In R. Kramer & T. Tyler (Eds.). *Trust in organizations: Frontiers in theory and research* (pp. 114–139). Los Angeles: Sage Publications.

Lewicki, R., & Tomlinson, E. (2003a). *Trust and trust building.* Accessed at www.beyondintractability.org/essay/trust_building/?nid=1210 on December 2, 2008.

Lewicki, R., & Tomlinson, E. (2003b). *Distrust.* Accessed at www. beyondintractability.org/essay/distrust on December 15, 2008.

Lewicki, R., Tomlinson, E., & Gillespie, N. (2006). Models of interpersonal trust development: Theoretical approaches, empirical evidence and future directions. *Journal of Management, 32*(6), 991–1022.

Lewicki, R., & Weithoff, C. (2000). *Trust, trust development, and trust repair. The handbook of conflict resolution—Theory and practice.* San Francisco: Jossey-Bass.

Lewin, K. (1943). Defining the field at a given time. *Psychological Review, 50,* 292–310.

Little, J. W. (1984). Seductive images and organizational realities in professional development. *Teachers College Record. 87*(1), 84–102.

Little, J. W. (1990). The persistence of privacy: Autonomy and initiative in teachers' professional relations. *Teachers College Record, 91*(4), 509–539.

Loewenwarter, P. (Producer), & Weiner, R. (Director). (1988). *The leadership alliance* [Motion Picture]. United States: Enterprise Media.

Luft, J. (1984). *Group processes: An introduction to group dynamics.* Mountainview, CA: Mayfield Publishing Company.

Mauer, R. (1996). *Beyond the wall of resistance: Unconventional strategies that build support for change.* Austin, TX: Bard Press.

McKennan P., & Maister, D. (2002). *First among equals: How to manage a group of professionals.* New York: Free Press.

McLaughlin, M., & Talbert, J. (2001). *Professional communities and the work of high school teaching.* Chicago: University of Chicago Press.

Miller, L. (2008, March 10). Stop your sobbing now. *Newsweek.* Accessed at www.Newsweek.com/id/117883 on January 9, 2009.

Mitchell, C. (2007, February). Principles of engagement: Building sustainable learning communities. *Changing Perspectives, 13–16.*

Mitchell, C., & Sackney, L. (2000). *Profound improvement: Building capacity for a learning community.* Runnemede, NJ: Swets & Zeitlinger.

Mitchell, C., & Sackney, L. (2001, February 24). *Building capacity for a learning community.* Accessed at www.umanitoba.ca/publications/cjeap on Februrary 20, 2009.

Newman, F., & Wehlage, G. (1995). *Successful school restructuring.* Madison, WI: Center on Organization and Restructuring Schools.

Nias, J. (1989). *Primary teachers talking.* London: Routledge Press.

Obama, B. (2006). *The audacity of hope.* New York: Crown Publishing.

Ouchi, W. (1997, November). *Tools for Schools, 3.*

Owen, H. (2008). *Open space technology: A user's guide.* San Francisco, CA: Berrett-Koehler Publishers.

Patterson, J. (2001). *Suzanne's diary for Nicholas.* New York: Warner Book Group.

Patterson, K., Grenny, J., McMillan, R., & Switzler, A. (2002). *Crucial conversations: Tools for talking when the stakes are high.* New York: McGraw-Hill.

Peck, M. S. (1997). *The different drum: Community making and peace.* New York: Touchstone.

Peters, T. (Producer/Writer). (2008, December 2). *The leadership alliance* [Television broadcast]. Los Angeles: Baseline Studio Systems.

Peters, T., & Austin, N. (1985). *A passion for excellence.* New York: Warner Books.

Peters, T., & Waterman, R. (1982). *In search of excellence.* New York: HarperCollins.

Reina, D., & Reina, M. (2006). *Trust and betrayal in the workplace.* San Francisco: Berrett-Koehler.

Richardson, J. (1998, April/May). Applause! Applause! Recognize behaviors you want to see more often. *Tools for Schools, 1–2.*

Rosenholtz, S. (1989). *Teachers' workplace.* New York: Longman Press.

Rosenholtz, S. (1991). *Teachers' workplace: The social organization of schools.* New York: Teachers College Press.

Rotter, J. B. (1967). The new scale for the measurement of interpersonal trust. *Journal of Personality, 35,* 651–665.

Rotter, J. B. (1980). Trust and gullibility. *Psychology Today, 14*(5), 35–38.

Rousseau, D., Sitkin, S., Burt, R., & Camerer, C. (1998). Not so different after all: A cross-discipline view of trust. *Academy of Management Review, 23*(3), 393–404.

Rubinstein, S., & Kochan, T. (2001). *Learning from Saturn*. Ithaca, New York: Cornell University Press.

Rudin, S. (Producer), & Linklater, R. (Director). (2003). *The school of rock* [Motion picture]. United States: Paramount Pictures.

Ryan, M. J. (2004). *Trusting yourself.* New York: Broadway Books.

Ryan, K., & Oestreich, D. (1998). *Driving FEAR out of the workplace: Creating the high-trust, high-performance workplace.* San Francisco: Jossey-Bass.

Sackney, L. (1986). Practical strategies for improving school effectiveness. *Canadian School Executive 6*(4), 15–20.

Serva, M., Fuller, M., & Mayer, R. (2005). The reciprocal nature of trust: A longitudinal study of interacting teams. *Journal of Organizational Behavior, 26,* 625–648.

Saint, S., & Lawson, J. (1994). *Rules for reaching consensus*. San Francisco: Jossey Bass.

Solomon, R. C., & Flores, F. (2001). *Building trust in business, politics, relationships and life.* New York: Oxford University Press.

Smith, M. K. (2005). *Bruce W. Tuckman: Forming, storming, norming, and performing in groups.* Accessed at www.infed.org/thinkers/tuckman. htm on December 1, 2008.

Smith, S. (1987). The collaborative school takes shape. *Educational Leadership, 45*(3), 46–50.

Sparks, D. (2002). *Designing powerful professional development for teachers and principals.* Oxford, OH: National Staff Development Council.

Sparks, D. (2004). Broader purpose calls for higher understanding: An interview with Andy Hargreaves. *Journal of Staff Development, 25*(2) 46–50.

Sparks, D. (2005). *Leading for results: Transforming teaching, learning and relationships in schools.* Thousand Oaks, CA: Corwin Press.

Spies, P. (2003). Promised land or assembly line. *Journal of Staff Development, 24*(30), 57–62.

Stephenson, S. (1994). *School-based planning: Talking and growing together.* Brampton, ON: School Success Consulting.

Stephenson, S. (2001). When your heart is in your dreams. *Register, 3*(3), 28–31.

Stephenson, S. (2003). Saying "NO" to the unimportant. *Register, 5*(2), 21–24.

Stephenson, S., & Thibault, P. (2006). *Laughing matters: Strategies for building a joyful learning community.* Bloomington, IN: Solution Tree Press.

Stoll, L. (1999, August). *The power of school culture in school improvement.* Paper presented at the Innovations for Effective Schooling Conference, Auckland, New Zealand.

Stoll, L., & Fink, D. (1996). *Changing our schools: Linking school effectiveness and school improvement.* Maidenhead, UK: Open University Press.

Telford, D., & Gostick, A. (2005). *Integrity works: Strategies for becoming a trusted, respected and admired leader.* Layton, UT: Gibbs Smith.

Troman, G., & Woods, P. (2000). Careers under stress: Teacher adaptations at a time of intensive reform. *Journal of Educational Change, 1*(3), 253–275.

Tschannen-Moran, M. (2004). *Trust matters: Leadership for successful schools.* San Francisco: Jossey-Bass.

Tyler, T., & Kramer, R. (1996). *Trust in organizations.* Thousand Oaks, CA: Sage.

Veeck, M., & Williams. P. (2005). *Fun is good: How to create joy and passion in your workplace and career.* Emmaus, PA: Rodale.

Want Loyal Workers? Give Them a Reason to Trust You. (2007). Accessed at www.industryweek.com/PrintArticle.aspx?ArticleID=13920 on November 11, 2007.

Weisbord, M. (1982). *Discovering common ground: How future search conferences bring people together to achieve breakthrough innovation, empowerment and shared vision.* San Francisco: Berrett-Koehler.

Wheatley, M. (2002). *Turning to one another: Simple conversations to restore hope to the future.* San Francisco: Barrett-Koehler.

Whitaker, T. (2003). *What great principals do differently: Fifteen things that matter most.* New York: Eye on Education.

Ziglar, Z. (1985). *Raising positive kids in a negative world.* New York: Random House.

Index

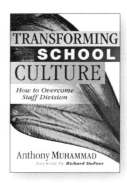

The Collaborative Administrator

Austin Buffum, Cassandra Erkens, Charles Hinman, Susan Huff, Lillie G. Jessie, Terri L. Martin, Mike Mattos, Anthony Muhammad, Peter Noonan, Geri Parscale, Eric Twadell, Jay Westover, and Kenneth C. Williams
Foreword by Robert Eaker
Introduction by Richard DuFour
How do you maintain the right balance of "loose-tight" leadership? How do you establish profound, lasting trust with your staff? What principles strengthen principal leadership? This book answers these questions and much more in compelling chapters packed with strategies and inspiration. **BKF256**

The Collaborative Teacher

Cassandra Erkens, Chris Jakicic, Lillie G. Jessie, Dennis King, Sharon V. Kramer, Thomas W. Many, Mary Ann Ranells, Ainsley B. Rose, Susan K. Sparks, and Eric Twadell
Foreword by Rebecca DuFour
Introduction by Richard DuFour
Transform education from inside the classroom with this accessible anthology. Specific techniques, supporting research, and real classroom stories illustrate how to work together to create a guaranteed and viable curriculum and use data to inform instruction. **BKF257**

Transforming School Culture

By Anthony Muhammad
Foreword by Richard DuFour
Busy administrators will appreciate this quick read packed with immediate, accessible strategies. *Transforming School Culture* provides the framework for understanding dynamic relationships within school cultures and ensuring a positive environment that supports the changes necessary to improve learning for all students. **BKF281**

The Handbook for SMART School Teams

Anne Conzemius and Jan O'Neill
Learn what makes a school team SMART and how you can collaborate to achieve positive results. This practical, engaging handbook shares best practices essential to building a solid network of support. **BKF115**

Laughing Matters

Susan Stephenson and Paul Thibault
Use the power of fun and humor to transform your learning community. Based on research that reveals the deep benefits of humor, *Laughing Matters* engages teachers with pages of laughter-inducing strategies for enhancing learning potential and increasing educator effectiveness. **BKF213**

Learning by Doing

Richard DuFour, Rebecca DuFour, Robert Eaker, and Thomas Many
This book demonstrates how collaborative teams can take action to close the knowing-doing gap and transform their schools into professional learning communities. **BKF214**

Solution Tree

Visit solution-tree.com or call 800.733.6786 to order.